Miss Brenda and the Lovelady Movement

Dr. Brenda Lovelady Spahn
with Jeanne Sparks Dean

PALMETTO
P U B L I S H I N G
Charleston, SC
www.PalmettoPublishing.com

Copyright © 2024 by Dr. Brenda Lovelady Spahn

All rights reserved
No portion of this book may be reproduced, stored in a retrieval system, or transmitted in any form by any means–electronic, mechanical, photocopy, recording, or other–except for brief quotations in printed reviews, without prior permission of the author.

Hardcover ISBN: 979-8-8229-3712-3
Paperback ISBN: 979-8-8229-3713-0
eBook ISBN: 979-8-8229-3714-7

Miss Brenda and the Lovelady Movement

Dr. Brenda Lovelady Spahn
with Jeanne Sparks Dean

To my cherished husband, Jeff, my five children, and my 32 grandchildren and great-grandchildren, whose unwavering love and boundless support illuminate my life. Your acceptance of me for who I am, without reservation or condition, has been a gift beyond measure during this journey. With heartfelt appreciation, I acknowledge the depth of your love and the profound impact it has in my life.

To my esteemed mentor, Joe Medina, whose unwavering guidance and boundless wisdom have been a beacon of light on my journey. I am deeply grateful for your steadfast presence, always ready to lend an ear and offer sage counsel, regardless of the hour. Your profound insights and spiritual guidance have not only enriched my professional endeavors but have also nourished my soul, guiding me toward greater clarity and purpose.

To my cherished friends, Kim and Sue Ratliff, who walked with us through every twist and turn of this extraordinary journey.

To every remarkable woman and precious child who has walked the halls of The Lovelady Center, your presence has unveiled the depths of my true purpose. In the shared experiences, struggles, and triumphs we've encountered together, I've discovered the essence of my destiny. You've been the catalysts for my growth, the inspirations behind my journey, and the embodiments of resilience and hope that have forever transformed my life.

"This Center and ministry have become what it is today not because of us, but rather, because of *Jesus*." Brenda Lovelady Spahn is the real deal. God spoke to her, she listened, she obeyed. I have been blessed to visit The Lovelady Center five times. I walk in the front door and there is no doubt Jesus is there. *Miss Brenda and the Loveladies* never left my heart after reading it. My heart made room for *Miss Brenda and the Lovelady Movement*. I will never forget it. Read it. You will meet Jesus with every word. And you will never be the same.

Janet Scherer
Women's Ministry Director
First Baptist Church, Kennett, Missouri

In her first book, *Miss Brenda and the Loveladies*, written with Irene Zutell, Brenda Spahn tells the inspirational and heartwarming story of the beginning of an incredible journey of faith, which began with seven women released from prison into Miss Brenda's "Wholeway House," her own home. That journey culminated in the most successful program for rehabilitating formerly incarcerated women in the United States. From a group of seven women, The Lovelady Center is now a major facility housing over four hundred women and some eighty children. Literally tens of thousands of women have been through the program, which serves not only those formerly incarcerated, but women dealing with drug addiction, spousal abuse, and homelessness. Now, in her second book, Brenda Spahn brings to life the stories of the women themselves, many times in their own words. Their stories can be funny, tragic, terrifying and inspiring. Although The Lovelady Center has as high of a success rate as any rehabilitative facility in the country, not every story has a happy ending. With unflinching honesty and unwavering faith, Miss Brenda recounts both the successes and the heart breaks, told always with love and compassion for each of the women whose lives she has touched, and faith in the Almighty who has guided the way. This is a story that will warm the heart and inspire the better angels of all who read it.

Dan Gordon
Head Writer of *Highway to Heaven*, and author of the book, *Postcards from Heaven*

I have never met another person in my life anything like Brenda Spahn. She's tough, courageous, funny, tenacious, kind and loving. She's each of these things to a tremendous degree. But above and beyond any of these qualities, Brenda Spahn is a woman of powerful faith who listens for the word of God to direct her in her life, and then follows it. No matter what.

It took this special blend of characteristics to make anything at all like the events of which you're about to read in this book take place. The existence and success of the Lovelady Center hardly seem possible and the events that takes place within the pages of this book sometimes seem like they can't possibly be true. But they are. I have been to the Lovelady Center and I have witnessed with my own eyes a few of the miracles that take place there. But, for the people you'll read about here in this book, and within the walls of the Lovelady Center, miracles happen many times over, every day, year after year.

For anyone out there in the world that has lost their way, this book is proof that there is hope. For anyone out there in the world who is doubtful of or frightened to follow the path upon which God is leading them, this book is proof of the amazing events that can take place if you have the courage to take that first step.

Brenda herself says that if she knew the enormity of the task she was about to take on when she started the Lovelady Center, she never would have had the courage to go through with it. But she took the first step, and then just kept taking the next one. So did her wonderful family, who have been with her in the effort every step of the way and so did the many former clients of the Lovelady Center who have gone on to make its mission their lives' work. Most importantly of all, so did the tens of thousands of women whose lives have been saved and whose futures have become bright to a degree most of them never thought possible thanks to Brenda Spahn and the Lovelady Center.

The story you're about to read in these pages has its share of struggle, sadness and tears, but far more than that it is the story of overcoming these things with the power of love, joy, friendship and family, and the tenacity we can find within us when surrounded by them. Most of all, it is a true story of faith and the boundless miracles that an adherence to that faith has the power to bring into the world.

Doug McKay
Movie Producer

The phenomenal true story of *Miss Brenda and The Loveladies*, and the Movement that followed, is living proof that our God is the God of never-ending love, miracles, and second chances. I know this first hand because I witnessed the anointing power of God working in and through my precious friend, Lovelady Center Founder Brenda Spahn. A "Whole-Way House" that has transformed and continues to transform the lives of thousands of women. Women who were born without a chance in life, tossed away by society, incarcerated multiple times or who'd suffered through addiction and abuse. Women in need of a real and everlasting opportunity for a purpose-filled life full of love, joy and peace. This second book, written by Miss Brenda and Jeanne Sparks, tells the stories of these transformed lives in gripping detail that is, at times, gut-wrenching to read - but which overflows with hope and heart. Time, as we know, is so incredibly precious in our lives. I can say though with absolute certainty, if you take the time to read this book, Christ will move your heart and open your eyes and ears in ways beyond what you could ever imagine.

Cindy Bond
Producer, *I Can Only Imagine,* and *Redeeming Love*

In *Miss Brenda and the Loveladies*, we read the sometimes joyful, sometimes heartbreaking, but always miraculous story of seven women released From the Julia Tutwiler Prison for Women in Wetumpka, Alabama, to move into Brenda's home for the hope of finding a new way of living. What drew out of that humble beginning was a faith journey that God used to create one of the largest and most successful prison reentry and drug rehabilitation programs in the country today. As Brenda said, 'In the beginning, I had no idea what I was supposed to do. I just knew I had to do something.' And what Brenda learned from those first seven women about the revolving door of the prison system, about life in the streets, and about the never-ending struggles of addiction became the foundation of the program that to date has helped over 15,000 women and 4,000 children. In the pages of this book, you will read the stories of many of these women. Stories that do not always have a fairytale ending, but stories that will touch your heart, and hopefully inspire you to look to where God may be leading you to step into your faith journey, the story that may lead you much farther and much deeper into God's vision for our world than you could ever imagine.

John A. McNeil
Board Chairman
The Lovelady Center

Contents

Foreword	i
Prologue	1
Introduction	11
Dreamers	20
Storms Brewing	28
City Hall	43
Castle Living	55
One Bite at a Time	64
Flea Market	77
Elizabeth's Story, in Her Own Words	84
Tar Baby	92
Peas in a Pod	100
The Heart of Lovelady	109
The Girl with No Name	113
I Was Baby Girl	119
Danielle's Redemption	126
Sadie	130
The Atheist	137
Tell It Like It Is	142
Bury the Past	150
The Client Rep	153
Michelle	158
Most Wanted, in Carmen's Own Words	173

Carmen's Redemption	180
Vivian	186
Changed, in the Changed Woman's Own Words	190
Weeping	195
Losing Shay	199
Epilogue	211
It Takes a Village:	215
An Acknowledgement to Our Volunteers	215
Lovelady Life in Pictures	225

Foreword

I am one of over 15,000 women who entered The Lovelady Center program. Born there in 1971 when it was East End Memorial Hospital, I have received life *twice* in that building. Like many others, I didn't believe I could stay sober for long, much less, for years. I didn't believe there was joy without a substance. I believed I had gone too far and had done too much. I am forever grateful that I was wrong.

When Miss Brenda first started pushing me, I did not always understand why because my deep disrespect for authority caused me to question her at every turn. When I wanted to start a "Lovelady Newspaper" for the women to read, really amounting to a gossip rag amongst us clients, she answered the request with a staunch "No," but insisted I had a creative talent that could be utilized. She decided I would no longer perform work therapy assignments in housekeeping and instead assigned me to Development to help build a media department. When the projects began, she wanted everything perfect; after all, *"we represent God in everything we do."* She pushed me hard, expecting my walk to shine a light continually to others, even under pressure—because in the beginning, I didn't always work well with others.

I look back over thirteen years of guidance, love, and friendship. Once my spiritual foundation was in place, the most profound thing she ever said to me was this: "Jeanne, you have to

Dr. Brenda Lovelady Spahn

find something that you love to do more than drugs *and do that thing just as hard as you can."*

I can tell you with certainty I have been utterly and permanently impacted by Brenda Lovelady Spahn. Some say she is hard. Indeed, she is blunt and fiery, and she pushes relentlessly—toward excellence. The fact is, had I seen just a drop of weakness in her that first year during our interactions, I never would have respected her. And in turn, I never would have trusted her. And if I never trusted her, she never would have been able to show me how to find something I love to do more than drugs and how to do that as hard as I can.

And I am just one of *many* she has forever impacted.

When she asked me to come alongside her and help with this book, I was honored and speechless. Who would have ever thought—after I had been homeless and strung out just a little over 13 years ago—that God would rebuild my life to *this* extent, in the very building in which I was born? It is an absolute truth that addicted mothers who choose drugs over their children *can* rehabilitate. To show that street junkies can once again contribute in important ways to society is my mission. I hope my story, as well as those from other "Loveladies," give stigmatized women who have made terrible choices a bit of hope—just as Miss Brenda and Miss Melinda have done for me.

Jeanne Sparks Dean
Integrated Marketing Communications
The Lovelady Center
Birmingham, Alabama

Prologue

Just as an ominous clap of thunder startled me awake from a deep sleep, I heard the phone ring. It was one of those mornings that I just wanted to sink down into the bed and sleep soundly—at least until 7:00 a.m. I reached for the phone while trying to become alert. Rain was pelting against the window's glass, and the last thing I wanted was one of those dreaded morning calls telling me something bad had happened. I am an early riser by nature but had just spent the better part of the week at the beach with my son Hunter and several of my grandchildren, as well as a helper for me. My ten grandchildren had worn me out and I was thinking only of some rest. I glanced at the clock and it was 6:03. I thought, "Maybe it's a wrong number." Then a soft voice asked, "Is this Miss Brenda?"

"Never heard of her," I wanted to say, as my voice answered, "Yes, this is Miss Brenda."

At that very moment the sky rumbled. It was like God was thundering at me: *"Get up and get going! We have business to attend to!"*

"We have a young woman who has been brought in with no identification," the professional-sounding voice continued. "Your business card was in her belongings. We were hoping you might be able to help us."

I was already scrambling for my clothes when she gave me the name of a local hospital about 20 minutes away. I practically flew out the door, yelling over my shoulder at my husband, Jeff, that I had an emergency and would be right back. I heard him make some smart remark about "right," and then he made sure I knew it was storming and that the driving conditions were bad. He's always on top of the weather, and always worried about me, especially during my many emergencies.

I called my daughter Melinda and asked her to go to The Lovelady Center (where she worked with me) in case I needed information on one of our residents. I so wanted it to be someone I didn't know, but then I felt guilty, because did that really matter? There are so many lives lost in the battle with addiction. Even if this was not one of "my girls" now, there was a high probability she might be someday. As I arrived at the hospital, I was directed to the floor nurse who had called me less than 20 minutes ago.

She explained to me that a Jane Doe had been brought in, and the hospital needed information so the next of kin could be notified. She then attempted to prepare me to identify the woman in the room. She explained to me that the girl had been put on a ventilator and was already clinically brain-dead. They needed to notify the next of kin in order to obtain permission to turn off the machine. Suddenly, I heard thunder again and thought "This is not going to be good." Even then I was not prepared for what I would find in that room.

The nurse motioned me through the door, and lying on the bed was a young, beautiful girl whom I recognized immediately. "Oh, no—not *Sarah*." She had just spent that very week with me at the beach, helping me with my grandchildren. No, I did not want it to be her. She was no longer the beautiful girl who had run on the beach with my grandchildren. Her face no longer was blushed with a tan but now had the bluish-gray color of death. Her face was so swollen. The beautiful hair that she and I had just colored was in a tangled mess. The only sign of life in her was that ventilator making her lungs expand. I do not like those machines at all. They play with my mind, looking like life is still present in the body because the breathing is up and down in a perfect rhythm.

What happened? She was doing great! This just was not possible. No, no, no! I grabbed the wall for support and then exited to the waiting room to call Melinda, who would have access to the vital information the hospital needed from Sarah's client file at The Lovelady Center. I had never been in situations I found myself in now. I was not used to all the deaths I was encountering. It wasn't really just the deaths, though; it was the drama surrounding the deaths. I was an only child and lived in a home where any drama was caused by me.

As I waited on Melinda's return call, I just sat there, wet and sick at heart, trying to make sense of the senseless. The nurse walked in and asked, "What are you doing here, Miss Brenda?" In my state of mind, I misunderstood her question. I told her, "You called me." She smiled and gently asked, "I mean, why do you do what you do for all these women?" Good question! *Really* good question! Before I could respond, I had to find the answer for myself. I just sat there, looking at her, puzzled. She offered a genuine smile and turned to walk away.

At times, we find ourselves questioning our life's purpose and whether we are truly on the right path. I found myself experiencing one of those moments. I could give her my entire life story—the good, the bad, and the ugly. I could tell her I felt that this was my purpose. I could tell her that someone had to do something about what was happening in our society. I hate hopelessness, I could even tell her that. I could tell her I felt God called me to this life. All of those would be correct answers. But did even I understand why I felt the overwhelming need to help women who had lost their way on this road called life? The same women I had formerly looked upon with contempt, I now counted as my best friends. I had urged my entire family to travel this road with me. It was a highway that had heartache, unanswered questions, and occasionally death littered along the way. It was a road I felt I had to navigate, against obstacles I never could have imagined. I seemed to spend many of my days fighting someone or something along this path. I had to fight city hall, neighbors, and friends. I had to fight racism, judgment, contempt, and, many days, even the very women I cared for so much in order to help them survive. By the time I was ready to answer the question, I got my second wind and that inner determination rose up inside of me. Where was that nurse? I was ready to give her the answer.

Before I found the nurse, my phone rang. It was Melinda. Suddenly, I was very glad the nurse had asked me that question.

As I had considered the question and searched for the answer, I had gained the courage needed at that moment. Sarah was gone, but she had two children who loved their mommy. The family had to be told that their Sarah was gone, and I realized I should be the one who called Sarah's sister to give her the grim news. After I hung up with Melinda I stood there and leaned on the wall for support. Finally, I dialed Sarah's sister Susan's number and waited for an answer. When she picked up, I could tell that I had awakened her, as she sounded the same as I surely did earlier. Could that have been less than 45 minutes ago? It seemed like many hours. Time is like that: We can just waste five minutes away, or in a blink something life changing can happen, and yet it is the same amount of time. I took a deep breath and prepared myself to change Susan's life. I was as ready as I would ever be.

Have you ever imagined how horrible it would be to get that kind of phone call? We dread the possibility and hope it never becomes a reality. Susan, who had been living with both Sarah's and her father's addictions, had probably gone over this call in her mind many times. She interrupted me before I could say anything other than my name.

"What is it? What has happened to my sister?" She bellowed through the phone. I knew in my heart this phone call was the one she had feared for several years.

I broke the news to her as gently as I could, and she must have thrown the phone down. I could hear her husband as he picked it up. I recounted the tragic news to him, as Susan had fallen to the floor screaming. The husband's voice was strained, and I could hear Susan in the background telling him all the reasons why this could not be true. I just absolutely *hurt* for those people.

"We can be there in about 30 minutes," the husband said, his voice breaking as his heart broke for his wife. They had custody of Sarah's two beautiful little girls. In my mind, I pictured them learning of their mother's death, and my heart broke all over again.

"I'll wait on you here." They also asked me if there was any hope at all that she would live, and I informed them of what the doctor had said. But because of who I am and how I believe, I said that God can do anything, although it looked very grim. I envisioned sweet Sarah with that swollen head and that death look, and I was not encouraged that she might live. I could only imagine how much those little girls were going to miss their fun-loving mother. Sarah had spoken about them nonstop while at the beach and was very close to regaining custody of them. I knew that Susan was planning on that, as she and her husband were looking forward to having their own family one day.

As I waited on the couple and Sarah's children, I relived our week at the beach with *nine* children. I had chosen Sarah to go with me because she had progressed very well at The Lovelady Center and was hoping to work with our children in her new life after graduation from our program. I love being able to show my women normal, sober living, and I felt the trip could be of real benefit to her. Besides, I was looking forward to seeing her interaction with children up close and personal. As we sat on the beach, Sarah told me her life story.

She came from a family of three children. She was the middle child, made good grades in school, excelled in sports, and was just generally very bright. Her mother and daddy divorced when she was seven. Her dad struggled with addiction and was unwilling to change. She was a real daddy's girl, though, and addiction did not break that bond. She was also extremely protective of her dad. It was easy to see that she really enabled her dad just by hearing her speak about him. The entire conversation was geared toward making excuses for things he did.

Sarah married right out of high school and had two children. Shortly thereafter, Sarah had a simple female surgery and was given opioid pain pills. The door to her addiction was flung wide open. That door changed everything. In the beginning, she failed to see the effect the addiction was having on her life.

Besides causing her to divorce, it knocked her off the track to accomplishing her dreams. She had worked full-time, was a mother and wife, and was determined to obtain a degree in early childhood education. That didn't last because eventually her addiction owned her. Soon she could not even get out of bed without a pill. Her marriage was over. Drugs had begun to destroy both of them. He totally blamed her, and it was all over. After realizing and admitting she had a problem, she became determined to detox herself, cold turkey. I questioned why she felt she could do that, and she said she wanted off so badly that it was the best way. We talked about how she wanted a quick fix because she realized she could no longer function without pills, but also could no longer afford it. She was determined to get clean, be a good mother, and work with children. She wanted the life she had dreamed of having.

Sarah came up with a plan. She dropped her kids off with sister Susan, checked into a motel, and was just never going to do any more pills. She would suffer for a few days, but then it would be over. She would be clean. She took the food she would need and kept no money at all, so she couldn't buy any pills. Her plan seemed to be working. She checked in with Susan each day. By day four, she was struggling but holding on, and she had not taken her car so she couldn't leave. Her dad stopped by to check on her, and it upset him to witness his daughter in such a terrible condition. Coming off opiates is an all-consuming pain, a bad ordeal. When someone is detoxing, it is ugly to witness. It is a gut-wrenching pain. But good ol' dad had the answer! He just shot her up with heroin. Heroin was "a cheaper route for her," Dad reasoned. He told her it would keep her from hurting, it was a better high, and she could still function. That was all lies. Soon she was spending all her days looking for heroin. Trying to find the money soon turned into turning tricks. Her descent into a virtual hell on earth began. I get so enraged when I hear this kind of logic. Sarah didn't even blame him; she thought he found her a solution to her problem. She told me she would do the same if he was suffering. I guess we all love differently.

Sarah never went back to pick up her children as planned. Susan took good care of them. Sarah lost her job and dropped out of school. Addiction is a full-time job. Life became unbearable. Her new relationship with heroin consisted of only chasing the next high. Sarah's family disowned her, except her good ol' Dad, of course. Dad understood. Sarah tried a couple of half-hearted attempts at rehabilitation, but just couldn't pull herself out of the hole she was in. She had a boyfriend and she thought that she was in love. She had several arrests, and the sweet "girl next door" became the girl no one would want next door. What Sarah did find were several serious legal issues. The judge ordered her to The

Lovelady Center for help. First thing we did was stop all contact with daddy dearest and the boyfriend.

Sarah worked the program exceptionally well. She had completed nine months, was such a lovely person, and was just as pretty on the inside as the outside. As we sat on the beach, she told me all her dreams. She had hope again. I remember one night as we watched the fireworks how she told me that it reminded her of her future life. She thought she had a bright future. We spoke of so many life decisions. She knew she was only one bad decision away from disaster, as we all are.

She held tight to the dream that her dad would one day be back in her life, as well as her boyfriend. I explained to her that, for a season, they needed to all stay apart. She could never be around that lifestyle again. Addiction is like quicksand; you get freed and you better not get near it again. She explained to me that she just never could give it all up. She loved her friends and daddy and was determined to help them get clean. She wanted her life with her dad and boyfriend. She couldn't imagine living without them. Her former husband wanted nothing to do with her or the children. He was into his own hell.

"Miss Brenda, I just don't want to lose *all* of me." She explained why she could not lose everyone. She loved her family and really loved life. I explained that life with drugs was not real life at all. I walked her through her new life with her kids living with their mother. Bells went off in my head, and I really began to focus on her developing new life. We had lengthy discussions about how she had to avoid previous friends and family at all costs. That one challenge had concerned me, but Sarah assured me she understood. She told me I was taking her words out of context. She laughed, and soon we moved on to other things. I've often wondered if there was anything I could have said to keep her on the right track.

She was trying to quit smoking, and chewed bubble gum constantly. I bought her a big bucket of bubble gum to aid her in the decision.

"It's either your teeth or your lungs," I had told her. She chose to chew away the nicotine cravings. While we were at the beach, her best friend Heidi (also a Lovelady program participant) called, and she and Sarah had made plans to go out to dinner on the following Friday night after we returned home. She was to attend church and class on that Thursday night, so I found no reason to deny her that pass. Our policy is to allow our women gradual freedom as they learn to live a sober, Christian life to its fullest. Heidi was another promising client. She had great family support. Heidi's mother had even taken Sarah under her wing, somewhat. I really felt good about these young women's decision-making abilities.

That following Friday evening, the two girls did go out to dinner and ran into Sarah's boyfriend, Derrick—accidentally or not, who knows? He had a friend with him. Derrick told Sarah that he had decided to enter rehab the following Monday morning, and he suggested they have a drink for old times' sake. Heidi said that Sarah was so excited that Derrick was going to go to rehab. I hate those "for old times' sake" excuses! After the drink, why not go to a hotel *for old times' sake*? Then, when the inhibitions are lowered because of alcohol, let's do one shot *for old times' sake*. With one shot of boy (heroin) on a Friday night, you will be clean by the next day if you are drug tested, as it is our Lovelady policy to screen randomly for drugs. Derrick knew the games to play to get by with getting high. So why not? Sarah chewed that gum like crazy the whole time.

When Derrick gave Sarah the shot, being the good guy he was, he gave her the same amount as he took, so as not to be selfish, of course. She had been clean for almost a year, so that amount was too much. She fell back on the bed while he went to the bathroom, and she began gagging on the gum that had become lodged in her throat when the high hit her. She was choking in a room full of people, with no one to help her because they were all too high. When they finally recognized that she was dying, they took off down the street and dialed 911. She was deprived of oxygen to her brain for a while. Heidi, the best friend, even took Sarah's purse with her, so as not to leave any identification in the room. She was scared and didn't want to get into trouble. "Good guy" Derrick left his "true love" alone to die.

We knew Heidi had been with her, and we needed to find her. We learned the entire story from Heidi. She felt ashamed and guilt-ridden. Heidi's mother was devastated. The death was investigated, but authorities decided to forgo charges against Heidi or Derrick. Nonetheless, Heidi was consumed with guilt and determined to seek out her former way of escape. She left our program. We reassured her that Sarah had been responsible for her own decisions, as we all are. I always say, "Any one of us is one decision away from disaster."

Susan walked into the hospital waiting room a complete wreck. Her husband and both children accompanied her. I must have looked shocked and totally unprepared. Susan said she wanted the children to see their mother one last time. I suggested she first go in and talk to the nurse and I would sit with the children. She took my suggestion. I could not bear the thought of those innocent children seeing their mother like Sarah was. My heart was breaking with all of it.

I made small talk with the 5- and 4-year-olds. Of course, I now have no idea what I said. I heard a faint scream and knew that meant Sarah was unplugged and had passed away. I could still hear the thunder. I felt God's sorrow and thought maybe the rain was His tears that day. I silently prayed, "I feel the same way, Lord."

That was in 2007 and is just the story of one Lovelady. There have been thousands. Thank God, most do not end in death. However, some do. The story of Sarah has haunted me for many years and for several reasons. I wish I had never bought that bubble gum. That said, the shot alone probably would have killed her and if I hadn't bought her the bubble gum, she would have just bought it herself. I wish I had not let her go on pass. If only I could have said something to stop her from wanting to be with Derrick. If only this, if only that. I just hate that this happened. This death had a profound impact on me. It was difficult to even tell my grandchildren, because they had really enjoyed being with Sarah. I find myself tearing up even writing about this. But life goes on, and there have been thousands of great stories to balance my heart.

The mountain that had to be climbed at the beginning of our ministry has been so high but so worth it. We've witnessed and experienced really hard times, but the miracles we see far outweigh the difficult scenes we face. However, in the beginning, even finding a place to house our troubled women seemed impossible. But God does the impossible every day if we get out of His way and allow Him to.

Introduction

> "How wonderful it is that nobody need wait a single moment before starting to improve the world."
> —Anne Frank

How in the world did this happen? How did you ever pull this Lovelady Center thing together? If I was on the outside looking in, I would ask the exact same thing. It is similar to someone asking for directions and when you pause to think about it, you suddenly have to say, "Well, you can't get there from *here*. You'll have to go all the way around, *that* way." That's us. The story of The Lovelady Center seems like an impossible, uncharted climb. That is how God works. He uses someone so insignificant in the scheme of things, equips them with what they need to do the job, and leaves them with no doubt whatsoever that it could not have come together without Him right in the middle of it.

I chased what I once deemed "success" for most of my life. And success to me was having all the material things and money that a driven person could possibly make. So when the IRS knocked, or more truthfully *barged in* like a tornado through the front door, I had been content with life. I had been totally content, driving down life's highway, gathering all the material things just as quickly as I could. And I am a fast driver! I had no idea back then that His equipping us had begun.

Dr. Brenda Lovelady Spahn

It was the very end of tax season when I pulled up to my office and saw the front of the building covered with agents who had guns drawn. I told my friend who worked with me for over 20 years and had pulled into the parking lot about the same time, "Oh my goodness, Joy! We must've been *robbed!*"

"It's okay, it's okay," I reassured the agents as I approached them from the parking lot. *"I own the office."* I was walking toward them with deliberate strides—my power walk, if you will—taking control of the situation and shuffling the keyring in my hand. They looked at me like I had four heads and told me, "Brenda, it's *you* we are looking for!" In that confusing moment, and the fact they called me by my first name, I felt a terror I had never felt before. *Surely there's been some mistake!*

My family and I prided ourselves in working toward the American dream. Part of that dream included becoming the largest tax business in the Southeast. We had completed well over 15,000 tax returns that year and were well on our way to becoming what we deemed to be pillars of the community. And we ran a tight ship.

"There has to be some *mistake*," I offered, now trembling as I tried to unlock the door with a wobbly hand. The IRS Criminal Investigation Department (CID) Agent, accompanied by FBI agents, rather loudly exclaimed that there was "absolutely no mistake, *Brenda*," again with just my first name because they apparently had been studying me enough to be casual with the salutations. Let me tell you, when that happens, a fear rises in you that just cannot be explained. As I fumbled with the key, I was commanded to "GET BACK, NOW!" and I complied. One split second later, a battering ram opened the door to my lovely office, and shakingly, all I could muster was *"Hey!"*

They commenced tearing my beautiful, well-kept office to shreds. If you have ever heard that an IRS raid is terrible, *believe it*. I really did not think anything we had done all the years we had been in business actually warranted this from them. They were so *mean*. They wondered why the garbage cans were all empty. They went through my refrigerator. They took *everything* and left my beautiful office in complete shambles. What on earth were they looking for? I immediately felt like a loathsome career criminal.

Dirty. Hated. Some agents were cruel with their treatment of us; others were kind and acted like they knew this raid was going nowhere.

One of our tax clients had told all manner of lies in order to get himself out of trouble with the IRS and throw someone else into the fire. A whistleblower of sorts. Looking back, I call it *God moving me to the place He had called me for many years anyway.* He took a horrible mess and used it for His glory.

I had the very best criminal attorney in Birmingham. He was a good friend, and I just *knew* he could get us out of our problem. He thought it was insane the way our family had been targeted, and I knew he was going to protect us during this mess. I know where I was the moment I received the devastating news that he had died: I was standing in a store, and I can still show you the exact spot where I was standing when the phone rang. We remember where we were when we heard President Kennedy was shot or where we were when the Twin Towers collapsed. Tragic news makes such a heavy impression on us. It was like that for me when I received the call telling me my good friend, the best criminal attorney in Birmingham, had died.

My sweet Melinda was pregnant at the time we received the devastating news and was terrified at the thought of going to prison. I have to admit, so was I. So, without the attorney I so depended on to end this chapter, I offered a guilty plea for unreported taxes on two clients, as well as failure to supervise. "Just get this thing over with, Mother, please," Melinda begged. By the time it was over, I probably would have pleaded guilty to just about anything to finish the chapter and turn the page of that book.

There comes a time in all of our lives when we have to decide whom we serve. If we are really honest, we discover it is ourselves. Aren't most of us that way? We want to stay within our self-defined boundaries, remain comfortable, and continue on our chosen path, never rocking the boat. We hope nothing ever pushes us off in an uncomfortable direction. That had been me, through and through. And I settled in and did what I felt was necessary to maintain a Christian life. As I went about my way, I made sure I kept a respectable distance from God because I had my own plans. I didn't tell God that; after all, we all say we know He is in control. When I was a little girl, my daddy would say, "Action speaks louder than words." That applied to me with God. I said one thing, but acted on another.

So when I finally decided to serve God with all that I had in me, I embraced the very thing I never would have planned on doing, to serve Him by serving hurting women who had no hope and no future. That is why I pleaded guilty—I felt that was His way. I wanted it over. "If you get us out of this, Lord, I will serve you the rest of my life." I prayed that over and over. I was given probation and had to wear an ankle monitor for a few months. Wearing that thing mortified Melinda, but it did not bother me at all. If I was out and saw anyone I knew, I showed them my ankle monitor. I went about my business and never even worried about me. Tax preparers would ask so many questions, and I knew that they all had been guilty of allowing people to give them information. We all had. I allowed myself to be the one who just might be an example of being more careful how they got the information on returns. I hoped so anyway.

Melinda and I were actually wearing ankle monitors when we were allowed to enter the work release program and minister. My mind and thoughts were even more consumed with the women in those days because they received devastating news routinely, and not just about how their lives and freedoms were always controlled by others. Some lost loved ones while locked up. The guilt and devastation just went on and on for them. I thought about how scary that would be. I thought about the choices they made that landed them in prison. I could have been one of them! I could have been in one of those uniforms with no hope in my eyes!

Their past mistakes and choices had defined who they were up until a certain point. Someone needed to step in and help countless women who had been confined in prisons, jails, and bondage. I had arrived at a point in my life where I just knew that if I did not heed the call I felt so strongly about, I never could be fulfilled in who God had created and called me to be. *And I had promised Him.* And He had delivered.

When the ministry was formed in 2004, I soon recognized ministering to the women locked up was not where I believe God was leading me. Oh, I loved ministering the way that Melinda and

I had grown used to—just praying and uplifting the women and then going about our way. After I left the work release center in Birmingham, I would stop and get a chicken snack and drive home as free as a bird. However, I felt He was leading me to minister to the women who had nowhere to go *because* they were no longer locked up in prison. I had learned that when a woman is released from prison, they seem to return back to incarceration quicker than you can blink an eye. They do not have a buffer that helps them make it on their own without crime, or that need to escape reality in some form.

I visited halfway houses and wanted to volunteer to mentor their female residents. But then I realized that was not what God had in mind. Someone had to minister to them up close and personal. I knew in my heart that someone was me.

We began our journey in our family home, on nine acres at the end of a road called Hob Hill. My original intentions were to house a few women who had been released on parole from prison—bad-check writers or maybe nonviolent bad-choice makers. *I had boundaries on whom we would serve, you see.* I even *asked* for those type offenders. I thought back to the halfway houses I had previously visited and decided "halfway" was not good enough. Instead, we decided to take it the "whole way." When the first women got off the Alabama Department of Corrections van in October of 2004, I was actually shocked to see what the parole board decided to send me.

"*Mother,*" Melinda had whispered to me as they were settling in, "these women are *violent*. We have *murderers* here." Indeed, their case files held the histories of women deemed unreachable. "Unable to rehabilitate." My goodness, surely there was a mistake. No, they assured me, these were mine to see just what I could do. I knew this was a major test and everyone was looking for Miss Brenda to fail. That was who I had become known as.

Even as I write this second book, I read what I have written and I am in awe that I listened to God and did it. There were days when I thought, "This is how Noah must have had faith because this is *crazy*," and I would find strength in that. I cannot express to you how thankful I am. The Department of Corrections (DOC) sent them, and we took them. I remember thinking, "How easy was that, to have pleaded with the State and be allowed to have a few women come live in my home and learn to live a new life?" That is when I found out it wasn't quite as easy as I thought. What I did not know is they sent me hard-core criminals to deter me and teach me a lesson that they thought I needed. However, that, in itself, was a miracle from God, because normally they will not send women out like that. So seven female inmates from Julia Tutwiler Prison for Women in Wetumpka, Alabama, were allowed to come live in my home with me. Six arrived by van that morning, and one more was delivered from the work release center in Birmingham.

I had a complete staff hired who were going to do the daily work. My idea was not to get my hands *too* dirty, just enough to know I was doing His will. I would set up the program and let it thrive through a paid staff. God would show me what He wanted me to do, and off I would run, doing it the Brenda way. So what happened? Every single one of the staff quit when my "girls" arrived and they got a good look at them. The people who "God had called" to work with former inmates got out of there as fast as they could, fearing for their lives. Granted, they looked scary, even to me. The first one off the van was a fearless bald woman ready to whip butt. Her name was Shay, and she was the ringleader of the group, telling the others that DOC would not take them out of prison and put them in a mansion. She thought she had it all figured out for herself and all the others. She was convinced they were all at my home to be maids to the rich white lady. Problem was I wasn't rich and she did not have it all figured out. DOC sending Shay to us was probably the most awesome gift anyone could ever give me. She and I became best friends. We were inseparable for so many years. She gave us an education that no amount of money could buy and gave me the sister I never had. You will read much more about our friendship in this book. My hope is that it encourages you to be open to new people you might not be open to at first. You never know what might lay in store for you.

We all just stared at each other. I saw immediately they didn't have a clue as to what I was trying to do, and they were right! I didn't have a clue. I had to come up with something. I saw immediately they had no real hope for their future but there were glimmers happening because they were just set free from one of the most dangerous prisons in the nation. But the felons I had *hoped* for were not found among "my girls" who arrived that day. There were murder charges, drug charges, theft charges, drug distribution and trafficking charges, assault charges, and other charges that shocked me. Those seven had a total of 124 years of prison time. I find myself still thinking about all those wasted years.

Melinda and I stood right together and gave them a welcome I did not feel. While everyone else said, "You are crazy, and this 'whole-way house' of yours is even crazier," Melinda said, "I don't know where you're going with this, Mother, but I am with you all the way." It reminds me of the story of Ruth and Naomi. It seemed my people were women discarded by society, and they immediately became Melinda's people too. The beginning of the ministry that is now The Lovelady Center is told in the book *Miss Brenda and the Loveladies*, by myself and Irene Zutell. The book details just how high the mountain was as we stood at the base looking up, along with the women who had no hope of climbing it anyway. It turned out to be much higher of a mountain than anyone thought it was going to be. And even knowing now how high that mountain was back then, I am sure I would climb it all over again. But some things are better learned as you go instead of their being unfolded before you from the start.

Originally, we served only women newly released from prison. Now we have opened our doors to all manner of troubled women. We offer hope, we meet physical needs, we educate, we rehabilitate, and mostly (and most importantly) we *love*. We love as unconditionally as we possibly can, God helping us. Our first and foremost plan is for every woman to see herself as God intended, to call herself as God sees her, and not to let her past define her.

I used to feel uncomfortable around troubled people. As a matter of fact, I would avoid looking them in the eye. Now I love them. Now they are my best friends. When I see a hurting person on the street while I am out in the community, I am instantly concerned for them. I say prayers for them. I stop and talk to them with no embarrassment. I have learned love is the bridge to hope. Hopeless women are given the opportunity to dream and hope again at The Lovelady Center.

We have women at the Center who have never had any opportunity in life, and we have women who have been handed every opportunity but somehow thwarted it. We have women who have turned to drugs to escape deep childhood scars and trauma, and women who began rebelling at a young age and never stopped until they found who they were in Him. I do not have all the answers for sure, but together, we search for them, find them, and introduce the women to the Only Way to complete wholeness, Jesus Christ. You may not believe in faith-based treatment. That's ok! You may believe other forms of treatment are better. We respect your opinions. But as for our Whole-Way House, we will serve the Lord. That is not to say that a woman must have a relationship with Jesus in order to complete the program. But she will be introduced to Him while in our program. We love no matter what she chooses. The most important thing is that she is free to choose.

When I first felt led to serve these women, I had no idea what to do. There are days when I still have no idea, but I do know this: *Doing nothing is not acceptable for me.* Melinda has skills that I lack. I have a vision. But a visionary can also be a dangerous person. Indeed, a visionary without boundaries can get out of control very quickly. Melinda is kind of like my boundary keeper. We also have a staff who are unsurpassed in dedication to leading these women out of addiction and crime. And they have skills that she and I both lack.

The Lovelady Center has become a beacon of light to lost women. Do we always get the results we seek? Absolutely not. Our yardstick for success is significantly longer than other rehabilitation centers. We do not count someone as successful unless they have completed our nine-to-twelve-month intensive residential program, have obtained employment, have made amends with their family or have regained custody of their children or are in good standing with them, have rectified all legal issues, have a solid transportation plan, have moved out of the Center, and have a relationship with Jesus Christ. People wonder what motivates us or what our drive is to take calls at 2 a.m., to sort through drama all day or to hear the most hideous stories of abuse that leave us sad and depressed. It is this: the changed lives. I *love* to see what God does!

Miss Brenda and the Lovelady Movement

Hugs are everywhere in the Center. Often, we hear people say that when they enter our door, they feel a real sense of the love we have for our clients. Most of our staff have been hired after graduating from The Lovelady Center. Occasionally, someone will forget their past and how far they have come from where they used to be and forget to give a new woman the benefit of the doubt. We promptly remind them who they used to be so they will not miss the opportunity to share their love and growth with others. It's called life experience. Some people are just more equipped in certain areas. That old saying about walking in another's shoes makes all the difference with our ladies, and 97% of our staff can say that they have "been there" when shown a problem a woman or, in many cases, her child, faces.

I have been asked, "When are you writing the second book?" referring to *Miss Brenda and the Loveladies* as the first. I have decided now is the time. But then the dilemma was to decide which stories—of the thousands—should be told. When cancer survivors hit the five-year remission mark, it is a great milestone. That means that 90 percent are still alive and in remission. I have used that same milestone gauge for every success story in this book. However, I decided to include some stories that are not successful. They are the hard truth of addiction and crime. Thank goodness we don't see many, but I wanted you as a reader to walk along with me and see the hard realities I see. I truly view every woman who allows us to assist her in changing her life as a miracle. We have bulletin boards in the Center aptly called "the Prisoner to Princess Board." When I am despondent, I will go look at those photos. They are created by using a picture taken upon arrival at the Center or the "before" recovery life, and a picture upon graduation, or the "after." Some of the "befores" are mugshots. Sometimes these pictures are almost unrecognizable compared to the vibrance shown in the "after" photos. Other stories are in this book that have just *impacted* me. They might not be "successful," but for one reason or another, I feel it might benefit you to read them, and may awaken a new understanding for "*those women.*" When you see what God can accomplish with the broken and what the broken can accomplish with God when trust is put in Him, you enter the land of the miraculous. Thank you for taking this journey with me.

Dreamers

"The world needs dreamers and the world needs doers. But above all, the world needs dreamers who do."
—Sarah Ban Breathnach

"Mom, this is borderline insanity! *Have you lost your mind?*" my sweet little sidekick asked, staring at me with her blue eyes open wide.

"No, Melinda, it's not insanity. I believe this is what God has for us," I answered, as nicely as I could. I will be honest, though, when things are not going just how I want them to or when I feel there is going to be lots of pushback, I tend to get a tad bit testy.

Knowing just how I could convince her, I said, "Do you have any idea how many lives could be changed in a place like this? Oh, my goodness, Melinda, just think!" In my mind, I had already moved into the building and was so excited I was practically jumping around. In actuality, the city had just evicted our program of 40 women from Hob Hill, our personal home on nine acres that I had incorrectly thought would be perfect for our Lovelady whole-way program. Now I assured Melinda that it wasn't insanity, standing in front of a huge, worn-down hospital that I neither could afford nor had the money to keep maintaining. However, I knew it could house hundreds of women at a time, and our plan had been never to have over 40 at any given time. So I was really not understanding my inward desire to have the building in front of us. Even just writing this I sound like a completely crazed person. But read on—don't judge me quite yet.

Miss Brenda and the Lovelady Movement

Now the "leader" of the first 40 women, Shay, stood beside me looking at me with that wide-eyed look that I had come to love. Shay had been the first woman to walk through the doors at Hob Hill. At that time, Shay had been a hardened-looking woman with steely eyes and a sneer and was almost completely bald. But the last year had given her an unbelievable transformation. She had gone from not even talking to me to sharing her innermost secrets with me daily. She was my best friend. Many times, when I looked at her, my eyes filled with tears when I remembered the horrible abuse she endured in her childhood and adult life.

And Shay knew there were 39 more women tucked away in our rental houses that could be sent back to Julia Tutwiler Prison any day if we did not find an answer to our problem. The city had decided that we were in zoning violation of the house. The code said no more than three unrelated people in one residence. There is no magic number if they are related, but even I couldn't find a way to make it work at Hob Hill. Tutwiler, the only prison for women in Alabama, was noted for being the worst and most dangerous women's prisons in the United States. And having the women be sent back to that horrendous place would have me looking crazy too, I had to admit. There were so many lives at risk, and I had no plan. This really was not borderline insanity; it sounded completely insane. But *was* it?

Melinda knew I felt God was leading me in this direction. The thing about my daughter is that she has the biggest heart of anyone I know, built for ministry and the changing of lives through introducing them to Jesus. We had begun the program with seven women, six being straight out of Tutwiler. The program had grown to over 40 women seemingly overnight. It had been an overwhelming success—so much so that it was gaining recognition. The recognition had brought attention, which brought our neighbors to know we all were there, and those neighbors got on the city and, well, you probably can figure it all out. Pretty soon, our great program was under attack and we were fighting a losing battle on zoning. We had to find another location or close. Closing meant sending all "our women" back to Tutwiler. The problems just mounted. Everyone was looking to Ms. Brenda, that's me, for a solution.

"I thought you found a small building over here to house the women. You said you never wanted to have over 40 women at a time. Don't you remember that at all? Isn't *that* the building you had in mind?" Melinda waved her arm in the air toward the teeny building I had already decided was not what God had for us.

"Please don't bog us down with those little ideas, Melinda. I had been tired and not seeing the big picture." What had I been thinking? That *teeny* building? I looked at the building she was pointing to across the street, and the truth was that *was* the building I had discovered and had come to visit. The real estate agent had told me to go to the big empty hospital across the street to obtain the keys to that small, reasonable building. He said a security guard would let me in and give me the keys.

So, as I stood there waiting for him to go get the keys to the small, reasonable building, I realized I had been led to the big, empty hospital that took up the entire block. What was *wrong* with me? I knew my husband and my family would surely be upset with me, to put it lightly. They would be so angry. They already believed housing the women in our home was crazy. My son, Beau, had just asked me that week, "Why don't you just retire and maybe rock your grandchildren or something?" I told Beau I could rock my grandchildren while I taught the women and I had been doing just that. But I had a burning desire to serve God, and I honestly believed the old worn-down hospital seemed to be where He was leading me.

The old East End Memorial Hospital had been a beloved piece of community history. Everyone in Birmingham knew someone who had been born there. It easily spanned a city block with 280,000 square feet and hundreds of rooms, an industrial kitchen, and an atrium with beautiful skylights that let in sunshine like the light of Jesus. The historic landmark had been an active hospital until the early eighties and had been rebuilt in a more urban area to become the new East End Memorial. The one we stood before had become a nursing home/assisted living still owned by St. Vincent's Health Systems. St. Vincent's was in the process of selling off its outlying properties as well as the old hospital. The nursing home had moved, and the hospice operation near the emergency room was in the process of moving that very day. St. Vincent's was buying the newer East End Memorial a few miles away and up the road from Hob Hill, and it would be St. Vincent's East. St. Vincent's was growing. Founded in 1898, it is Birmingham's oldest hospital and second in size to the University of Alabama in Birmingham (UAB).

People call it intuition, destiny, fate . . . I call it *God*, pure and simple. Every hair on my neck stood on end as my mind grasped the possibilities! I knew in my heart of hearts that this old, worn-out building was part of the plan the Lord had for us.

My husband, Jeff, just listened intently as we spoke about it. Melinda's twin brother, Matthew, came and looked at it and seemed to buy into the idea. He's a dreamer and visionary like his mom, so nothing really surprises him where his or my *vision* is concerned.

"Where do you plan to get the money for this little venture of yours?" Jeff asked me in a sarcastic tone. I asked him to go speak with the owner of the big, empty hospital and just ask him that if I gave him a decent deposit, would he hold it for me?

"Why, I bet they would just *give* us this old building," I added, and watched them all roll their eyes. I then promised everyone that if God didn't open the door for the purchase, I would drop it. I just kept thinking, "They should just give it to us."

I knew with my entire being this was where the Lord was planting us. When I was a little girl, I used to pretend I lived in a big, beautiful castle, when in fact I had lived in a small travel trailer. This building was certainly big but not so beautiful—yet. I did not see the building as old and worn; I saw it in its grandeur of yesterday, and its possibility for the future. I was already building and changing it in my mind. At that moment, Solomon's Temple could not have been grander in my eyes.

"Just please go get it under contract," I said as I was calculating how much down payment they'd want, what the payments would be, and a list of other concerns with my castle purchase. In my mind, I still believed they would just give it to us "to change thousands of lives. I wish they could see just what it could do for the city and just give it to us." "Just stop it, Brenda. They don't need the write-off and are not going to give you the building." But I was building up the sales pitch. Jeff had known me for so many years and had been with me through many of my dreams in business before we married. He knew I thought we would be given the old hospital. I was building the arguments in my head. "It's just sitting there wasting away. No one else would ever want it. It's in a bad area. Repairs are too expensive." My list was growing longer by the minute, and without my realizing it, so were the obstacles. The mountain was so high even I questioned if it could be climbed. And yet, I believed this is where we were headed. My faith was going to have to rise to the height of the obstacle.

Jeff came home the next day from visiting the hospital board. "Did they give it to us?" I could tell when I asked the question that it irritated Jeff, so I shut right up. "No," he said, "but I do have your contract." I jumped up and ran to hug him and thank him. I realized he had worked hard for that contract. And the price seemed reasonable to me at $1,240,000. We had to put $40,000 earnest money down and close in 90 days. I thought that was excellent. Now all I had to do was come up with one million, two hundred thousand dollars in 90 days. I had a whole 90 days and a whopping $40,000 to my name. My stomach was churning as I was considering what I was already saying. But wait! I wasn't in this by myself—*other believers would help me!*

Alabama is right smack in the middle of the Bible Belt with so many believers! I just *knew* raising the funds for such a needed women's ministry should be a piece of cake. I couldn't wait to get to the phone and begin calling everyone I knew and describing the wonderful ministry they could be as big a part of as they wanted. They would be so excited to help all of these hurting women who came out of that dreadful prison!

"Hang on, Honey, you know not everyone is going to be as excited as you. They're not just sitting around waiting for you to ask for their hard-earned money, standing there with their checkbooks in hand, waiting on someone to come along. They might not be all warm and fuzzy about helping your *prison women*."

"Oh ye of little faith," I answered Jeff. "Birmingham churches are going to be so excited to help us help these poor women leave their pasts behind them and move forward into a stable future!" I said it without allowing a shred of doubt in my mind. "They will become assets, not drains on society!"

"You don't have to sell me on this, Brenda. I'm right here with you! You're just preaching to the choir, now!" Jeff boomed. I knew that, too, and I guess I was just practicing the points I wanted to make.

I was off and running, never being able to gauge correctly the mountain I had to climb. I was thinking it would be a small little hill. In reality, I was standing at the bottom of Mount Everest, and as it turned out, I was the only one really excited to start climbing. The first thing I did was begin calling churches to see who might want to help me make a difference in these women's lives. After three days of calling, I did not have a line of pastors backing up the street waiting to give like I thought I would. After all, isn't Matthew 40 all about helping the least of these? I convinced several pastors to come take a tour. I had friends visit me, and got them to talk their pastors into taking a quick little tour of our life-changing building.

Well, those wonderful pastors came and those wonderful pastors went. I was so prepared for the tours of the building and was so excited to walk them around and cast the vision. One day I asked the pastor of the largest church at the time to give me just 15 minutes to walk around the facility. I saw him come through the door and he already had a big frown practically covering his whole face. I stepped right up there with my practiced speech about what God wanted and how our mission had to be for the poor, sick, unclothed, *and* the people in prison. He looked at me like I had four heads. However, I was not to be deterred. I led him all around.

Once in a while, I would see a little mouse out of the corner of my eye, or at least *hoped* it was a little mouse, rather than a big rat. I would quickly say something and catch his eye so he might not notice it. I had become very good at getting the attention to eye level. When we got to the old emergency room, I relayed my vision for the Childcare Services for our future graduates. It was to be a money-making area. There were desks all around, and I was trying to climb over them to turn on the lights for him to see better, even though he didn't seem to want to see better at all. Just when I moved a desk, a mouse ran right in front of his feet and I assure you he saw *that* one. You would have thought Bigfoot had just appeared and growled "Boo!" Before I could even turn on the lights, he took off down the hall like a bullet shot out of a gun.

Back then I could still run, but there was no catching him. Just as he was almost to the door, he turned and said, "Brenda, this is the craziest thing I have ever heard. You cannot just put a load of women in this building. You have already upset the neighborhood where you live, and I don't see how you possibly think *this* will work any better." The truth was, he was correct. I had to fight the neighbors surrounding the nine acres of Hob Hill, and it had not worked to have our program there. I never wanted to have to move our program somewhere else. I was perfectly content with what God had already done. But I had the answer to the neighborhood zoning issues. No *way* that would bite me again, right?

"Well," I shot back, "if not the churches, who will help these women ever change? Is there no hope for them? They have *nothing* when they are released after serving their time, and when they go home, they *still* have nothing but the same old stuff that got them into trouble in the first place!" I realized I had raised my voice and followed him out the door. "A community to teach skills that they have somehow missed or had never even been taught is a *must* for them! I minister to these women every day, and they deserve so much more than what they have and even more than what I have to offer! They need people like you and your congregation to come alongside. We have to do this, or *someone* does; it is our mandate as Believers." I just rambled on and on as I followed him out of the building down the sidewalk. I felt my eyes tearing up. "Lord, why are you driving me to do this? I just got my credibility back from that stupid raid and now here I go again," I mumbled to myself as my heart was breaking for our women, my daughter, and myself even if I didn't want to admit it.

"Lots of luck with your endeavor, but we are *not* interested. You are always welcome to attend our church," he said. With that, he opened his car door and got in. I just stood there to see if he might look back. I was still standing there when he pulled away. He never even glanced back. The truth was he was right in telling me that. I know that now. I had felt the same way until the Lord pulled me in this direction. Back then, though, I was just desperately seeking help because I did not know which way to turn and which direction to go.

The older guy who worked for the hospital as security watched my walk of defeat. As I entered the door to come back in, he felt the need to tell me, "He sure didn't stay long, did he?"

"No, he didn't; thanks for noticing," I said under my breath. It wasn't his fault the pastor did not have a big vision for women in trouble. I took a deep breath and did my best to get in a better frame of mind.

But I will admit that visit did take me back a bit. I went home with a long face. I really hated to tell Jeff and Melinda that it just wasn't a good fit, that it just wasn't exactly what we were looking for, that we simply needed to find out what God had for us. They pressed me for more information, but I just held it to myself.

We had scattered all the women out to the various rental houses Jeff and I owned, and they were always waiting with hope for me to tell them that everything was going to be fine. A few still lived with Melinda. They were so excited about the new building and were calling to see how the visit went. We had all been praying about the giant castle that they were so excited about moving into. To say we were disappointed was an understatement. In addition to the letdown and worry, Jeff was on my butt about no rent coming in from the rental houses that the women were now occupying. How was I ever going to tell Melinda that this was falling through? She believed everything would be fine because I said so. But I was beginning to understand that this was so far out of my realm. I just needed to go somewhere and throw up. Every mother who has ever given their child hope should understand the responsibility that then comes with it.

I can tell you this: I was just *not feeling it* that evening. I feigned a headache and went to bed, ready to curl up under the covers and escape the reality of the disappointing day. As Scarlett O'Hara says in *Gone with the Wind*, "I can't think about that right now. If I do, I will go crazy. I'll think about that tomorrow. Tomorrow is another day."

All I had to do was find my $1,200,000. The Lord had it somewhere—I just needed to find it.

"Tomorrow will be better," I decided, pulling the covers up to my neck. Thunderstorms were coming in, and I wanted to check the weather.

Storms Brewing

"If you want to enjoy the rainbow, be prepared to endure the storm."
—Warren W. Wiersbe

Have you ever noticed people will remind you of things you already know? It suddenly stings, like a thorn in your foot. Sometimes I think my husband reminds me of things just to aggravate me. "Brenda, I know you don't want to hear this, but the contract with the hospital is running out in a few weeks."

"You are right, I *don't* want to hear it. So just don't say it again." As if I wasn't already keeping up with that date like the countdown on New Year's Eve at Times Square! As far as the building, had I just missed God on that and it was time to own my mistake? Perhaps He really had intended that little building across the street to be our new home. At some point in your life, you have to face reality. If everyone is going south and you pass them going north, it may be that you are going in the wrong direction. Living by faith is a slippery slope, indeed. There is no wiggle room for error, especially if you are doing something out of the ordinary.

We were 55 days into the 90-day contract for the purchase of the building, and I was no closer to having the money than the day Jeff brought the contract home. He was trying to make sure I knew what time it was on the clock of my life's goal. Realistically, I was no closer to my goal, but in my mind I was almost there. Sometimes I have a way of walking confidently into something that has yet to happen, as if it already has. But I did know what time it was—*every hour, every minute, and every second.* It was a loud ticking in my mind as the hands moved to the next number.

After about three of my "grand tours," I knew I was going to have to spend more time at our new "home." I called and spoke to the man who had signed the contract with Jeff. I asked him if I could move my office into the building. There was a gift shop enclosed in glass in the very front of the hospital. It was close to the front door, and it had a good view of the important areas of the building.

"Why don't I just save us both some time and tell you to go ahead and move your office in, because I know in the long run I will say yes." I merely told him "Thank you," completely ignoring that he might have been sarcastic. So I was allowed to convert the former gift shop into my new office space.

I went to an office-supply store and bought just what I needed. They have these giant notepads that have sticky glue at the top, like someone would use in a presentation. They are just like those little yellow sticky notes, but are gigantic. I bought several of those and an easel. I began coming up with a ministry plan. I would write my ideas on the pad. I would tear off that page and stick it up on the wall so that I was surrounded by my plan. Everyone who came in could see what was going on and I stuck them up everywhere, so I could show my plan to anyone who might be interested.

When I know God is moving in something, like this big, beautiful hospital just waiting to be filled with women needing a second chance at life, I am *relentless* until I get it done. However, I was sailing on uncharted waters. I can only imagine how settlers felt going to California and not knowing what would happen to them. I prayed and prayed for direction and just hoped I was getting *some* of it right. I thought, "If only I could find a single ministry that was even similar to what we are trying to do!" I even met with several local rehabilitation programs, and to my great surprise, *they suggested I drop my plans.* I felt just like those settlers. I encountered opposition all around me, everywhere I turned. The really hard thing is standing alone and feeling so lonely. Melinda was always with me, but she's my daughter and we were partners in this endeavor. If there was any reluctance on her part, she never told me. When I was feeling lost with no hope, I would think about the many lives that could be changed. I moved my personal office from our office building into that grimy little gift shop. Though I cleaned it until it was spotless, I felt like I had gone from my nice, good-smelling office to a dungeon. Even so, my excitement was overwhelming. The huge sticky pads glowed against the dreariness of the space—and I just loved it!

Everyone tried to talk me out of moving my "headquarters," but I guess I was plotting out my territory like those settlers. My thinking was sort of like the pioneer days where homesteading meant that land was claimed by simply moving onto it and planting a flag: "*Claimed!*" I just moved onto the property, never intending to leave. In my mind, moving there would make it ours.

There I was, day-in and day-out, sitting in that little glass shop, running our ministry just like I ran things in my old office. I filled those big, yellow, sticky notepads with plans about how many women could be housed in the building and on which floors, where classrooms could be located, program information, projection of income, accounts payable, and anything else I could think of. It just went on and on. I taped the plans of the rooms of the hospital on the glass alongside the plan, and I would use little pink sticky pads to dictate how a room might be utilized. Pink sticky notes for girls' rooms and yellow for administration. With all the things being accomplished, it surprised me that those colored sticky notes seemed to cause the most curiosity.

People would come visit me or see me about other business matters and I would give them the grand tour like I already owned the place. Sometimes I would get lonely and sometimes I would even get a little scared in that big, old place. The guard was there with me, constantly asking me questions and eventually joining me in the countdown. I think he felt sorry for me. He said he had never met anyone like me, and I don't think he meant it as a compliment. Most of the time he didn't believe we could pull off the closing, and that was a realistic assessment—it *would* take a miracle. I would give him a little pep talk and I could see that shine in his eyes. He did so want to believe. I told him he would have a job when we closed on the property and the building became ours. After all, he knew every maintenance person and would be so much help, especially in heading up security at the building. He had worked in the building for over 40 years, and it was home to him. He had been very upset when the hospital staff moved to a new location. They had left him to protect the building. The thought that "his" building might have a new tenant was refreshing to him, although he did admit to me that he wasn't keen on the future residents. I laughed and told him to think of it like a hospital for troubled women. That seemed to make him feel better.

One day I decided to go into every single room. That morning I expressed that desire to Jeff and asked if he wanted to meet me and have a look. I had seen most everything but had not made a point of covering the building in its entirety, every nook and cranny. I had limited the tours to the grand areas and avoided what would be the women's rooms and communal areas. Jeff was already irritated with me for moving my office over to the building. He felt it might be dangerous, and everyone agreed with him. To say they felt it might be a bit premature is a vast understatement. "You never know who might have made themselves a home there," he warned me. "Oh, Jeff, don't be silly," I fired back. "There's a security guard, and no one would dare come into the building." After a quick stop in my office, I took off solo like a hunter going on safari. I even took a snack, a drink, my flashlight, and, of course, my cell phone. It was like I was going on a picnic into a temperature-controlled unknown. I was ready for action.

I started on the fourth floor, which actually spans only half the area of the building that the other floors do and has about 35 rooms. When the hospital was expanded, the doctors added that floor for their wealthy patients. I kept thinking about how I was putting women who had been in trouble in those rooms now and how Jesus probably liked that. I know I sure did. I've always been for the downtrodden, the ones whom others chose to ignore, the ones who needed to learn how to live a new life. I knew I was going to spend a great deal of time at the hospital when we finally did move in. I chose a really nice corner room for my family and me. With a great balcony and a little area where I could talk to a client in private, it was as good as I could hope for in the building. I was excited.

Dr. Brenda Lovelady Spahn

On to the next floor! The third floor had some former surgical rooms, and let me tell you, they were *more* than a little creepy. I talked to the Lord a good bit weaving through those areas. I went into room after room where people had faced hard times and hard choices, usually with their families waiting only a short distance away, dreading hard news, facing heart-wrenching pain, moving on to the next life. As I navigated my way through those rooms, I thought of our clients and the new lives I prayed they would find within those walls. I was excited for them and would be praying my heart out for the clients and changing lives, and then reality would hit me right between the eyes and I would breathe a big, almost overwhelming sigh of fear. Such an emotional roller coaster I found myself on. I would just put one foot in front of the other, hoping I did not break a leg stepping into the hole I was digging.

I went to all the rooms on the third floor, probably 75 to 90 rooms, most of them two-man rooms. I saw them with pretty curtains and comfortable beds with matching comforters, dressers, and lamps. I could envision the women carrying their Bibles into the room with them and stretching out on the bed to read after a day of work and classes. That was with my imagination, or "spiritual eyes," and then I would blink and see with my natural eyes. I would see the trashed rooms and stinking, dirty carpet. The emotional roller coaster would crank up again.

On to the second floor I went. More surgical rooms. The gas lines in the floor still worked. Some still had gurneys and operating tables in them. There were back halls and all kinds of secret ways to get around and circle back to main areas. Those hallways were probably convenient for the doctors to come and go. There were some kind of big hooks falling from the ceiling, and I really did a double take on those, trying to see what they were. A big, vacant hospital can be a wee bit scary, to put it mildly, when the lights aren't on and there are no patients or medical personnel going about their way.

I was thinking about all the people who must have passed away as I looked at all those gurneys and again got a little freaked out. I thought I heard a mouse or something and really didn't think much about it. I turned down one of the secret corridors and got a tad turned around. Well, actually I got as lost as I could be, and as I was trying to figure out how to get out of the maze, I opened one of the unknown doors and ran right into a man shining a flashlight at my face, totally blinding me. I practically jumped out of my own skin and turned around and ran like I was in third grade. The man followed me shouting, "Brenda, it's me!" I just kept running until I found my way out. I glanced back and there stood my husband. I hit him on the arm and just screamed and screamed at him. "I was just checking on my little explorer," he explained with a laugh. I told him nicely (not really) *never* to check on me again. It was two days before I could finally laugh about it.

I explored, drew out our plans on the sticky pads, and frequently called Melinda to get her opinion. She always had a gracious plenty of opinions. I am very grateful that I managed to raise independent children, but they can be tiresome. I taught them to think for themselves. However, when I am trying to sell them on a particular point and they are not buying into my point, I can get pretty feisty trying to drive it home. It does me no good because they are all independent thinkers. Go figure.

There are many days now when I wonder what on earth I must've been thinking, if not for believing beyond all doubt that God was in the plans for Lovelady. Writing this has been so hard for me. I know in the end it turned out all right, but I really cannot imagine what I would do if I had it to do it over again. Would or could I even have put this together? Absolutely not. It was all God. I believe that it is ordained for a certain time, and I felt the call and the need. That is where faith comes in. Martin Luther King said, "Faith is taking the first step even if you don't see the whole staircase." I feel like faith is something that just grows inside of us. The more we see Him do, the more it grows. It grows to where it has to be for His will to be accomplished. At some point, we have to allow that faith to overtake our natural mind. We have to let our minds work in unison with our faith. We all need other people in our lives who do not think exactly like we do, so we see more than one side of a situation and have more than one idea on how to get things done.

Everyone's thoughts on this huge endeavor really did matter to me. Beau, my oldest son, was very hesitant about the whole idea but was still supportive. Though he was still living in Gulf Shores, he was absolutely resolved to help all he could from a distance. I knew even in the beginning that this ministry had to have family involvement. It would be too consuming, and I needed to have my family with me. As a mother, I feel that was and is a priority if at all possible. But, in hindsight, I think Beau was glad he was so far away. He could just say "Okay, Mom." However, those around me were telling me I had lost my mind, that something had never been done like this, that I did not have the experience or training, that the women might be dangerous, that there would be fights in the building, and—then the *big* problem—that I did not have the money for the $1.2 million building. The issues just kept mounting. I kept climbing but was not getting anywhere.

When I was overcoming my obstacles, the financial problem loomed over me like a cloud. Because I had called so many of my friends, word had gotten around that I had *really done it* this time. I had a difficult time with my Christian friends not giving me any support. I understand it now, but back then, I saw the plan so clearly and I wanted others to see it also. *What are you thinking,* others would ask me, and I really did not have the answer. Right when I would overcome my fear of one thing, another would pop up.

I remember vividly the time I discovered the power bill averaged $25,000 a month. All the while, I was trying to keep the 40 clients calm and kept reassuring them prison was not in their future. The facts, as I uncovered them, gave me a sick feeling, and I constantly doubted the plans I had would work. I told the Lord that it would have to be Him who opened the doors because I simply could not find them. It was like I was still lost in those dark rooms. And I was still scared. I want to say that I just sailed through this time, but it would not be true. *Scared* is a mild term to use when recounting my fear. Looking back, I honestly do not know if I could do it again. But just when I thought of quitting, it's like God would give me a small nugget to keep me calm and moving forward. A tiny little nugget would be like a drink of water in a desert.

Our country faced a lot of bad weather around that time. A terrible hurricane was brewing along the Gulf Coast. Because Jeff and I lost our beach houses to a hurricane in prior years, I paid close attention to any coastal weather. The news reports said the hurricane we were watching was not as bad as we thought, but it was going to hit the coast around Louisiana. When you live or have property on the coast and the weather guys finally pinpoint where the storm is hitting, most everyone else lets out a sigh of relief. Everyone is relieved the hurricane is hitting anywhere but where they are. Then the hurricane goes ashore and you feel so sad for the ones who are in the direct path. I always felt a tinge of guilt—survivor's guilt, I guess.

The hurricane was a medium one, but then they threw in that it might overwhelm the levees and it could be a problem. The levees did fail, and all hell broke loose on those poor people in and around New Orleans. Katrina arrived and many of the people were losing all they had in the world, and I had been so selfish worrying about my extra houses. I cried watching the people walking on the interstate to get away and find a safe place outside New Orleans. It was terrible. I called Melinda, and we started figuring out what we might do to help. I can say that in all honesty, even with all I was facing, I was looking for a way to help the New Orleans people. The television would show people walking on the side of the interstate carrying their meager belongings left from Katrina, and I just would feel so bad for them.

As I sat on the edge of my bed, rubbing lotion on my hands, I was waiting on the rain to slow down to go to my "hospital office," and I was just so anxious. Anxious for the Louisiana people, anxious for our clients, and anxious for my own self hanging out on the side of the mountain. I had already gotten my "The clock is ticking, Brenda. What are you going to do?" speech for the day. I will say the thought came out of nowhere, but I know it didn't. It didn't just pop into my head. It came from deep within my heart: *"What if I could house some of the Louisiana people in the hospital?"* What *if?* Of course, the fact that we did not own it yet never occurred to me. It was ours, as far as I was concerned. I wondered if this was God's way of solving three problems. Could this be a light in the dark tunnel where I was traveling? This solution could be a triple win for all of us ... the hurricane victims, our clients, and me. Hope in the hopeless situation for all of us. God made me very resourceful, and this was a resource for us. I began putting in calls to FEMA fast and furiously. They were so busy. Everyone I spoke with was more confused than the last one. What a mess! I guess when something is so big no one can figure out what's what. It seemed FEMA just could not wrap their heads around the huge problem. I finally gave up! Giving up to me was putting the phone down and praying for God to handle it. It's strange how prayer works, and it would make so much more sense if we would pray first every time. You may do that, but invariably I work myself silly and then pray—opposite from what it should be. I especially was feeling time slip away from me and felt I could work faster than I could pray. That sounds so lame.

Then I got *the* call. The man on the phone from FEMA told me he had gotten my number from the hospital, but as far as I was concerned, God had dialed my number *for* them. He asked if they could rent the building from the hospital directly to house Katrina refugees since I couldn't close on the building. He knew my contract would be up in about 20 days. "What in the *world* would make you think I'm *not* going to go through with the purchase by the deadline?" I said to him. He stammered around, finally saying the officials at the hospital had told him so. "Well, I don't know why they would think that. Why don't you come on over here and let's talk about this?" We made an appointment for the following day at the hospital.

Sure enough, they showed up and I gave them my "grand tour." I almost felt bad for them as they walked through the door. They really thought they were coming to see a ready, equipped hospital—one with beds, furniture, televisions, kitchen equipment, and the incidentals that make life better … just normal everyday things that any reasonable person would expect to see when he or she entered the doors. The FEMA guys looked like they were going to turn and run. However, I told Bill, the security guard, that if they tried to get away to lock the doors. I almost laughed out loud at his face as he nodded intently. I do believe he was prepared to lock them in, if need be.

They were looking for an equipped building ready to house their evacuees. Instead, they saw a trashed-out, vacant building. The first day they came, it was like the mice were having a party. I halfway expected to see the mice scurrying along wearing party hats and tooting horn blowers. I had never seen them out like that. My "grand tour" was not grand at all. It was terrible. They kept saying they needed to leave, that they had another place they needed to go. Bill and I glanced at each other, like we were trying to decide on the locks or not. I actually got tickled. FEMA looked like I had invited them to a broken-down, threadbare, trashed building. They were just not feeling it.

They had every excuse in the world for why it would not work, and I had every reason for why it would. It was too much work. It had too much wrong with it. It had no furniture. You name it and he found it wrong with the building where he and I *both* envisioned housing victims. Finally, he said, "But you don't own it." I explained to him, "When you pay me the dollars we agree upon, I will have my down payment for it and they will hold the mortgage. We can even close both deals on the same day." I finally lured them into my "office" with my big sticky notes. I was drawing faster than fast, making lists, formulating budgets, even selecting the furniture we'd need.

I was actually working up a sweat with my presentation. I then laid it out there for the men. It was not going too great when I finally said those words that scare Jeff: "I'm just going to be honest with you," and I saw Jeff cringe. He always gets a little nervous when I just blurt out the truth. He says too big of a bite will choke a deal. I told them about my women, how I had to fight to keep them. I told them that I was a faith walker, and I just laid it out there. They thought for a moment, and finally said that it would work for them if I could make the deal work with the current owner. They asked about the initial $40,000 and I told them the hospital had it already as a deposit and could just keep it. At that, Jeff looked like he was going to lose his lunch, but I kept going. I asked Jeff to see if, after keeping the $40,000 of our money, the hospital would allow FEMA to pay the $100,000 each month on our mortgage and we would get the deed. Jeff really thought I had fallen right off the cliff with the idea of getting any of it forgiven or given to us. However, he agreed to talk to them about it. I really wanted him to present the plan so I would know what any issues would be and so I could overcome them with my next conversation. I knew that we were presenting an interest-free deal for a year, but considering what they had and we had it seemed plausible. They would pay the closing costs. After going back and forth with the purchase of the building plans, this is what was presented: $1.2 million guaranteed by the Government of the United States of America, or as we call it, FEMA. You tell me where they're going to get a better deal than that? One little tidbit is we also had a separate contract for maintenance, insurance, and housekeeping. That was the important thing for me, as it gave me the funding I needed for the credit cards we were using for all the extras required to get the program on its feet. Being a FEMA facility gave me lots of perks, such as utility deposits.

Right in the middle of getting ready to scream with excitement, I realized the FEMA guys were getting concerned about those other incidentals like furniture, pots and pans, TVs and linens, pillows, and, and, and. The list got longer. All of a sudden, 500 pillows seemed like a lot. We had only one week before evacuees would arrive. We could do it, I just knew it. About that time, I looked down and remembered Melinda and I had just gotten our ankle monitor bracelets off, and I knew if God had orchestrated that, we absolutely could do our part and get all the work done. The white-collar criminal who thought her life was over was negotiating with the Federal Emergency Management Agency of the United States Government to house their evacuees. My life was just starting. I felt the very reason for my existence was to help and show others a new life. It mattered not what had brought me to this point. I knew this battle was not mine; rather, it was His. I was filled with excitement and remembered all the doubts I had but felt them all just wash away. Yes, we could do this and get the building ready for those people who needed a temporary home. My excitement was contagious. The FEMA guys were excited too. I found it difficult to believe then, and as I write about the miracles we were experiencing, I still find it incredible now.

I'll offer a recap: A woman who found herself in trouble with the IRS starts going to prison to minister to broken women. She decides then to open her home to those women coming out of prison. Her home grows to 40 women. She gets in trouble with her home zoning board, so she finds a small building to house the said women. The key to the small building is across the street, in an old hospital. She walks into the old hospital to get the key to the other building. She instantly feels the old hospital is really where she is being called to house the women so they can begin the program. The cost of the hospital is $1.2 million. With only $40,000 on hand, she puts together a contract with the hospital for 90 days. The clock starts ticking. No prospects for the money are in sight after calling all the preachers and churches and anyone she could possibly think of calling. There are no prospects at all. In a separate part of the country, a hurricane starts brewing. It goes ashore as a category three, hits New Orleans head on, and the levees, which were not supposed to give way, break. New Orleans and all the residents are flooded, with no place to call home. Louisiana is declared a federal disaster area. FEMA is called in. FEMA begins looking for housing for the evacuees. The woman calls FEMA to offer assistance and can not reach anyone notable. FEMA calls the woman to request her signature in order to discontinue the purchase of the hospital she was buying to house women. FEMA visits dilapidated hospital and somehow agrees to house the Katrina victims there if lengthy list of provisions can be met. A contract is met with the hospital owners for $40,000 down and $100,000 a month with no interest, to be paid out in a year, the same amount as the contract FEMA offered to lease the location to house the evacuees. The lease would be paid directly to the new hospital system guaranteed by the United States of America via a separate contract for various other needs such as housekeeping, insurance, and utilities.

    If I were to look back and attempt to number the miracles that happened that made everything possible, I would be unable to. FEMA was the key to us getting into the building. God did not send a hurricane to those precious people in New Orleans, but He sure used us to help house some of its victims. And that was the key that unlocked the door to the new location.

    So, in the meantime, our sweet women loved what they were seeing. They had a home. They loved being a part of something so important and being able to help people at the same time. They were part of a bonafide miracle. Those nasty carpets started getting cleaned within two hours of the FEMA men leaving.

    This was a home they could take part in *building*. Tiffany, who was second only to Shay in our very first group of women, took one cleaning group, and Shay took another one. There was always so much competition between those two that running between them to check on progress was almost more than any of us could do. We literally worked around the clock. There was one other snag, though: *We still did not have one single piece of furniture*. I had committed to FEMA just what would be in every room: beds, dressers, nightstands, and lamps. Each room would also have a television. My son, Matthew, the dreamer, called a friend of his who introduced him to hotel liquidators, and in one day he had 18-wheelers of used hotel furniture brought in. One of the trucks arrived in the middle of the night, and we went to the building at 1:00 a.m. Matthew actually had to call *several* liquidators. It seemed pieces of a puzzle just fit into the proper place. He actually found a Marriott close by that was remodeling and got all the linens there. Well, look at us go! Nothing but the best for our evacuees. Matthew went around and collected all of the family's credit cards. Matthew had to use all his credit cards, all of mine, all of Jeff's, and all of Melinda's, but we finally had every television, mattress, bed, nightstand, lamp, sheet set, and towel that we needed. We had sofas for the common areas, and chairs and tables in the dining area. He found the sheets, blankets, towels, and even pillows. I was so excited and this was another nugget that proved God was in this endeavor. We even managed to make this huge endeavor fun. Everyone was hiding from Matthew because he would just walk up to us with his hand out and we knew it would be time to hand over the credit cards. My wonderful family never even asked about when we would pay it back. I knew that had to be done, so I immediately put another $75,000 on my financial list. My goodness, that list was growing. As excited as I was, my heart beat wildly as I read it for the hundredth time.

    Several churches around Birmingham offered to help, and everyone met at the Center to unload all the furniture. These were the same churches who were so skeptical about the project. They may have been skeptical but they realized God had to be in this movement. If nothing else, they saw this as a way to help the Katrina victims. We had every room set up just in time. We bought all the televisions from Walmart and were so excited that it was all coming together so easily—in such a short time. We looked so professional when the FEMA people showed up, and they were simply amazed. The same guys never came back until the day before the evacuees arrived, and I asked them why they hadn't checked on us. The guy in charge told me he never once doubted after he made the deal. We all stood and watched as they inspected, looking as proud as we could.

The entire operation was so amazing that it was hard to believe. I went to the attorney's office and closed the deal in that office with FEMA and then immediately went to the next office and closed on the hospital. The seller paid all closing costs, kept the $40,000, and all I had to sign was the note and that the FEMA lease proceeds went to the seller. At the end of the 12 months, we would own the building. Unbelievable! Even as I write this, I still find it hard to believe how this whole thing came together. *Only God.* And when He moves, I follow. I will follow Him anywhere. I talk so big. Is that speaking about something as if it already was or faith walking? I do know this, I read about mountain climbers often. They amaze me, and as I lie in my nice, comfortable bed I wonder why they climb those mountains. Every single climb has some really dangerous footing. Every decision they make concerning their climb could result in death. I can't climb Everest, but every day we each make decisions that could result in all matters of consequence. My walk of faith seemed to have hazardous footing at every step. However, I just kept climbing. I always know I don't see every bit ahead of me. I just take the next step and keep going. It's His way, and I never know what may lay in store. But now we were in our building and so happy about it. What was coming?

I quickly recognized that our FEMA guests were very similar to our women. They were all scared about their future—and rightly so. They did not know each other and were very untrusting of one another. They didn't want to lose anything more. They didn't want to hurt anymore. They all came from a point of desperation. We became trustworthy to the evacuees. Our clients became beacons of hope for our New Orleans guests.

Before you could turn around, I discovered our residents were ministering to the New Orleans folk. The women were giving them hope, just like they had been given. It took a lot off the busy FEMA guy's schedule, actually, to have our women on board and loving on the people as much as they did. FEMA and the City of Birmingham set up offices in our devotion area. I thought back to just a few weeks prior, when the building had been in such a sad disarray: no furniture, just all that space, sad and lonely, serving no good use at all. Now it was home to so many who had no home. And while it might not be beautiful yet, it was shiny and clean. Problems would arise and quickly a solution would be found. How amazing that was! I also thought that the City had to be seeing how wonderfully it had come together. The new reports would speak about Birmingham's FEMA facility, its organization, and the civic pride in it. Our name was vaguely mentioned—FEMA and the City got all the credit, and that was fine with me. I felt we had made the news a little too much lately, so I felt good about that. One day as I stood and overlooked the setup, I thought how great it was that we all were working in unison to give help where it was needed. I thought about how the town had been, and now just look at us, all working together. I was so naive. I was living in a dream where life was so good and everyone loved each other, and I believed the City was finally behind us.

    FEMA had opted to have all the food catered. My Loveladies, who were really good cooks, began making a special dessert each day, enough for everyone in the building. Everyone loved it. Soon, there was a line each day of the New Orleans residents right outside my office. FEMA wanted to know if we could take some of their residents into our women's program. When we took someone into the program, we moved them to the fourth floor, where the Loveladies were housed. They would go to class just like the Loveladies. The refugees were changing their lives, and we were helping them find their future. FEMA's intention was emergency housing and basic humanitarian assistance. Those practical needs were absolutely being met. As the FEMA officials watched, however, the victims were receiving so much more than basic emergency aid. Their hearts were being healed as well.

    However, I have also learned that just when you take that sigh of relief, trouble is most likely headed your way. Katrina had come ashore and was over, leaving destruction and pain. But another storm was brewing for us, one we named "City Hall."

City Hall

"Do what you feel in your heart to be right—for you will be criticized anyway."
—Eleanor Roosevelt

One day, while FEMA was in the beginning stages at the Center, I walked out of my office to go down the stairs. I had spoken to Jeff, who was going to meet me downstairs to go over several items we needed to work on. I arrived a tad bit early so stopped to observe what I was seeing. I thought back to a few weeks prior, when the building had been in such a dilapidated disarray. No furniture, just all that space, sad and lonely, serving no good use at all. Now it was home to so many who had no home. And while it might not be beautiful yet, it was shiny and clean. Problems would arise, and quickly a solution would be found. I thought just how amazing it all was. I also thought that the City had to be seeing how wonderfully it had come together. The news reports would speak about our city's FEMA facility, its organization, and the civic pride in it. Our name was vaguely mentioned—FEMA and city officials got all the credit, and that was fine with me. I felt we had made the news a little too much lately anyway.

    The stairs were between our offices, and Jeff and I always seemed to meet in the middle. Standing at the very top of the stairs so no one could go down them was a man holding a walkie-talkie speaking very loudly.

Dr. Brenda Lovelady Spahn

"I told you that crazy, redheaded bitch is the one they say owns the building. I just verified it. The mayor is going to have a fit." I was so shocked I almost fainted to hear him speaking about me like that! He did not even *know* me! I had not seen his face, just the back of his head. I knew I was not loved down at City Hall, and that was putting it mildly. They thought I was out to ruin the town by housing a few women prisoners? Our state was overrun with crime, and our only women's prison had been overflowing with women. Our one women's prison, Julia Tutwiler Prison, was finally sanctioned by the Department of Justice for its inhumane conditions—but back in the early days, abuse and neglect ran amok there. No one dared to believe Birmingham could be part of the solution, as the crime rate in the city has been and still is one of the highest in the nation. All they could see was the darkness; they were not interested in what we could do to brighten the situation. I was so taken aback by their short-sightedness.

I know what they thought: *"We had shut her up and taken away her ability to house 40 women and now she has gone and gotten one of the buildings we wanted and will have hundreds of felons housed there."* They were really upset with me. I even felt a little sorry for them. Well actually, I felt sorry for myself more. I looked like a really smart person playing chess, knowing every move to make, but the truth was, God was the one playing chess with them. All I was doing was moving the chess pieces where I totally believed He was showing me. I looked to be something I was not. My entire life had been meant to serve God by serving those who needed a second chance. Often it was the first chance they had ever been given because of the lack of parental guidance, poverty, abuse, and other atrocities they faced in childhood. He had raised me up for such a time as this. And during this time, I had the fortunate opportunity to see the well-oiled machine that is FEMA up close and personal. I count it an honor to have been able to see our government come to the aid of its people.

I immediately looked at Jeff, hoping he had not heard, but one look at his face and I knew otherwise. I was hoping he had developed a quick onset of laryngitis or something that would prevent him from saying something hostile, so before he could go confront the man, I hurried up to the guy myself and tapped Mr.

Miss Brenda and the Lovelady Movement

Big Mouth on the shoulder. I guess he assumed he was just moving over for someone who wanted to go past him because he just backed up a bit without even glancing at me. I stepped around him and kindly told him, "You can probably tell I'm that 'crazy redhead' who they correctly say 'owns the building.' Can you talk to me directly, or do you just talk behind people's backs?" His face turned as red as my hair, and for a split second, I thought he might explode. I could see the smoke coming out of his ears. I immediately recognized him from television. He may have thought I might be crazy before, but I knew when I got through with him, he would have no doubt. But just as I was preparing to tear into him and let him know more about me than he probably needed to know, it was like a calm settled in my spirit and I just walked away. (Now that was another miracle!) As he walked off, I heard him mumble about being under FEMA protection. *"Looks like FEMA saved you for a year."*

Now is as good a time as ever to let you know that I am a real work in progress. In the beginning, all those many years ago, I was an even bigger work in progress. You know what they say about redheads! I am a natural flaming redhead with a temper to match. I used to love a good scrap. Not so much now. God has calmed me down. Nevertheless, I did then what I just hated to do and that was to take a deep breath and walk away.

I knew I did not want Jeff to get started on Mr. Big Mouth and I surely did not want any more trouble out of City Hall. "Why would you say all that stuff about me? You don't even know me or what we are trying to do. We will actually do the city a big favor by giving women a home who would otherwise be on your streets!" Then to my great shock and complete disbelief, the man practically pushed me down the stairs as he walked forward to take a step down, never saying a word. I mean *not one word*. Jeff and I stood there in complete shock. I followed Mr. Big Mouth, but he went out the front door like a crazy person himself, never looking back. I had a sinking feeling in the pit of my stomach that we had not seen the end of him. He may not have been looking back at me then, but I was sure he would be looking my way again very soon.

We settled into day-to-day life at the Center with all the people from New Orleans. We were so busy I never had time to worry much about city officials. When I was a little girl, my mom told me "What you worry about never happens." I took all that my mom said to heart and especially what I knew to be true in my own experience too. Every so often, I would get a nasty letter from the City. I discovered they had wanted our building because they had made plans to build some kind of homeless shelter program themselves. I guess I'm the type of person who just does not hold a grudge. I would just let go of it. In my way of thinking, that's what would eventually happen at the city level and we would all be one big happy family, providing for those needing help together.

But right now, those officials were pretty put out with me. I can say one thing with absolute certainty: Those guys were not raised by J.K. and Catherine Lovelady. To reinforce my position, I called our attorney. He assured me, "Without a doubt, you are correct in your thinking. As long as FEMA is operating in the building, the City or even the State cannot say a word anyway because a federal emergency trumps anyone's preferences." So, I was right, FEMA trumps all other entities.

Just because we were standing firm in our position did not matter to the city officials. They kept sending letters, one after the other. They said the building was never zoned to be residential. It was zoned to be a hospital.

I went to my "do not open" drawer and found all that mail where I had stuffed it and put it out of my life, temporarily. I quickly read over the letters and saw that the first one said to vacate the building, but the second one said after FEMA evacuates the building then vacate the premises. I thought to myself "They must have found the rule book between letter one and letter two. Oh well, that's a worry down the road."

Still, we were improperly zoned for how we intended to use the building, according to them. Zoning ordinances are local laws that define how property in specific geographic zones can be used. Residential zoning, which is what communal living in a program required, was not the same as hospital zoning. And I had a sinking feeling they would not rezone us with a wave of the hand and let us keep helping the women. FEMA had a lease for a year, and that offered us protection.

Miss Brenda and the Lovelady Movement

FEMA asked for a meeting on a Monday morning, which was not at all unusual. Everything was going great, so I strolled right into our meeting with no concerns at all. We were about six months into our lease, and things were coming up roses. Roses are so beautiful, and we love the flowers and aroma but don't think about the thorns until we grab one. I grabbed a thorn that Monday morning at the meeting. FEMA told me things were going better than they had hoped. There was just one little problem: We all did such a great job, helping and relocating our evacuees, that after the first six months, FEMA was leaving. What? I had another six months on our lease! They couldn't go yet! I was so naive, yet once again, I asked the FEMA person, *How do I get the rest of the lease payments?*

My mind was already thinking how I could ramp my plans up by a few months and all would be well, maybe even better. The FEMA guy looked at me like I had four heads and explained that FEMA does not have to make any more payments once they end the occupation of a location. Mind you, no one mentioned this little clause in my contract. It took me two days to mention this to my sweet Melinda, who was just now settling down to a "normal" life, or at least normal for *my* family! I called the attorney, and we talked about the closing. FEMA had been so careful to make sure they could use the facility longer, we had not even talked about the possibility of their leaving sooner. By the time I delivered that news to Melinda and the others, I was all settled down. I learned we just had to roll with the punches and keep breathing. My blue-eyed beauty took the news like a champion, her faith never wavering. I could've stood a little of that hope, but the remaining $600,000 was staring me in the face, plus insurance, utilities, trash, and a sundry of other things. And when I say leave, I mean within three days it was like they were gone ... vaporized. They had bought these little trailers for them and were putting them in there.

I realized God's wisdom in bringing the displaced people to us. The day they loaded up to leave our building brought many teary eyes. I was surprised that two of those eyes were my own and even more surprised to see two more of those teary eyes were Shay's. Just as they were getting ready to load up, Shay handed each person a bag of homemade goodies. I whispered to Shay that some of those folks were diabetic. She glared at me and stated, "They can just take their shots!" I was going to explain that was not the way to treat diabetes, but she glared at me and I decided to let it go. "Choose your battles" always rang truest concerning Shay. When she did something for others, we just got out of her way.

We were even awarded a medal for the way we took care of the evacuees. Our Center was considered one of the best places for the Katrina victims to recover. City Council members came out that day to shake the hands of the refugees. They spoke and waved to the press as if everything was their doings. But that's ok—we helped a lot of people. And God knows the truth. I slept very well that night knowing we had helped them. That was our last good night of sleep for a while, though. I was dreading the battle I knew was coming with City Hall. I knew it was coming and there was nothing I could do to stop it.

Even today, when I watch any kind of war movie and the soldiers know the enemy is coming and they all have that dread in them, waiting for the soldiers to come into view over a hill or mountain or something, I can relate. I know it sounds dramatic, but I know that watchful dread. If I did not have all the women to concern myself with I would have felt less fearful. When you are responsible for so many others, it's a different concern and set of fears altogether.

After we got the FEMA notice that they were leaving and we learned how great we did, I was so proud of the Loveladies and everyone who had pitched in to help. We had a big celebration. The church that had helped us held a service for us, and we presented *them* with the medal we had received. Before the doors on the FEMA van were shut and before I could really sit down and take it all in, a city employee hand-delivered another letter to us. I ignored that one by placing it in the "do not open" drawer, and two more were delivered as certified mail.

I still can remember the Sunday afternoon that I decided to face it head-on. I had preached that morning in our sanctuary, to our women, on standing and holding onto the truth. I was more determined than ever in holding to what I viewed as my destiny.

Miss Brenda and the Lovelady Movement

So we topped the stairs and met in my office. We had the best zoning attorney anyone could ask for. He was also one of the godliest men I had ever met. I had faith that whatever he said would be right.

He listened to every word and just looked over all the documents that we had received and that I had put together to state our case. He had read the newspaper articles on how the City had handled our Hob Hill situation. He told me that they still could bring about all kinds of issues for us. I already knew that to be fact.

We were in an old building, and there were hoops they could make us jump through and it could get ugly and costly. Gee whiz, why did things have to be so hard when I was trying to do the right thing? I thought of all the trials the disciples had to go through to help and do good for people, so I put on my big-girl panties and said we would fight to the finish line. At that time, I had no idea that a finish line could be moved time and time again.

While all of this was taking place, a friend of mine who became a friend of the ministry from the State of Alabama came and sat across from me and told me the latest rumor: *Our women were throwing dogs off the parking deck.* I knew that was the biggest lie ever and could not imagine how someone could come up with something like that.

We investigated the matter. There was a little dog who would come up to the second floor of our parking deck, jump to the concrete railing, and then jump into a dumpster on the ground level, maybe 10 feet down, to dig in the garbage bags for food. One day, our women heard the dog barking as they were outside smoking and had gotten him out of the dumpster. We do not expect our women to quit smoking while trying to quit drugs, and many in our population go outside to smoke. Anyhow, the little doggie would do this repeatedly, day after day, searching for food to eat in our dumpster. The women even started throwing good food in there for the little dog. They nicknamed him Dumpster Diver because many of them had gone "dumpster diving" before, and made jokes about it. "Dumpster diving" is looking for salvageable things in dumpsters behind stores.

I went and watched this doggie show for myself. It was not a long jump at all. But I am sure if someone did not know the exact location of the dumpster, it could have potentially looked bad to them just passing by . It's amazing to me how some people tend to judge others in the worst way. Or they like to make up things to spread drama and claim their little five minutes of fame.

We had to deal with all the entities anyone could name: elevator regulators, the fire department, rescue department, gas department—more than I could have imagined. Some days it would feel like they were lined up to get through our doors. The poor health department was sent in so often for unfounded community complaints that I felt sorry for them. They never found anything wrong with us or the building except for a few small instances.

Jeff had to meet with representatives from various organizations day in and day out. I listened to it at the Center and then heard more about it at home. Jeff just could not accept what was happening to us—and for good reason! Why was it so difficult to help people? We had gone through it at Hob Hill. He could see only injustice in our circumstances. I thought the good reports would help us, but the zoning fight raged on.

I dug in my heels and met with the City several times to go over exactly what I felt was the right thing. After I had met with our attorney, I told the official I thought we could handle it by him telling me what to do so we could save the city and state money. He was all for that. I would be so humble and kind and soft-spoken; after all, that's another lesson from Mom. There again, it didn't work. Then I would get a little louder and make my point a little more, and that didn't work either. The City must have a different rule book than my mother did, I decided. Finally, things were getting heated up.

There is a wonderful donor in the ministry. His name is James, and he's an extremely well-connected man at the state level. He told me that he would go with me to the next meeting. I was so tickled I thought "Man, we have this in the bag." I thought because he was so well connected, they would be impressed. He and I worked so hard and had all the code books for zoning with those yellow sticky notes marking all the important points of our presentation. We were ready! I was so excited. Finally! The city officials were going to get to know me, and that I was just trying to help women, which in turn was helping the city.

Miss Brenda and the Lovelady Movement

I told James we would be meeting with a city attorney. Our appointment was at 3:00. We got there about 10 minutes early and were sitting outside the conference room. We saw people going in there one right after the other, and I told James there must be another meeting in that room—I wondered if we were going to be redirected somewhere else because that meeting looked pretty important. Finally, at exactly 3:00, they asked us to come in. I thought there had been a mistake because no way were we to meet with all those people.

I have never seen such a hostile group of people in my life, including the meeting when the program was located at Hob Hill. People can really get riled up and not even listen to a word of explanation! They would not even let James or me say a word. This was not my first hostile meeting. When we were trying to maintain our home at Hob Hill we had to attend a neighborhood meeting and it had gone badly also. I had thought, though, that the neighbors just didn't understand the legal issues. Since these were city staff people, I believed it would go better.

At any rate, all those people who went in one after the other were all there for *our* meeting. James looked shocked, and I felt like throwing up. I felt so bad for getting him into the mix of all those problems. I finally realized it was like a contest to them: *the City vs. Lovelady*. I thought pretty ugly things too. And no, my mom didn't teach me that; I learned that all by myself. James did great and I did great too, even if I do say so myself. But the people acted *terribly*. We would make a good point and they would shoot it down, even if the point was sensible.

After the meeting, I received another nasty letter. At that point I determined I needed to bring our attorney into the mix. He put us on the agenda at the next City Council meeting, which ended up being standing room only. All the neighbors in the neighborhood had been invited, and you would think surely *some* would stay home, but it looked like all of them showed up even though we were the only issue on the agenda. The neighbors thought their houses were going to decrease in value just by our being in the area.

The "show" started and I was so proud of our attorney. He was outstanding. He presented our case and I just knew that we were going to be approved and it was going to be over that day. In my mind I thought, "We should have pulled out the big guns a long time ago." The Council members were the only ones who got to vote, but I have since learned that the Council just goes with the majority of the neighbors because that is how they get elected. The Council never even tried to explain our mission to the people. They just let the people talk. One by one, people would walk up to the podium and say the craziest things. I had to listen to lie after lie.

The lie that surprised me the most involved a precious older woman who had spent about 40 years in prison before coming to Hob Hill. She was legally blind, and we took her to ophthalmology appointments to have her vision corrected. She had been a seamstress, and I visualized her at a sewing machine in the heat of Tutwiler Prison, hunched over close to the threading needle so she could see. African American and having been given a raw deal, she had spent 40 years in prison for manslaughter. They had not even proven beyond doubt that she was the driver of the car that ended in a man's death. Anyhow, her children wanted to celebrate her first birthday free in 40 years and rented a limousine to pick her up from Hob Hill and take her to dinner. Instead of me being able to show the City Council how happy that poor, old woman is now, and how she is receiving good healthcare now, the only people allowed to speak about her said that she was a prostitute who was picked up in a limousine to go turn a trick. So I was leading a prostitution ring out of Hob Hill. There were more equally disturbing lies, ranging from theft to drug dealing to prostitution. You name it, suddenly my women were engaged in it. I was absolutely shocked that anyone would even think that I would allow such vileness under my roof and label it Christian. And I couldn't even raise an objection to it in the meeting. It finally came time for the vote, and I squirmed. We lost! How was it possible that they believed that crap?

Our attorney found more points, and we went to the City Council one more time. He had found the point of all points, actually. He discovered that the very first zoning for our building was for dormitory living. The building was originally built in 1927, for residential housing for Howard College nursing students. It was zoned originally to house people! We did not even need to change the zoning! It had never changed in all those years. Well, we certainly had this in the bag now, didn't we?

As I write this, I get mad all over again just thinking about all the time and money that nightmare cost us and, in turn, cost our donors. When the vote came in that last day, I didn't even get my hopes up, because I knew in my heart of hearts we would lose. They really had no rationale in turning us down for the zoning—were they just waiting me out? Trying to outlast me? Without FEMA, I had no money coming in to pay the remaining $600,000 on the mortgage. Were they thinking they could just hold out and keep denying my zoning?

By this time, the zoning issue at Lovelady was being played out in the media. I remember thinking over and over, *All the lives being changed in that building and all the media was reporting on was about our zoning fiasco.* What a mess! By then, everyone knew we did not need a zoning change and yet everyone also knew the Council would always vote for us to leave!

I had moved that precious old woman, who could now sit up correctly to sew because finally she could see, into a large room on the fourth floor. We bought her a new sewing machine. She would just smile so big. No prostitution ring, no tricks. Just Jesus. I vowed never to give up. I knew the city thought that sooner or later I would, but it just wasn't going to happen. Not ever! I knew in my heart that the precious old woman who was about to graduate from our program and go live with her loving children was worth the fight. I knew some of the staff thought I was just being stubborn, but sometimes you just have to stand your ground and when things look grim *you just keep standing there.* So I stood and stood. Poor Melinda stood right alongside me. I say "poor Melinda" because she was having to listen to others in the family wanting her to talk me into just moving on to Gulf Shores and retiring. *The city wasn't going to relent anyway.* But, she just stood right there with me. It was very hard for the family to watch the battle. To make things worse a good part of the battle was played out in the news.

One day, the mail was brought to me. There was yet *one more letter* from the city. I laid it on my desk, intending to put off reading it until the following day, and that's just what I did. It was not even sent certified, which was strange. I slid an opener along the top seal and unfolded the letter.

"It has been determined the current zoning of the property is correct and acceptable for the usage of your facility. If the property is sold, please advise the buyer of zoning restrictions which may apply. Thank you. We wish your ministry the best." It was never in the media. There was no write-up in the newspaper. I never gloated. I never even said anything unless someone said something to me, and then I would simply relay, "It ended up being okay."

No fireworks, no "We're sorry," no anything. Just one little letter. All of this for one little letter. Yes, you can fight City Hall and win, if *Right* is on your side. By the way, that first rude city official and I became friends, but that's another story.

Now I just had one teeny, tiny problem: *Where in the world was I going to get $600,000 plus the other items, which totaled about $730,000?*

Castle Living

"Home is a shelter from storms—all sorts of storms."
—William J. Bennett

After FEMA's Katrina evacuees were able to move on with their lives, we began in earnest to create the very best program we possibly could. Melinda, Shay, and I began to put it together. We based it on what the women needed to learn for a new way of life. We were like The Three Musketeers: the crazy redhead, the innocent blonde, and the Black know-it-all street professor. We were a force. I was putting every idea I had into the program while on the flip side consuming myself with the St. Vincent's $600,000 mortgage and playing catch-up with the other bills left for us to pay. My days continued to be an emotional roller coaster. Trying to be tough, gentle, and persistent in keeping things rolling was so hard, and I hope it didn't age me too much. Besides just my emotions, the work was very laborious. I felt much too old for all I was trying to do. Jeff would tell me, "You're burning the candle at both ends." "What end, Jeff?" I would think but never say.

In the meantime, Shay was like a search engine for the underworld. I never had any idea how much was involved with living a criminal lifestyle. It required so much to remember, so much effort. One day I told Shay, "It looks like it would be much simpler to just do things the right way. To try to find money for drugs for each day with no job would wear me out!" I know what the vast majority of women do to get the money they need to buy their drugs. I have been astonished to see just how much money flows through their hands. Of course, the men were robbing people and various other things they could do to get their money.

A typical opioid habit costs about $200 a day. Oxycodone has overtaken the pill addiction. I actually had one of my clients who was taking 60 norco (hydrocodone) 10mg pills a day. Her dad finally locked her in her room and sat outside her door listening to her scream for days. When she was brought in to us she looked like she was going to drop any minute. Oxycontin (OC's) had finally been stopped, which has helped, but that help came a little too late for thousands of addicts.

A typical opioid addict starts with hydrocodone and then moves to oxys, then to heroin. The heroin addict will then possibly go to methadone and the meth clinics to save money or to try to get help, but the cycle goes on and on. The line outside a typical methadone clinic appears like a cast of a zombie movie. There are drug deals and prostitution right in the parking lots as they line up to dose. They have to show the nurse dispensing the drug to them that they have swallowed, so as not to be able to sell what was in their mouth outside in the parking lot.

Melinda and I received quite an education from our women about the drug life. We learned a great deal about opiate addiction, as well as other choice drugs. We committed to be the ones who would help anyone's drug-addicted female family member. If someone needed assistance, we would provide it in any way we could.

"You are so right, Ma," Shay answered. "If I could just have all that time back that I spent chasing a high, I would live to be an old woman." I have thought about that statement so many times. I loved her so much, and she had suffered so much abuse from relatives when she was a child. She had raised herself from the age of 11 living in the back of a biker bar with a group of prostitutes. She lived with them from age 11 to 16 working the streets. At that time, the court decided to help her. She was bitter when they first took her off the streets. They put her in group homes, where she promptly ran away over and over. She had lived all her years in hotels, in the back of bars, three prisons, and even in the back of a parked 18-wheeler for a few months. She had told me that she had a living room and bedroom set up in the back of the big rig. She had longed for a home for so many years. If any of us could just take back lost years, it would be wonderful.

When I was a little girl I imagined that one day I would have a castle. Shay and I would talk for hours. I lived in a small camper with my mom and dad until I was in the fourth grade. I told my children and anyone who would listen about my dream castle, and that's when Shay decided it was her dream also. "You can't just steal my dream," I told her, laughing. "I'm not stealing your whole dream—you're just going to have to share it with me. There are lots of rooms in the castle, and I only need a few." We would laugh about our shared dream often, and if I was ever too hard on someone, she would threaten me with the "lock you in the tower" speech.

I told her about being an only child and how lonely I had become. I always dreamed of having lots of children, and so she became my child. She did want a family and at that point had no relationship with her family at all. So when Shay heard the castle story she quickly became part owner in the castle in her mind. She had her very own wing, and she had no intention of moving out. One day I overheard her tell a messy person that if she didn't get her room clean Shay was going to move her out of her castle and she would put her right back on the street. She saw me listening to her and changed it to "Please clean your room. You must treat this as your castle. After all, your home is your castle." Then she smiled a sly little smile at me and walked off.

She might have allowed people to move into our castle but she would never share *me* with any of the other women. I was *her* mom, and she did not want others to call me Mom. She barely allowed my own children to call me Mom. I would laugh so hard at some of her antics. Melinda would just hate it if she had to leave Shay and me alone. She always said we changed things if she left, which of course was true. My motto is "If it's not broken, break it because you may be able to put it back better than it was." That's exactly what I do: I try to make things better and better. Saint Augustine said, "The awful catastrophe is not the end but the beginning," and there is so much truth in that!

We all had much to learn about our old building. One man already knew the building inside and out and all its equipment. I had located the former head of maintenance. For a small fee, he would come show us how to repair something if it broke and would teach our maintenance guys how to do it. I kept him on speed dial. We all would wait our turn to talk to him and learn what we could. But if you ever want to hear constant negativity or continual hopelessness and gloom, go buy an old building and house a ministry in it. Such-and-such is going to go out if we don't have one-two-three right away... This is how much it'll cost... No, they don't have that part anymore—where's a good machinist... If so-and-so breaks, Mr. Inspector could shut you down....

The few men we had helping us committed to learning everything they possibly could about our old building. We were always very careful to select men who would respect our women. I was quickly beginning to understand why everyone had an aversion to us owning this big, old building at first! This was a *huge* undertaking. However, I believe the Lord prepared me my entire life for this monstrous challenge, which is probably why I saw it as *wonderful*. But I let everyone know very quickly that *this deal right here belongs to the Lord*. We are just running behind Him, trying to keep up!

So I would go through times of deep, unwavering faith and times of extreme worry—because if we closed down, the women would go back to prison. *This had to work out.* When I discovered the costs of maintenance for the building, even just basic preventive maintenance, I got a sick feeling in the pit of my stomach. I almost fainted, actually. The boiler, elevators, commercial kitchen equipment, sprinkler system, and chiller were all foreign concepts to me. Every time someone said a building word, my response was always "How much does it cost?" When anyone is walking in faith, it is natural to have those thoughts in your head.

I worried endlessly, barely sleeping. All of a sudden, during one of those late-night worry spells, it hit me: *Either God is in this ministry and He knows what's best, or it's all just on me.* If it's all just on me, we need to pack up and go home. But if it is all up to *Him*, this ministry is going to make it, despite our best, inexperienced efforts! I always say, "God has put this together, in spite of us." People are so quick to tell me how wonderful we are, and I am so quick to make sure they know that Lovelady has been put together by God and Miss Brenda is just honored to be along for the ride.

I received much inspiration from a man in England who had an orphanage. His name was George Muller. He never had enough food or milk and was just like me, moving in faith. There was a Sunday when he had zero milk for the children. He instructed his cook to put the glasses on the table, and of course she explained to him about having no milk. George said he knew that but insisted she put the glasses out. Sitting around the table, they all prayed. About that time, there was a knock on the door. There stood the milkman, who told George the refrigerated truck just broke down and asked if the orphanage could take all the milk he had while it was still good. They filled the children's glasses and the refrigerator also.

I am used to being shocked at the way things happened for us. Something would break, I would be stressing over it, praying about it, and someone would hear about us and stop to see if we needed any help. When we inquired about what skill set they held, they would be just who we needed for the current problem. George Muller and his book would come to my mind, and I would consider those children sitting there and that alone would encourage me and lift my faith.

Plumbing was a different issue. You would have thought the plumbing woes were planned as sabotage! The things that sometimes would be flushed down the toilet made our maintenance team believe the women were trying to flood the place on purpose. The plumbing would be backed up and the men would have to "snake" it out, a snake being a flexible auger used to dislodge clogs. They would find all manner of toys, diapers, and other unmentionables in the plumbing system. They would have to snake the pipes or disconnect them, with the icing on the cake being that all the sewage would rain down on whatever was on the floors underneath. We would have to use the wet/dry vacuum to suck up the mess and then clean the floors.

To be truthful, I vacuumed the mess only when they could find me. I just couldn't stomach it. When the plumbing went out and things got a bit nasty, Melinda and I would get very busy with other things really quickly or just downright *hide*.

In the beginning, when Jeff came back from the Gulf to spend time with his wife who chose castle life over beach life, he would get in late at night, muttering to himself. I would pretend to be asleep so I didn't have to partake in what was becoming a routine. *Not one time* did my ploy work. He made so much noise coming in that it sounded like a herd of elephants—to make sure it would wake me. Our nightly routine consisted of me kindly and gently asking him how everything came out and if the problem was fixed. He would give me a 45-minute lecture on women and their total disregard for maintaining a good plumbing system. I would tell him I was sorry and that it would not happen again. I would tell him the same thing the next day and the day after that too. Jeff had come home from his beloved beach house to help with the Center, and he was so much help.

Melinda and I would explain to him that most of the women were not used to minding the plumbing. Either they had not been in one place long enough for it to matter, or they were accustomed to flushing State or County facility toilets, which could handle much more than our old building. We have plumbing classes regularly, and most of the women listen and do better now.

One night, about one in the morning, the entire second floor west wing flooded and seeped through to the medical department, which was under the second floor. "Brenda! One of your women climbed up and hung a wire clothes hanger on the sprinkler in her room." It broke and flooded the rooms on that wing. Jeff then suggested, when I prayed to God, to maybe send women who might be more careful of what they put in the toilet or hang from the sprinkler in the ceiling. "I'm tired of sewage raining down on me." All I answered, I'm embarrassed to admit, was "I certainly will." I felt so bad not just for Jeff but for all the men who tried to keep up with the plumbing.

We started out in the building, post-FEMA refugee occupation, with about 75 women. The 75 quickly grew to 150 to 200 to 250 and finally 300. We scurried trying to keep up. We did not look at imposing limits on how many we would take into the program back then. We had the room. Currently we have over 400 with really long waiting lists. That does not count the children.

Starting the Center with a plan and then having FEMA pull out early left a huge financial hole for which we weren't prepared. Truth be told, we started the Center on nothing but faith. Of course, in my world there *is* nothing but faith. Still, it would be wonderful if the finances were sitting in the bank waiting only for us to stroke a check and pay the bills on time, with smiling, happy women attending classes and no worries in sight. That would not be reality though. Reality was FEMA pulling out early and that brought in a world of grief. Often I would think of that day they were leaving and I could hardly breathe. My mind could not wrap around their leaving when I had a contract with them for a year's lease. Oh well, I also could not wrap my mind around a resulting little problem, a mountain I saw no way of climbing. Every day I made a teeny tiny little inch up the mountain and then would slide 6 inches downward when I thought of all the money I owed for this wonderful building that I loved so much. All I could think about was that the Lord was probably sick of me pestering Him about everything. The grand total owed for the building at the end of the FEMA departure was $600,000 plus the catch-up.

"Mother—" Melinda started, handing me an envelope. My heart skipped a beat.

"What is it, Melinda?" I took the envelope from her and realized it was from the power company. Oh my goodness, what else? My heart skipped another beat. If Melinda could not even speak, I didn't even want to open it. It was a bill for part of a deposit still being owed plus the current bill, saying we had to pay $25,000 within a few days. There were two things I desperately needed immediately. One was spiritual, and one was physical. I knew God would provide, but I needed that assurance that can come only from Him. Faith must grow in you and overcome the need for which you are believing. I needed finances I could touch with my physical hands. I did not intend to let the Lord off the hook one inch. I put a mattress on the floor under the cross in the chapel, the absolute center and heart of the building and, aptly, the heart of Lovelady. I decided I would stay there and pray until we had the financial breakthrough I knew we had to have for survival. We all must come to a place of rest sooner or later. I simply could not find mine. It happens to us all. I think that $25,000 was mine. I just knew in my heart that all would be fine, but it was difficult when all the employees looked to me for their salary and we did not always have it. Not only did the power company, understandably, wish to be paid for the electricity we had used, but also the gas company wanted their part and the water company wanted theirs—so, I decided to sleep in the chapel until something happened. I needed to see God move a mountain for me. NOW LORD, please.

The staff never complained one bit about going without pay during the difficult times, but I knew they had bills to pay and things happening in their lives also. So yes, *it had come to that*. Melinda stayed in the chapel with me when she could, praying hard and long for breakthrough. Shay would stay with me occasionally, but we never told her the size of the miracle needed. I felt weak in the knees, and Melinda felt the same, so I knew Shay would have fallen on the floor clutching her chest and I would have had to call 911 and be at the hospital all night if we had told her.

About that time and on a side note, when a little money would come in and our sweet Chief Financial Officer, Rosie, would try to decide which bill to pay, I earned the nickname "Moses" for repeatedly giving the order *"Pay my people!"* I will never forget the day a large statue of Moses was donated to our facility—the staff rolled that huge thing right up to the elevator and placed it on the third floor, not far from my office. The inside joke relating me to Moses is unheard of now, as we no longer miss paychecks, but it was hilarious at the time.

Moses is still standing right there in the same place, all these years later. He is missing one hand. I put a scarf on him and covered up the missing hand. I just love having him there, and when some of our more affluent donors look at him, I laugh and tell his story. I have discovered that our affluent donors have the heart of champions and there is virtually no difference in the haves and have-nots. Birmingham is full of the most giving, philanthropic people ever. The Lovelady Center is in the perfect place.

Hiring people who believe they are called to work in ministry is much harder than hiring people looking for employment for income's sake. People who work for a ministry truly work for something *other* than the white picket fence dreams for which most Americans strive. I certainly understand the security and luxury of the American dream. But if we were to have placed a classified ad for job seekers back in those early days, it would've read something like this: low pay, long hours, difficult people to manage and inspire; you may be asked to serve additional hours for emergency situations such as relapse, the receiving of crushing news, or basic drama resulting from immaturity of years of stunted emotional growth; occasionally, you could be asked to meet at 2 in the morning to assist with waking everyone up for random drug testing; emotional roller coaster experiences as the women you pour into decide to go back to a life of drugs and crime or make other horrible choices; an occasional heartbreak when a beloved client overdoses and dies. I am positive that the job search sites would have recommended different verbiage be used in the descriptions, maybe something more appealing. The point is, most people would've passed on answering the ad. Nevertheless, we prayed fervently to acquire the very best person for each position, and every day it seemed we needed more people.

At the last moment, but in more than enough time, the Lord made a way for that one important power bill to be paid. A wonderful man walked in with a $25,000 check. He always makes a way when it's His ideas in the first place. For some reason, even with all the miracles I have seen, that mountain moving $25,000 we just had to have filled my soul with joy I cannot explain. We had to scale many more huge mountains, but that smaller one gave me the shoes I needed to scale the ones looming ahead.

One Bite at a Time

"Love begins by taking care of the closest ones—the ones at home."
—Mother Teresa of Calcutta

Melinda and her husband, Shawn, sold their house, and we all lived together at Hob Hill for a while. Melinda has three children, and I also had one at home. That means we had 10 people living together. Good thing we were all related or City Hall might have had something to say.

I remember that time as being wonderful. We had so much fun! Jeff was still in Gulf Shores much of the time, but the rest of us just had a nice family time. People talk about sacrificing for ministry work, but somehow I do not look at it that way.

We would have parties at the house, and Melinda and I would enjoy cooking for the clients and our families. We would have services outside in the back and even baptize in our pool. When I look back on those days, the sacrifice of a normal home life, finances, and personal time never enter my mind. *Building something with God gives you a fulfillment that you cannot get any other way.*

Shay was always front and center. She would come up the driveway just flying in the big van, drop off a load of women, and then hurry back down the driveway to go pick up another. They all looked relieved to have made it to Hob Hill. During this particular time, Shay felt like she was in charge, and clearly she was. She worked diligently to keep us all straight. She affectionately called Jeff "Pa" and would just sit and listen to him. Then she would tell him how wise he was. I would tell her "Just keep listening to him and maybe *you* will wise up." Shay would roll her eyes at me. She was a professional eye roller! Then she would tell me to go back in that kitchen and make some more seven-layer salad and L.A. caviar. Sometimes I would just go back in the kitchen and do as the boss ordered.

Annette and Tiffany, having been with us since the start, still work with us. They both think we could not make it without them, and they are probably correct. At least they would be hard to replace. Annette finally admitted that she was the one who had caused such turmoil when we were still in Hob Hill. She had put ants in Shay's bed. When they visited Hob Hill at the same time, Shay would usually become upset and get all fired up again. They would just glare at each other and make rude comments.

We began to hire more graduates of the program as staff. They would come to us and tell Melinda or me that they felt called to the ministry. We would pray, listen, watch their decisions, and consider what they could bring to the table for others—and then we would jointly decide what to do. It's one thing when someone feels they are hearing from God, but, in my opinion, it is something *you* need to hear from Him too.

And still, Shay would always put in her two cents' worth. Melinda and I used to have so much fun with her. We would tell her the tallest tales just to hear her rant. We would exaggerate or maybe just make general statements. Well, to be honest, I would mostly be the one telling her the tall tales, and then Melinda would spoil it for me.

One year we were having a party to celebrate her birthday, which to Shay was as monumental as a national holiday. Can you believe I had forgotten it to begin with? Someone had told me that Shay thought we were giving her a surprise party since we had not made the big deal that she thought we should.

I had someone run to the Center and grab me the "biggest" cake there. Many bakeries kindly donate items to us instead of throwing them away, so I was hoping for a sheet cake. They finally arrived back at Hob Hill, struggling with carrying in a huge wedding cake!

I had my icing tubes ready and waiting. I wrote her name and "happy birthday" on that wedding cake and put a little color here and there like speckled flowers. It was very pretty but was extreme overkill for a birthday. Well, let me say, *overkill for most of us*. But it was not overkill for Shay.

When she walked up and saw the cake, she didn't miss a beat. She picked it up all by herself and walked straight to her car with it! I followed behind her hollering, "What are you *doing*?" I mean we hadn't even lit the candles on that cake and she just swooped it up and walked out with it!

"I'm taking it to my daughter's house so she can see it! She has got to see this cake!" Tears filled my eyes as I glimpsed into the soul of the woman standing there. She wanted them to see how important she was to me—to all of us. She wanted them to know Miss Shay was wanted. And she wanted to share that moment with them and give them the cake.

One day I was at the work-release center giving updates about our program in the new location and I was able to meet the new chaplain. I was so impressed with her. We chatted for a short while. She was very curious about the new Lovelady Center that all the women were talking about, that began as a whole-way house. Everyone called her "Chap." She was and is one of the godliest, organized, loving people I know. So well spoken, so intelligent.

I invited Chap to the Center for a tour the following day. Sure enough, she came. I showed her the Center and everything we were talking about doing in the future, but I had a seriously ulterior motive for asking her to come see my castle. Chap had credentials needed for the counseling department we had yet to set up.

Melinda was a tad uncomfortable about me just jumping up and offering an Alabama Department of Corrections employee a position with us. She recognized that we had to have counselors, but she felt I was a little out of line, being that we needed a good rapport with the State to continue to bring women out of Tutwiler.

Miss Brenda and the Lovelady Movement

Many times she thinks I am out of line, and sometimes I truly am. But for the most part, God directs my path and I try to stay on it.

Chap's hands were tied within the prison system. She could counsel only at certain times, and she was to call the person she was counseling by her last name only. It was like everything in that dismal place reminded a woman that she was no more than property of the State, even in a counseling setting. Can you imagine? "And how did that make you feel, *Miller?*" There was no chance to get comfortable and deep. An officer had to stand by the door the entire time she counseled an inmate. Also, the door had to be open and other officers could hear because Chap had to use a front office, exposed to everyone in the area. Now *how* is a woman supposed to share her innermost feelings with a counselor when it cannot be personal?

Chap felt she was called to minister to prisoners once they were released from incarceration, so when offered the opportunity, she accepted a position to counsel the women at The Lovelady Center. She is incredible. When she first began with us, she was the only counselor and now she's Director of Counseling and is over an entire group of incredible counselors. She has complete freedom to help our women and has completed degrees to better enable herself to help them. We get a report from her monthly about her entire department and the progress of each counselor, the department goals and successes, and any obstacle she deemed worthy of leadership instruction. Her department is like a well-oiled machine. You can give someone complete freedom to create the perfect environment of trust and nurturing when their heart and mind is focused on the best interest of those they serve. Chap has been with Lovelady for more than 17 years. Dr. Debra Jones ("Chap") for sure has been one of our greatest blessings. I called the warden after she accepted the position and told her what I had done, feeling a bit guilty for taking someone so gifted and professional from the inmates there. She said it was fine and she wished Chap the best. That was about 16 years ago. God gave us the best person for the job, and we have never looked back.

Sometimes you just have to jump in the deep end and start swimming, and for our cornerstone-like employees, that's exactly what we did, trying hard to keep our heads above water. God uses a mix of personalities in His body to carry out His work. My "counseling" approach is a bit different: I want to just grab everyone's phone and break it when they sit in front of me carrying on about what made them break a rule.

So many times it comes down to them thinking they will die without a phone but it was in the manual what would happen if there was anything inappropriate on the phone. Back then, we had flip phones. I cannot tell you how many I have broken. Now, you need to know I only broke those of women I felt were in jeopardy of staying on a path that would eventually take their life. People forget we are fighting for people's very lives here. Sometimes drastic decisions call for drastic measures. Finally the Alabama Department of Corrections asked me to quit breaking the phones. So we decided counseling was not my strong suit. Laying down the law might be, but counseling was not. I left that area to Chap.

One day when we were first moving in the hospital, a lady came in. She seemed a little strange to me. She spoke softly and walked slowly. She was the polar opposite of me. If I am as fiery as people say, she is absolutely not. She came and found me as I was overlooking the move. She told me that a mutual friend recommended her to visit me. I have so much respect for our mutual friend I simply said, "Great," even though I was so busy. I asked her what I could do for her, and she told me she wanted to live at the Center with us and teach art. *Teach art*, I thought to myself, *and live here in this building?*

"I'm sorry, but I do not need an art teacher, and if you have never had a drug problem you probably don't want to live here," I replied, having a hard time envisioning her with our women. I apologized again and offered that if I needed anyone, I would call her. She walked off, and I silently questioned what my good friend who sent her must have been thinking.

As I stood there reflecting on all my issues, I began to pray and ask God to send who we needed. I don't want to say, "God said this" or "God said that," but as plain as day, it seemed almost audible to me. "You just sent your blessing out the door." What? Now, I am not a fast runner, but I'm faster than Ms. Teresa and out the door I flew to catch her.

"Wait! Don't leave! I changed my mind. I do need you," I said loudly to her up the sidewalk. We talked as I walked her up to the fourth floor, and I felt a gentle nudging to give her the best room that I had been eyeing as mine to stay in. I declined the nudging and gave her the second best in the entire building. I took the best, and Hunter and I stayed about half the time at the Center. Oh my goodness, after I moved things into my new room, I had the hardest time. I felt that same nudging about the room situation. Every time I passed her room, I felt guilty. I reasoned with everything in me.

"I've given up so much, I want the special room. It's my right. There are two or three of us here, and she is only one person," I argued to myself. Finally I realized that it was useless and I just gave her the big room. She did not want to move. I ended up moving her myself and fixing her room so pretty, and I resigned myself to the small room. She is a little weird, but most people think I am too. She has given more than she has ever taken. She does teach art to the women and the children. She is one of the most special people I know, and I love her a great deal. Everyone calls her Miss Teresa. She has been with me since we moved into the building in 2005 and I hope will be with me until God finishes with me.

Because I had hip problems, I had a scooter to help me get around that big building. Gosh, I loved that scooter. Miss Teresa went everywhere on her scooter. She had used her scooter for years for genuine needs. I really did not need mine until I had hip surgery or if I was walking around the building a lot. I know it's bad to say, but it was so handy and you can get so much done with one. I had a very good time at night on the fourth floor racing around on my scooter. It did make Teresa anxious, and I tried to behave, but I might have been a wee bit reckless on occasion.

I was always trying to get Miss Teresa to race on her scooter. Well one night she finally said yes she would. All the girls were standing around cheering us on. I finally told them they could not cheer for a particular person. We kicked the race off. I held back to give Teresa the lead, and my goal was to barely let her win. I was being more than a little reckless, I am ashamed to say, and had my pinky finger sticking out and drove too close to the door frame. It broke my finger. The race was over, and Teresa won. It hurt so bad, but I did not tell Melinda anything! The girls loved my being there, playing with them. They taped my fingers together, and I was off and racing again. It is most important to show the girls that there is fun without drugs being involved. Of course, there are probably smarter ways to show them than racing on a scooter. My scooter days were coming to an end. But we had a motto: "What happens on the fourth floor stays on the fourth floor."

The last time I got even a dab reckless at the Center, Melinda was leaning over the devotional area railing with her right leg behind her, kind of kicked back. She was wearing a skirt. I was intending to scoot by her and let the wind move her skirt to take her by surprise. The scooter made little noise, and I planned to move carefully—or so I thought. I went zooming behind Melinda and got too close to her and clipped her foot. You would have thought I broke her leg the way she carried on. Anyway, my scooter days came to an abrupt halt with that accident. I hung my head in shame. But we all got over it. Melinda limped a little for a day or two, but then she was fine. I had a hip replacement, so I needed to walk anyway. We sold the scooter.

The same person who caused mayhem on the scooter is the same person who prayed all night in the chapel for the Center. Not just once but many times. Over the years, various women have joined me. It inspired all-night chapel prayer that eventually grew into different "prayer stations," and activities in the chapel centered around long prayer times. All that prayer has made all the difference in our ministry and program; after all, *it had come to that.*

I wanted to be at the Center day and night, as did Melinda. Jeff was in Gulf Shores most of the time, driving me crazy about hurrying up and going down to the Gulf to see him. I was like a juggler, keeping several balls in the air. In truth, I had told Jeff that I would be down at the beach with him a great deal. I did not intentionally tell him an untruth, mind you—I still believed I'd get this thing rolling and there'd be lots of help and staff. That just wasn't happening yet.

Especially with the furnished room on the fourth floor for Hunter and myself, it soon became apparent that I lived at the

Center and just visited home or Gulf Shores occasionally. Hunter was my 6-year-old. We had adopted him at birth from a girl on the street. Hunter loved staying at the Center, and we would lie in bed when Jeff was out of town and pretend to be in different places. It was priceless. Instead of being an intrusive time, it became a time he and I would come to love. The internet and such did not work on the fourth floor. Being at the Center day and night was just what we needed to do in the beginning. After he would go to sleep, I would talk with the women or we would play board games. I was happy, they were happy, and Hunter was happy. Sometimes when Jeff would come home and I did not feel I could leave, we all three would just pile up in a double bed. While it sounds unorthodox, it worked for us. Then daytime would come and problems along with it.

Shay soon became the queen of intake. She wanted to "make sure" the women we accepted were the women she felt God had sent to us. She never turned anyone down. Her bark was so much worse than her bite. Shay and her department completed each intake procedure, explaining what was expected, and saw to it that all necessary paperwork was signed. In the beginning it never occurred to us to have children with their mother. It did not take long for us to discover that women had to be able to reunite with their children if they were to be rehabilitated the whole way. We had to adjust the current program to include the children, which in turn opened up an entire separate program. However, if we were going to have the best program, we had to include children.

With more women and children, more employees were needed. We had to have more help. However, we had a real problem. No funding. That is when the rubber meets the road. That is also when it became important to have only people who are committed and who know they are called to the ministry. We made a commitment to pay everyone, but we also made sure everyone knew it might not be on the exact day that was planned.

I personally made the commitment that I would never get my check until everyone else was paid. Melinda made the same commitment. I was scared about that promise sometimes because by then we had sunk everything we owned into this project, but

I never failed to honor it. Melinda, Jeff, and I put our checks in a box. Once in a while, we would get to pull one of our checks out of the little box.

It seems crazy to say this but the Lovelady Center's financial position formed a real family who looked out for each other. Deep bonds formed, helping each other and sharing resources while waiting a few weeks on paychecks and hanging in there with the ministry. It was a wonderful feeling for everyone to pull together with a common goal. That goal was to change lives. I can say with certainty that only the strong survive in that atmosphere.
And God answered the prayers. The money came in. It always seemed to work out. He would come through right at the last moment. One time we had already told our staff that their pay would have to be given out the following week, only to receive an enormous check at the very last minute. We started calling and texting the staff to come back and pick up their pay. They never complained about the disappointments but certainly were dancing with joy over the pleasant surprises.

I felt it was very important for our clients to see good men. There was an older minister who visited us regularly, and I did so enjoy talking with him. He told me all about his family, and especially his grandson. He absolutely loved his grandson so much. The older pastor's daughter was an addict and struggled. She came to the Center and then would leave. She could not commit to staying and completing the program. The older minister died, and then she died as well.

One day, I was talking with a pastor who came by to visit me. As I was speaking with him, I realized he was the grandson of that incredible older minister. Immediately I knew he would be so good with the women, and I was thrilled to meet him. I had looked long and hard to find a pastor who could understand our clients. This young man, Lestley Drake, did understand. He told me that his mom had met the Lord while at the Center. I just really liked him. He told me all about his wife and his kids. He was very happy with his life.

"Would you be interested in coming to work here with us in a pastoral capacity?" I asked him, and he told me no, because he ministered at various churches. I asked him just to try it please for three months and see how he felt. He has now been at the Center for 13 years. I am so honored to have him there, an example to our women and children. He has been a true inspiration to our clients. He counsels, teaches, preaches, and hosts all manner of special events. He teaches classes and creates tradition. We have several events based on Jewish holidays into which he puts a great deal of heart and time.

And I'm really not very good at fundraising. I would much rather the Center be completely self-reliant than to constantly have to ask people for donations. We now have the most wonderful development department. That department solicits donations and applies for grants—and what a blessing they are. Professional people are given the opportunity to give, to be blessed in their own lives by blessing our women and children.

People need to know their money is going to a good cause and their finances are going to a ministry that does with the funds what it says it will do with the funds. There was a tremendous learning curve for me, however, because with hundreds of women and children, something is always happening that has to be financially addressed. I learned the correct terminology for what had to be financially addressed in our daily life back then was aptly called "putting out fires." God always comes through, just not always the way we request. His ways are not my ways, and I am wiser and a better person because of it.

However, somehow we would always have enough to operate and that is a miracle in itself. Many people have commented, "This just does not work on paper." They then acknowledge that it works only because of the Lord—truly, He is the *only* way we make it. Those long, overnight prayer sessions are some of my favorite memories. I would feel so good after each one. It was in those sessions that various parts of the ministry came to be and that new, fresh ideas were born. Sometimes it is good for us to know that the only hope we ever have is to go to Him in prayer. It works every time, but remember, we might not get the exact answer we want. We might not even realize it was the answer we received, but sooner or later we will know *it was the answer we needed.*

People visit the Center for advice in their own program— they come for tours and attend meetings to learn best practices.

Most already have an established nonprofit recovery ministry, but some come to us wanting to start something like The Lovelady Center in their own area or state. They ask us so many questions. I tell them what we have gone through and the difficult times we have faced but always end the common speech with "If you feel God tugging at you, just go for it, and make absolutely sure you are ready!" I knew back then that God had called me, but my plans for all the good Christian people to come in and help me do it just did not happen when I wanted it to. Maybe that makes it even more plain that it was only the Lord helping us stay afloat. So *would* I once more willingly go through everything again? Then I think of the women I have known, some of whom you will meet in the following pages. *Yes, I would do it all over again.*

However, the mountain of debt was always looming over me, and Melinda and I still kept much of the worry to ourselves. It was on our balance sheet, but so much was going on and the remaining money for the building was still needed. I know our people felt at times that they were on the Titanic. Sometimes you just feel there is nothing that you can do. I was functioning, but even with all that prayer, every time I had a visitor, my heart beat a little faster. One day, I received a call from downstairs that a "Sister" needed to see me. I thought the Catholics wanted to be volunteers for the Center, so I hurried down to escort her myself to my office.

She was kind and soft-spoken. I instantly liked her, and she became my friend. Then she told me she was from St. Vincent's East. I thought, *"Oh no, she has been sent here due to the money we owe."* So, I just threw it out there in complete Brenda fashion: "I'm sorry about the money we owe you; I don't know exactly what to do. I am believing the Lord will work it out."

"Oh, Miss Brenda, I'm not here about the money!" Sister Diana went on to explain that she simply wanted to talk about possibly holding Mass at the Center, and of course I said yes, visualizing any women who may be Catholic kneeling with this sweet woman. We decided to begin the services the following Friday. I had been to only one Mass in my life, and I had enjoyed it immensely. She asked me questions about FEMA and the lease being broken. We talked about everything this program could become. It was a great visit with a great friendship forged very quickly. When she left, she hugged me tightly and planned to be back on that Friday.

As promised, Friday arrived and Sister Diana and the priest were there, holding Mass with about 15 girls. Later, it grew to about 40 women attending. Sister Diana asked me if she could bring all the other executives from the hospital to see what was being done at the Center. I must have looked like I was going to faint, but I thought, we will just meet them and explain where we are, trying to raise the $600,000 we still owed them, as St. Vincent's Health Systems still owned the mortgage on the hospital.

The next day came, we gave them the grand tour, and I will tell you it could not have gone better. Everything was like a Hallmark movie. Every kid behaved, the elevators worked, the food smelled right, and all employees and clients acted like ladies. Shay was there, running ahead of the tour just to check around every corner to make sure all was well, orchestrating what they would see.

"Shay, stop it! Just let them see whatever is there," I would whisper. I told her later that transparency is always the best. If there was a mess around the corner, oh well—that's life.

I didn't know what would come from the meeting. I was just hoping for a little more time or easier payments or something, but I'm telling you Sister Diana could read my mind. When she and the men sat at our table, she asked me what I could use for help.

"Well, you guys are in a unique position. We owe you $600,000. Anything you could do to lower this money would be a major blessing." And heck, I just went for it and continued, "If you would like to just give us the building, you would be helping save thousands of women's lives." I said all of this without blinking an eye, but I was kicking myself under the table for being way too bold. They were still very cordial and left shortly thereafter. I almost threw up when they left. Had I asked too much of them? Why in the world did I ever think they would just give us the building? Yet, when I asked, I knew that I had to speak out boldly.

The very next day, Sister Diana came to meet with me. By then, when the receptionist called me about her, she would just say that Diana was on her way up to see me. I met her at the door because I had a surprise for her. Years before, when I had money, I had visited Vatican City when I was in Italy. Now, I could not afford to visit the other side of Birmingham. Nevertheless, while I was at Vatican City, I bought an expensive piece of mosaic art that was very beautiful. All pieces were signed by the Pope and had a Vatican postmark on it because the Vatican is a country itself within Italy. As she walked in, I told Sister Diana I had a present for her, and she replied that she had one for me also. We laughed and I said, *"Me first!"* I shifted the art from my hand to hers.

"How did you know that this art I hold in my hand has been a dream to own?" she exclaimed as she was reading the back. She said she could not take such a gift. I told her I had felt led to give her this most precious gift since I had met her.

"I just love you and really want you to have it," I added. "Please, take it." She came around my desk and gave me a big hug. She was such an honorable and loving person. She was still crying, so to break the moment, I said playfully, "Now where's my present?"

I was looking all around where she was sitting and in the top of her bag. I stood up again, peering around her as she sat down, smiling. It took me a moment to comprehend what she meant when she said, "You're standing in it, Miss Brenda."

Flea Market

"Our greatest weakness lies in giving up. The most certain way to succeed is always to try one more time."
—Thomas Edison

At one of my nightly prayer sessions, it came to me that we needed to write our own destiny. We needed to get busy with some money-making businesses and become more sustainable. And because of my background that's all I know. You need something, you find a way to work for it.

The first way was to make denim jean purses. Worn denim jeans had been given to us, as well as bolts of fabric. Someone gave us plenty of sewing machines. The purses were really cute and sold like crazy. However, after the sale of all the purses, it was not cost-effective to buy the fabric to sew more. I kept hoping someone would donate more fabric, but it was not meant to be. So the great purse factory closed its doors.

After that, I decided we would set up a flea market in the parking deck. I can really come up with some ideas, determined to make our finances work. The flea market was doing great. Then business just *stopped*. I could not figure out, for the life of me, what could have happened! One week the parking deck was full of people coming to shop, and the next week, *no one!* Some of my sweet girls grouped together, coming to give me some uncomfortable news.

"Okay, ladies, what's up?" I asked in the most intimidating way I could muster, having fun with them, never even considering it was about my flea market. "Well, Miss Brenda, we can't work in our flea market anymore."

"What seems to be the problem?" I asked, getting up from my desk.

"Best you come see for yourself," they answered. I headed down the stairs as they all stomped down the stairs behind me. I was going to solve the problem, and I mean I was going to solve it right then and there.

When I stepped through the double door that opened into the second level of our parking deck, an absolutely *horrible* smell hit me. I immediately knew what it was. *Cats!* How did this happen? They had made a home in my flea market! It seemed every cat within a hundred miles had found themselves a new comfy home. One of our girls had actually been feeding them, and of course they all loved the nice soft litter: *my merchandise!* There was a cat smell on everything. We had no way to wash all of those clothes. I was so upset, not just because of losing my flea market but for all the people who had given us the clothes in order to sell and make a profit for the Center.

We found a local ministry that gave clothes to those in need, and the next day they were so glad to come get all of it. I made sure they knew what happened, but the ministry assured me they would get the smell out. So the great flea market closed its doors.

Never one to give up, I was looking for a "tiny" building to rent the next morning, because I was going to open a "tiny" thrift store. I found a small building that we could afford and signed a year's lease. It took exactly six weeks to fill up the store. Racks that had been given to us were wall to wall—no one could shop in there because it was so crowded. I hit that chapel floor on my mattress for a few nights of prayer, and yes, it had come to that again. I realize you are probably saying, "What did she think she could possibly know about starting a thrift store?" What knowledge I had about that subject could have been put on the point of a pencil. I knew *nothing!* However, I am enterprising and fully believe "faith without works is dead." I pray like it's all up to God and work like it's all up to me. Besides, "build it and they will come." I felt like if we used all our resources and showed we were serious about thrift stores, a way would open up for us. The truth was, I had never spent much time in a thrift store and had been to only a couple of garage sales.

One of our board members called me because he wanted me to meet some friends of his. His ministry has a huge network of people with resources, and he has helped connect us to people with means. We made an appointment to meet the two couples he wanted me to meet. Of course, I love to tell people all about our wonderful Center and our precious women, so I was excited. The next day, that wonderful board member, Don Ankenbrandt, came to the Center with Ronnie Giles and his wife, Dean. Ronnie's son, Greg, along with his wife, Ann, were with them.

Ronnie was the jovial one of the four, and his personality was so friendly and he just made you feel like you had known him forever. What I did not know then was that these people would be instrumental in our future sustainability. My money-making business was about to take flight.

I casually asked them what business they were in, anxious to share with them how they could be part of our vision and change lives. Thrift stores! God had connected us with the thrift store gurus of the world! Oh my goodness, I did everything but jump in their laps. That was one of the most wonderful meetings I've ever been part of in my life. I told them about my recent dilemma with the crowded, tiny thrift store that was already problematic, as well as the failed, cat-smelling flea market in our parking deck. They just laughed and laughed.

"If I can secure a larger location, would you consider teaching us to build a successful store, since you do not have a location in this state?" That is my personality—just throw it out there. They assured me that they would. I must have lit up like a Christmas tree because Mr. Jovial smiled and leaned in as I asked the big question: *"What do you think it will cost?"* I held my breath, not even having close to any idea.

When Greg answered by saying $350,000, I told them it might take me a little while to get the money together, but my wheels were already turning over ideas. After we finished up our meeting, I hit my knees one more time. I prayed God would open the door for us to find the money.

The next day, Greg called and said they were looking for a location! *Location, location, location,* he told me, and I immediately thought of my tiny, little "location" just a few blocks from the Center. I also thought of that yearlong lease I had just signed on that tiny, little "location." But even *that* could not put the fire in my belly out. I was so excited—we were going to make it! He was thinking *location, location, location.* I was thinking 350, 350, 350. I explained to Greg we didn't have the finances in place just yet. He said they had decided to loan us the money and would take the payment out of our net sales, and that they would teach us the entire business. Oh my goodness, if I could have gotten through that phone line, I would have hugged him so big!

I was jumping around like a complete nut. I can get so excited. All I could think of was how the ministry would be on the road to being self-sufficient in the happenings of two days. The teeny, little thrift would be growing up to a big one. Oh, and that lease? I called and the owner told me a guy had come in the day after us and offered him more money for the rent. Not only did the guy want it, but also he wanted the racks and the merchandise. I gave him a price, and he bought it and took over the lease. All of this happened within four days.

Greg had agreed to loan us the money and teach us the thrift store business. "Give a man a fish and you feed him for a day. Teach a man to fish and you feed him for a lifetime," as the idea for alleviating poverty and creating sustainability goes. The Giles family *taught us to fish.*

It was like God just moved the mountains that I had been standing at the base of, looking up at the top. The new lessee called and wanted to know how soon we could move out.

"Tomorrow would be good for us; is that soon enough?" I was so relieved, so excited about the future that was laid out plain as day in my mind, and making a mental checklist to begin tomorrow's project of moving out. In reality, I just went and got the cash register and cordless phone.

At the time, we put the rest of our clothes in storage that we had at the Center. I felt it was more than we could ever sell in any thrift store. We now sell that large amount on a good sales day. The Giles family found the absolutely perfect location. And our reward for all the hard work and fast maneuvering, moving out of that tiny, little location and into the perfect, department-store quality location? The first day open, we made more than all my other days flea-marketing and tiny-thrift-storing and denim-pursing times three.

It took us six months from that day to the grand opening day. I thought it would take about two months. I was so completely out of my league, to a ridiculous level. Racks, hangers, tags, complete renovation of the building, cash registers, jackhammer, security systems, signs, collecting merchandise, trucks, scales, balers, collection boxes, forklift, and on and on. The Gileses have thrift stores in several states but never had any in Alabama. They held classes for our women to teach them the business of sorting and pricing the merchandise. They even set up a call center for us. Jeff oversaw the renovation for the store. He worked so hard, and I was so grateful he knew what he was doing. The girls from the Center helped and were like a collective proud mom as they saw the store coming together. One of our clients, Elizabeth, never missed a day working, and she fell in love with the business. She is a real worker, having entered the program in 2009 and graduated right before we opened the store in 2010. She is a manager of all managers. You will read her story in our next chapter.

I just watched everyone in awe. To this day, I still call Greg and Ann with any questions. The store ended up costing more than we thought. The Gileses were not surprised. They did a contract with us and taught us the accounting end of the business. The store is in the same location and has proven to be extremely profitable for the Center. It is a great place for our women to learn and for us to teach them the value of a hard day's work. We called Greg and Ann when we found the second location, in 2016, and we would never go anywhere without their stamp of approval. We had paid back our initial loan, and the bank loaned us the amount for the new store. This time we knew what to do and how to do it. Ronnie Giles passed away a few years ago, unexpectedly. Attending his memorial service, I noticed the incredible amount of people who were there. The line was around the block. I was not surprised by the line of people waiting to pay their respects. He was the real deal. We owe this incredible family so much, and I know we can never find a way to repay them.

Our thrift stores are not like others. I guess it helped that we had zero knowledge of retail sales, like having a clean slate on which to learn from the best. Our stores do not resemble a common thrift store, however. They are more like a department store, all nice, neat, clean, and organized. Retail atmosphere at thrift store prices!

Many Lovelady program graduates decide to work there after graduation. It is a great experience because our women are out front and learn how to operate in the real world with a legitimate job. Rather than being hidden away, out of the public eye, we take the opposite approach and have our women mingling with the customers. The stores are really happy places, as well as busy and thriving. I receive calls every week with someone giving me a good report on one of the women who have gone over and above what the customer expected.

One of the Lovelady goals is for the public to embrace the women who are restoring their lives. It is defeating for a transforming person to be shunned by others. Sometimes it is hard for us to understand just how much it hurts for others to look down on us. That stigma is something my women have to deal with already in life, so acceptance from the customers in the stores—from the general public—goes a long way to build the confidence a woman needs.

I feel like that is one thing the women love about me. They need people in their lives who are *real*. They have lived a criminal life full of lies and deceit for so long, bending apart everything they are in order to keep getting high, and that *truth* is what they are looking for in a person.

Occasionally, someone negative will come into the store and make a negative remark about my women and I will set them straight quickly. The girls just love when I take up for them. And you know what? *I mean every word of it.* I love them, every last one of them, and they deserve to be treated with the same respect that anyone would want to be treated. Ninety-nine percent of the time our customers love our women in the store. It gives the public a new awareness of who the women are and the girls no longer are nervous about what people think. We call it our win-win.

And every few years we'll decide the stores need a facelift and man, we go at it. I gather a crew together, and we work and make a huge mess that we scramble to fix up before opening time. We figured out a way to get all the carpet up without moving all the clothes racks, covering all the inventory with tarps. We painted every wall and floor, and even pulled a forklift in to pry up some of the former business's red rubber lining running up all the aisles and former walkways. When we were finished, the store looked like we had added onto it because it looked so much bigger. It is always an amazing outcome because our wonderful women join me in the work.

I really want you to get to know Elizabeth, the manager of all managers, the best of the best. She now oversees both stores, with each store having its own manager. Elizabeth is a remarkable person and does a phenomenal job. Having someone who has walked in the same shoes and run the same race as the women in the program makes a huge difference. Her story is in the following chapter.

I am so proud to tell everyone that while we are not completely there yet, we are about 70% self-sufficient. Most of this high percentage is due to the Lovelady Thrift Stores.

Elizabeth's Story, in Her Own Words

"You just can't beat the person who never gives up."
—Babe Ruth

I was born in Alabama to a father who drank all the time and a mother who was addicted to pills. By the time I was five years old, they were divorced. My daddy got custody of my older brother, Nolan. My mother got custody of my sister and me. My sister is eight years older than me. I was the baby of the family. We went back and forth from Dad to Mom and back again throughout our childhood.

My mother moved into a trailer park where she met a man named Skip. She and Skip soon made it official and then moved us all in with them to the small town of Odenville. I was young, and even with my parents' problems I was still pretty optimistic, so I didn't know things were about to take a turn for the worse. My mama graduated from popping a few pills in order to get moving in the morning to a full-blown addiction. Having an addicted mom was no joke. Every day we had to gauge Mom's mood so we would know what we faced. There are no good days in addiction, but some days are more tolerable than others.

Around that time, we also learned that Stepdad Skip had Post Traumatic Stress Disorder. I didn't really know what PTSD was, but it didn't take me long to discover the symptoms and how he released stress. He released the stress he felt from whatever had traumatized him by beating me. I have always been a feisty kind of person. I'm not exactly mouthy, but I'm certainly not wimpy either. My brother and sister never were beaten like me. I learned violence at such an early age, and that violence would linger with me, sort of lying dormant in me, until later. That ugly head of violence would rise up fairly often and get me in trouble in school. I really did not know another way.

I learned all about drugs and much more from Mama and Good Ol' Stepfather Skip. One day, my brother and I were watching television when a woman knocked at the front door. Stepdad Skip opened the door and quickly walked the woman to the bedroom. Nolan and I just looked at each other, waited a minute, and peeked around the corner where we could see what was happening in there. We were surprised to see them making out in a frenzy. Her top was off, and his hands were all over her. We didn't think he saw us looking, and we backed out to the kitchen to call Mama. Man, were we wrong about him not noticing us catching them together! He stormed into the kitchen with a snarl on his face, jerked the phone out of the wall, and went right back to the bed with the woman.

My mom rushed home, running up to the door with a great big belt in her hand, and rushed down the hall into the bedroom. She was screaming at the top of her lungs and began hurling and slinging that belt, whipping them both on any body part she could make contact with. That set Nolan and me off, with pent-up rage against Stepdad Skip, and we began screaming at the top of our lungs. The woman escaped the bedroom without her top and took off out the front door. I really think that scarred me for life, and I am not just saying that. When a little kid sees something like that, it doesn't leave you. I was about seven years old.

Skip and Mom began fighting. He slammed her back into a chair and broke a few of her fingers. Then he began punching her in the face like a man would punch another man. I jumped in there trying to protect my mom from the large man, who punched me in the eye and knocked me across the room. He hit me so hard it knocked me down and I lost consciousness as I fell to the floor. When I was able to stand, Nolan put me on his back and ran next door to our neighbor who was a very good man. He was a preacher. He was the first good man I ever met.

"He's trying to kill my mama!" I have always been the "mouthpiece" of the kids in the family. Nolan was older and much larger than me, but he has always been quieter than me. As quiet as he is, I am as loud in comparison, always was.

The preacher called the police, who got there in a flash. I was so excited that something was finally going to be done about him! Even at my young age, I had endured so much physical abuse. It also was mentally overwhelming. I remember wondering why he would hit and hurt me more than the others. It was probably my mouth. I was so tiny, always the smallest in my class, and always the loudest. Whatever the case, I believed it was my fault.

I was thrilled with excitement because the police were finally going to put him in jail, where the bad people belonged. But they didn't even arrest Stepdad Skip! I was so disappointed. It was the eighties and rural Alabama, and all they did was make him go to a motel for one night for a cooling-off period.

He had sex with a strange woman while little kids watched and then beat his kids and wife brutally, *and they didn't even arrest him*. My eye was already swollen shut, and I was covered with bruises. They made him agree to stay overnight in a motel room, "away from the victims for the night." But he was back in less than three hours making up with my mom.

I had the blackest eye ever, swollen, and my head hurt so bad. My feelings were so hurt that my mom was more worried about my stepdad than her little girl. She told me to lie at school and tell them I fell down the front porch steps. That was my first lie to the authorities, and it rolled off my tongue easily as pie.

My older sister had just moved out of the house when Skip had his playmate over for a visit and beat us all black and blue. Suddenly, all the housekeeping and cooking became my responsibility. I remember having to stand on a chair to reach the stove, cooking for my brother and me. I hate to cook noodles now because I cooked so many of them, so many boxes of macaroni and cheese. By the time I was eight, I never got to play again. I cooked and cleaned like a grown woman. Mom would do her drugs to forget her pain, and look the other way from all of my stepdad's antics.

Skip was offered a job in Sulligent, a small town near the Alabama-Mississippi line, so we packed up and moved away. They painted our new life for us. We were going to be the perfect family. Mom was going to cook and stay home, and he was going to work. He became a 9-1-1 operator, and we settled into community life, with he and my mom even volunteering for the small-town fire department. Skip and Mama both got their EMT license to be paramedics. He portrayed us to be the perfect family with him at the helm as the perfect dad, and life went on the same way it always did. The perfect family was just a facade. Almost nothing changed. The big change was he didn't hit me around the head anymore. My bruises were all covered up by my clothes. He just hit me all over my body.

Time just rolled on. When I was a teenager, Mama lied and told a company I was 15 (even though I was 14) so I could get a job to help pay bills. Behind closed doors, we lived a hell on earth. Mom did not get beat on so much anymore, but I got plenty of beatings. Skip went to school to learn to be a drug officer, with his wife on drugs. She doc-shopped, visiting one doctor and then another for the same prescription, and was high or passed out most of the time. Skip eventually stopped hitting me with his fists. Instead, he would grab my hair and throw me down, telling me he was making me "tough." Well, he certainly did that. I have always been a scrapper.

Skip would get mad and throw everything on the floor, out of the cabinets, and off the counters and tabletops. Even though he would throw things and make messes on the floor, we had carpet that we were not allowed to walk on with shoes. He would actually make us all crawl on our knees across the carpet. Can you imagine needing to go to the bathroom and having to crawl on your knees to get there? When he would have one of his tantrums, we learned to clean up any glass on the carpet because when we crawled, we would get cut on the little shards. It was a miserable existence, one that I believe he enjoyed subjecting us to.

I did not ever want friends to visit. They all thought I had a great stepfather because he was so careful to maintain his reputation. One night, a friend came over to see me. I went to the door and was talking to him, already putting my shoes on to go outside and visit. Stepdad Skip loudly commanded me to get him a glass of milk. I took my shoes off and calmly walked across the carpet, rather than crawling, and glared at him with everything in me. If he had made me crawl right then, I really don't know what I would have done. I got him his glass of milk, walked to the door, and left to go walk around with my friend. When my friend went home and I came back in, I closed the door. Skip picked me up by the hair and threw me on the floor. I scrambled away from him and finally dialed 911. He was so shocked because I had said I was going to do that many times in the past. I had threatened it so much that no one believed I would ever really do it. Had I known it would be the last time he ever laid hands on me I would have called the police on him years before. This time the cops were getting a little wiser. They scared him. No matter what he said, they would look at such a tiny girl and say something else mean to him. He never hit me again.

My mom left Skip for a little over a year. She stayed on her pills but got on cocaine. She was doing it night and day. She offered it to Nolan and me. Nolan tried it and found it to be the answer to all his problems. My poor brother loved it, and he and Mom found a new way to bond. In truth, my mom just used Nolan to help her have plenty. It would take years and a trip to prison for his drug use to run its course. Mom talked me into trying it, but I didn't like it. I walked away from it all and moved in with my sister and her husband, staying in school and working part time. I began to start partying. I finally just gave up and quit school, a decision I would come to hate later in life.

Mama committed to and completed a short stint in rehab to try to get off the cocaine and pills. She then moved back in with Skip to try their love just one more time. She begged me to return to live with them in their new fairy-tale existence. In spite of all that we had gone through, and maybe partially due to the trauma we shared, my mother and I had a very strong bond. So I went back to live with Good Ol' Stepdad Skip and my mother in Walker County, Northwest of Birmingham. Somehow, Skip had become the Chief of Police in a small town there. I was shocked.

I was doing so many drugs I really had no idea who I was. I lived in a fantasy world, and no one could tell me what to do anymore. I walked tall and went through a phase where I carried a baseball bat around with me and was not afraid to use it. My life consisted of drugs, violence, and men. I believe Skip was afraid of me, or at least afraid of what I would do to his reputation. We hated each other, but he no longer said a word to me. At that point, Mom would just hang her head when he started in on her, finally beaten down enough I guess.

Mama, Nolan, and I did plenty of drugs, and I graduated to the needle with OxyContin. I began to cross it with crystal meth, in order to speedball. Mama became my best friend, my only friend, my drug-buddy, our newfound drug bond forming quickly. I walked around with my baseball bat, drugs in tow, hating every man I saw. I was a mean human being. I would pretend to be in love with a man and then steal all his money and anything else I could get my hands on that he owned. I was arrested many times on conspiracy, assault, drugs, and a list of other charges. My rap sheet is as long as I am tall. Of course, I'm not very tall for a person, but that's a long rap sheet. Mom, Nolan, and I were best friends. This sounds so bad but Nolan and I felt responsible for keeping Mom on drugs. It was such a sick relationship. There was no "mom" in this situation. It was three junkies with one being so weak, the stronger ones had to take care of the weak one.

I met a good man who sold pot but would not touch another drug. I stayed with him so I would have a roof over my head. But he was so good to me I felt myself loving him. I still had no other friends besides Nolan and my mom. Somehow, I had managed not to get pregnant until I was 24. I have no idea how I avoided getting pregnant but am so glad I did. I made a vow to clean my life up when I discovered I was going to have a baby. We got married for the baby's sake before he was born.

In all the craziness, I wanted so badly to support a baby sober. My husband helped me stay sober during my pregnancy, and when my time came, I had a beautiful baby boy. I loved him so much, and to this day it makes me sick to know I began using drugs by the time he was three months old. I had no idea how to be a mother at all. I lost him to foster care by the time he was five months old. When I lost him to foster care, I really turned the drug-use dial up to warp speed to escape the pain. My husband

and I divorced. I do not know how I managed to stay alive and not die during that period. I was so lost, had no hope, and didn't care if I lived or died.

One night, during that time, I prayed a real prayer for the first time in my life. I asked God if He was real, would He help me get off drugs. I had no understanding about how God worked or how He answered prayers. And although I wasn't praying to go to jail, that is exactly where I wound up.

Two days after that prayer, I got arrested on an assault charge with that baseball bat of mine. I was looking at prison time. I have no idea what the judge saw in me that no one else had ever seen, but he did. He sent me to The Lovelady Center, a program in Birmingham. The number of women and children at the Center was smaller than it is today and I was blessed enough to have day-to-day contact with Miss Brenda. She saw right through me, introduced me to Jesus, and convinced me that I had a future and could have a real life if I would just slow down and listen to how it can be done.

I gave up drugs right then. It was so strange to let go of them so fast, but that vast hole in my soul was filled with love instead of violence and drugs. It was amazing. I finally found the peace I so desperately needed. I got my sweet baby boy back quickly, and he was allowed to come live with me at the Center. My life turned from terrible to wonderful so fast when deciding to follow the Lord.

One day, I looked up and there was my mom! It happened just like that! She had left Skip and wanted to change her life too. Nolan was the only one still caught up in the drug life. He went to prison for two years, got out, and went back. This cycle lasted for many years. When he got out the last time, my mother and I just walked him into Miss Brenda's house and begged her to do something.

She reminded us she worked with women only, but we told her we wouldn't leave until she said she would help us. It wasn't long before my brother joined in and changed his life. He and Mom had watched me and decided it was possible to change too. Instead of a drug-led family, we became a God-led family. I had a few bumps in the road, but those bumps became two beautiful babies. I became a proud mother of three. But I never used drugs again. My problem was not just drugs but also men, though I had despised them for so long because of Stepdad Skip.

I worked very hard and was on the opening crew of our new thrift store. By the time we opened the second, I was the manager. Now, I am the general manager over both! I am so excited that every day I get to pour into the lives of our women who work with the thrift store who once led a life like I did. Every day, when I feel that anger rise in me, I am forced to remember who I was at one time before I met Jesus.

I finally met the man I knew God had for me. We own a beautiful home. We have our own cars to drive to work, and our children are in football and cheerleading. It's hard to believe that I am a ballpark mom! We have a new baby daughter. My husband works with the thrift stores too, and I am so thankful for my life. I am so thankful that God heard that prayer and sent me to Lovelady. Without Lovelady, I don't believe my life would be where it is today. I love this ministry and am so thankful to work here and show other ladies how they can find the love and hope that I have.

Tar Baby

"Change is painful, but nothing is as painful as staying stuck somewhere you don't belong."
—Mandy Hale

One day several years ago, as I was walking through the thrift store, I saw a very attractive woman. Actually, I could not miss her. She had a presence about her, being over 6 feet tall with blonde hair and blue eyes. I noticed her accent sounded like Jeff's. It is abnormal to hear a Californian accent in Jefferson County, Alabama.

    I have a Southern accent, as do most of our women. We Southerners tend to notice accents, probably because people notice ours. At any rate, Cindy was *different*. I watched her around the other women, and I could tell that they liked and respected her. I asked Elizabeth about her, and she told me pieces of Cindy's story. I was most intrigued at what I heard.

    Cindy was born in California to high school sweethearts who married. Her mother was 5 feet, 10 inches, and her father was 6 feet, 7 inches tall. Dad had a good job working for the state, building roads. He loved motorcycles, and the couple would ride on the weekends. They were excited to have their first baby, a little girl, but Dad really wanted a boy. When Cindy was born, the second little girl, her dad did not hide his disappointment in the matter. The third baby was yet one more daughter. Deciding they would have no more children, Dad chose the middle daughter to be the son he always wanted.

Around that same time, the dad was hurt on the job when a pole fell on him. He had been a very good provider. The pain from the injury opened the door to an opiate addiction. Opiates can be a wonderful solution for genuine pain, but they also can destroy lives if a person is prone to addiction, and he was really prone. Those wonder drugs can destroy so many lives. I see it daily at the Center.

Dad never worked another job after that. He bought an expensive motorcycle. He loved the motorcycle, even parking it in the living room. He would sit Cindy in the shiny black seat and let her pretend to ride it. He doted on Cindy and did not even try to hide that she was his favorite. He had her help him work on cars and motorcycles, calling her "My Little Monkey Wrench."

It was not long before his addiction led him to become an active member of a violent motorcycle gang. He traded the love of his life, his good job, and fatherhood for life in the motorcycle gang. His marriage dissolved. His name became "Animal." He totally changed, literally overnight. Cindy's mother left California and moved to Montana. After Mom left with her children, Animal's life *really* changed. He became an "enforcer" in the gang, increasing his involvement in all the gang's illegal enterprises. An enforcer is just what it sounds like—it isn't good at all. Animal went to prison on a 10-year sentence for armed robbery and became involved in the Aryan Brotherhood, a white supremacist prison gang.

Meanwhile, Cindy had already become too much for her mom to keep in line and by the age of 16 had already been to drug treatment once. She wore the "black sheep of the family" label like a badge of honor. Her sisters disliked her immensely.

As soon as her dad was released from prison, Cindy wanted to go live with him. Her mother was relieved to see her daughter go. Cindy had become so bad, and her mom could not rein her in at all. The mom had remarried, had two sons, and was just *busy*. Cindy was more trouble than her sisters could've ever thought about being. Like most people, Cindy's mother thought that going to prison would actually rehabilitate someone, a common misconception believed by hopeful loved ones when their family members get into trouble. The prison recidivism rate in the United States is the highest in the world at 44%. Animal had at least four round trips to various correction centers.

When Cindy first arrived back in California, her dad began teaching her the ropes about life in a motorcycle gang. Evidently, she was a quick learner. In no time at all, she was not only riding bikes but shooting heroin, and became involved in various other gang activities. There was one solid rule in her father's house: No man could have sex with her. It was a rule she wished he would bend, but he held strongly to it. After all, he was her dad. And we all know how dads protect their little girls. He basically made it crystal clear to Cindy "No sex, but you just shoot all the heroin you want." The members had to help Dad keep up with her, and she was treated like a princess.

To be on the "safe" side, Dad insisted that only he or his best friend could shoot her up. She overdosed a few times, but they always brought her back around. They didn't take chances with the princess. They always had something nearby to remedy an overdose.

Once in a while, she would get antsy wanting a bit of freedom from the few rules she did have and would leave for a few days. She would roam around, seeking new friends, new experiences. There were some women in the gang, but she wanted to meet new people.

By then, Cindy's nickname was "Tar Baby," as the heroin they were distributing was the black and sticky, smokable kind. Cindy was also known for being a great fighter, something else that made her father proud. If there were any women who needed correction, the guys would put them in the backyard where Cindy was waiting to work them over. She never lost a fight and would hurt the females pretty badly. She was a real force. Knowing her now, I just can't picture her hurting another human being for sport. She is so gentle and loving, but very tough.

One day, Dad had someone shoot up a girl with rainwater to show Cindy how someone could just hand over a syringe and she would never know what was in it. He told her about cotton fever from shooting up stuff and its possible consequences. Some call it trash fever. It could kill her, he said. At the very least, she would wish she were dead. Dirty dope is a reality in the dope world; so is shooting up bacteria from using cigarette filters to soak up the liquid in the spoon through the syringe. But addicts will use anything to get the drugs in their bodies. It's supposed to filter out the bad stuff that may give you trash fever—but how anyone could believe a cigarette filter will kill bacteria I will never understand. The girl who was shot up with rainwater did not die but was very ill for days.

One of the bikers had a girl who he felt had wronged him. He decided to punish her by stuffing her in a car trunk for the day. At the end of the day, the girl was almost dead because it had been so hot. Another one overdosed, and the guys simply put her in a car and dumped her at a park. Bodies were a reality to Cindy. Pain was a reality. Crime was a way of life.

In a single day Cindy saw more illegal activities than a large percentage of our clients have seen combined. There would be stretches of time when Dad would have to go to prison. During those times, Animal's mom, Cindy's grandmother, would keep up with Cindy as best she could. She lived next door to them and was a major enabler. She would help her son anytime funds were low. I guess it was a case of "the family who steals and does all other activities together stays together."

During one of Dad's trips to prison, Cindy got with one of the gang members. With dad out of town and safely tucked away behind bars, Cindy had time to get pregnant and have her first baby—a boy. Dad finally got his boy, so he was beyond happy, actually, surprising everyone who formerly believed he was going to kill the father of the baby. In actuality Cindy almost killed the baby. She overdosed on heroin when she was six months pregnant. Under the guise of saying Cindy had toxemia, the doctor put her in the hospital for a month to save the baby. Cindy was given opiates to manage withdrawals, and finally at 32 weeks they took the baby. Right at three pounds, he was born as healthy as could be. Daddy was so proud—he had a baby boy to bring into the family business!

Cindy stayed in California with her son until he was 3 years old. Animal's mom took care of the child while Cindy ran wild. Eventually, Cindy felt the time was right to leave California, also wishing to be away from the father of her son. She loaded up and went back to Montana.

Cindy's mom did not meet her with open arms. In fact, Cindy actually had to convince her mother to allow her and the grandson into her home. Cindy sold the idea to her mother and also decided she was going to change and leave her wild ways behind.

Cindy met a guy in Montana and began a serious relationship with him, and had another baby boy. She was happy—for a little while. This was the first time that Cindy had been clean. As I listened to Cindy's story, I had the hardest time wrapping my mind around believing that the woman sitting in front of me was the crazy, wild biker chick being described.

She was on pretty bad terms with her sisters. However, when she decided later to leave Montana, she left both her boys with them, her mother helping the sisters. Her firstborn son was then 13 years old and not happy with his mom. At some point in their lives, many boys change from wanting their mothers to never wanting to see them again.

When Cindy arrived back in California, she found it exactly as she left it. Everything seemed much the same, yet different. She got back with her first son's father, John. Eventually, their son moved from Montana out to California to live with them, but there was no white picket fence or happy lives—they all three ended up in trouble. John got into serious trouble, so he and Cindy went on the run. The son went back to Montana. Her dad died during this time period, and that was a heartbreaker. No matter what, he was still her father and she loved him with her entire being. She went into deep mourning and was more than happy to put California behind her.

Cindy and John ended up in West Virginia. The road ended there for John because the bondsman caught up with him there. Being on parole already, John was about to do another stretch in prison.

When John was taken, Cindy walked to the bus station and put all her money on the window ledge and said, "I want a ticket to the farthest place I can go on this." She did not even ask where, and when she got on the bus she discovered she was going to Winston-Salem, North Carolina.

That is where the wind blew her next. She got off the bus in Winston-Salem and within less than a day met Bobby and quickly got into a relationship. You just can't believe this stuff. They had shared interests, including a love for every type of drug. She stayed with Bobby for a relatively long time, and they decided to go to Florala, Alabama, because her mom had moved there a few years prior with her husband. Cindy's sister had moved south to the Panhandle of Florida, and their mother had wanted to be close to help raise the boys.

Finally, living in Florala, Cindy was arrested and facing some serious drug charges and had to sit in jail. While she was there, she heard about a place called The Lovelady Center, which helps women who want a new life. She was 48 years old at that time and had used drugs almost *every single day* since her teen years—those not spent incarcerated, anyway. She had never been married. She had no family but her mom, who told her she dreaded seeing her. She had two boys she didn't even really know. She had some serious prison time coming her way. She hated the world but hated herself most of all.

She told me that she just sat in jail and thought hard the entire stay. Going to prison did not bother her—it was really just a right of passage in her world. She was not afraid of anything. But one burning thought needed to be sorted out in order for her to hold onto sanity.

The women in jail were all talking about Lovelady, and that name stuck in her head. When she called her mom, Cindy asked her to see about this unique program for women. Cindy had no information or knowledge about the place; she just liked the name. Her mom filled out the application for her online. She heard there was usually a waiting list, and she didn't tell any jail mates that her mother had applied so no one else would be inspired and take her place.

When she stood before the judge, he announced that she would be enrolled in drug court, though she never asked for anything other than prison. As the name implies, drug courts are specifically for persons with an addiction that causes them to break the law. These court programs offer individuals the opportunity to enter long-term drug treatment and agree to court supervision, rather than receiving a jail or prison sentence. As soon as she could get to a phone, she called The Lovelady Center to see if she had a bed ready, and learned that she did! She had her mom take her as soon as she was released. Upon walking through the door for the first time, she immediately began to cry. The front desk girl thought she was crying about having to be at The Lovelady Center and said, "Don't worry, you will love it." Cindy said she never doubted that. She just felt a peace she had never felt before and knew this place was something different.

Cindy called her probation officer before she handed over her cell phone and told him she had come to The Lovelady Center, and therefore had to leave the jurisdiction to which she was probated. She admitted to him she would have run if she had not come to Lovelady. He told her he would handle the legalities of it all, and that Lovelady staff could test her weekly for the courts. He told her The Lovelady was the best program he had seen and he was very happy for her.

Once in the Intake Department, she filled out her paperwork, was drug tested and tested clean, had all her belongings searched, and answered a lot of questions. Then a staffer asked if she had any questions for them.

With tears streaming down her cheeks, that burning question in her mind that had filled her thoughts in jail finally came spilling out: *"Can you tell me if I have lost my soul?"*

Cindy said she knew the moment she entered the Center's doors she felt overwhelmed with an immediate peace she had longed for most of her life. Cindy was escorted down to Phase One, where she would spend a month with other new intakes in a secluded part of the building, nurtured and loved on, introduced to Jesus, and taught about addiction and sitting still. Phase One has a committed, God-led client representative who puts everything she can into helping the women see they are worthy of a normal life, that the relationship with their children can be restored, and what to expect from the 9- to 12-month program they are entering.

Cindy was not a short program kind of girl. She experienced her changed life in stages. After the first few emotional days, she settled in and grew according to the program's guidelines. She was actually a house monitor to some ladies in one of our programs. Cindy always liked the idea that her drug use never hurt anyone but herself, no matter how many times we told her differently. One night, on Cindy's watch, we had to dismiss a young woman for having drugs in the Center. We always strongly suggest anyone being dismissed stay on the sofa until the next morning. The young lady declined to stay and had some guys pick her up and give her a ride. Of course, she immediately used drugs, and the guys thought she had died—they just dumped her body in the middle of the road. A Lovelady graduate happened to pick her up and took her to her mother's house, where paramedics were called. She survived. But under Cindy's "watch" as house mom, it affected her deeply. She saw her drug use for the real diabolical poison it is. Cindy was forever changed in moments like that, with Jesus opening her eyes to the truth about drugs. She reconciled with and apologized to her children and family and has never looked back at that old life again.

Today she is a manager of one of our thrift stores and lives in one of our graduate houses. She lives an amazing life and knows just what Amazing Grace really is.

The rest is history. Cindy, of course, answered her own question: She had *not* lost her soul.

Peas in a Pod

"If you are offered a seat on a rocket ship, get on; don't ask what seat."
—Sheryl Sandberg on the best advice given to her

As Melinda and I maintained the executive positions, Shay prided herself with being the first person anyone saw when entering the program, other than the receptionist who pointed a woman to Shay's department when she arrived. In the beginning, that receptionist position changed on a day-to-day basis, depending on who was available. So the actual face of the ministry who people saw as a constant was Miss Shay, and believe me, she took her position very seriously.

The Intake Department is on the floor where a person enters the building from 2nd Avenue, the main entrance. We call it "Second Floor" because we count from the atrium view, where all three levels can be seen. There is a basement level, where our Education Department and after-school tutoring classrooms are located, as well as our gym and aerobics classrooms.

In the Intake Department, Shay would send out letters of acceptance when a woman applied to come into the program, and also directed women to another program if we were not a good fit for them. Her department would answer questions from courts and attorneys as to what Lovelady offered, and sometimes women would just walk in with their bags, looking for a place to change their lives. More and more responsibility seemed to fall on Intake, and Shay loved every bit of it. Sometimes it seems we would have a meeting and Shay's department would end up with one more thing to do. I would talk to her about it, and she would explain to me that no one else was able to do what she could do and no one else cared as much to make sure things were done properly. Frankly, there was so much to do, and we just let her run with it.

This was the time in Shay's life that she believed God had set apart for her—the reason she was born. She was always there because she lived in the building. Concerning some issues, Melinda and I would laugh and ask Shay what she wanted us to do and by golly, she would tell us! God and the Center had become her world as she worked on the relationships with her daughters.

Shay and I disagreed fairly often, but she taught us so much. I feel like I have a Master's degree in the underworld now. Mainly our arguments would be about how mouthy she would be with the women in the program. She would tear into them over the smallest thing. I explained to her that we had to meet them where they are, not where we want them to be. No one ever got over on her. Melinda and I watched her every move, learning. She had been in prison, jails, juvie, and the streets for 90% of her life. She had street smarts that Melinda and I lacked. She could call people out when they were trying to pull fast tricks on us or manipulate a situation.

In the first years, an innocent-looking woman was ordered to come into the program by a judge, and when she arrived, she rambled on about getting clean for her little girl. I fell headfirst into her rubbish, knee deep. I believed her—hook, line, and sinker. We thought Shay had taught us all her tricks and I had one-upped her this time by believing that innocent girl standing before us.

"Ma, she's lying," Shay said. "I can see it in her eyes." The girl just continued to wail about wanting to change. I looked into her eyes as Shay kept going through the girl's meager belongings she brought with her, and my heart broke.

"Enough is *enough*, Shay!" I exclaimed, rather sternly, as Shay reached up into the woman's hair. A different kind of fear washed over the girl's face as she struggled against Shay, dipping away from the search and out of Shay's reach. I knew she was looking at prison time and Lovelady was her only out—the judge had sent her to us as an *alternative* to prison if she could complete our program.

"Aha! I found it, Ma! It's in the scrunchie of her ponytail!" Shay exclaimed. She held out her hand and demanded the scrunchie from the girl, who immediately obeyed, tears streaming down her cheeks. Shay turned the scrunchie inside out and found a little tear where small, white baggies had been stuffed into an unraveled seam. "Meth, Ma. It's *meth*." Shay held out her hand in my direction this time, waiting for me to observe the tiny bags. The baggies looked like miniature sandwich bags with a closable seam at the top. They were filled with icy-looking shards that people crush and snort, smoke, inject, or ingest for a speedy high that can last for days. I knew all too well that Methamphetamine is an evil drug, producing paranoia, psychosis, extreme weight loss, and permanent damage to the body and teeth if used for long periods of time.

How can someone know, just by observing behavior, that a person is hiding drugs somewhere on themselves? That was our Shay. She was also sad to see the girl go, but off to jail she went, crying the whole time and begging us to please just let her stay. We cannot risk someone bringing drugs into the Center. As bad as Shay and I felt for her, we just could not risk her settling in and somehow getting drugs brought in to her, possibly pulling her clean roommate or others into the mix. She begged us all the way up until the police walked in, *"Please, I have a little girl."* We make hard decisions at The Lovelady Center. I cried and prayed for her that night when I went to sleep.

As the girl was being loaded into the patrol car, shackled and headed to Jefferson County Jail to eventually be processed into a prison stay, Shay had every right to gloat and say "I told you so." I actually expected it. She touched her hand to mine as we stood there at the front door watching the patrol car pull away. "She'll be ok, Ma" is all she said. We later found out the young woman had used all her chances and had been sent to prison. She was sent away for three years. It's so sad to think she had freedom in her grasp and traded it for a quick high. When she got out of prison, the trail went cold. We hope she is doing well.

Miss Brenda and the Lovelady Movement

Getting busy over the next few days, Shay and I decided the Center would never be clean until the carpet was pulled up, so we gathered a team and off we went. I am the worst to dive into a situation without seeing how deep the water is. In my defense, it never could have happened except the way that it did because we cannot just close down and renovate. We are open, *and busy*, 24/7, 365 days a year—so there is never any time like the present.

The same carpet had probably been there for thirty-plus years because the building had been a hospital and, for a while, an assisted living facility. There had been carpeting throughout all the main areas and rooms. When we pulled pieces up, it was just horrible. Some days you could barely see in front of you because the dust from the carpet hung in the air.

Poor Melinda, who never gets sick, ended up with the flu, strep throat, and a double ear infection all at the same time, after having pulled carpet up for three days; the sickness and filth hidden under the carpet was just horrific. Once we got through the outer layer, however, pure beauty was discovered, much like the sweet women helping us. Shay and our little team found beautiful floors underneath the mess.

We had a great time, learned some hard lessons about renovating as nonprofessionals, and started turning our old hospital into the castle our princesses deserved. I had renovated residential houses before, so I thought "No big deal, right?"

We got off to a rather slow start, though, on our painting. We had so much paint that had been donated, so never one to waste a dime of donated funds, I decided to mix all the paint together in a huge tub. It was getting a little too dark for my taste, so I sent my little minions to grab a few gallons of white and we would put it in the dark and have a much lighter color. In the meantime, Matthew had stopped to visit for a few minutes to see how the renovation was going, so I told my "painters" I would be right back and to wait on me. I led him around and finally downstairs, bragging about our pretty paint colors. My elves had already put the white gallons into the dark to surprise me, and they did surprise me! They did not know then, and still do not know, that you cannot mix latex and non-water-based acrylic together. Dear me, what a mess! It took several hours to get paint remover to get the paint up and off my little ladies. Lesson learned on my part. I never let anyone put paint together again.

We painted the entire interior of the building. Shay had a joke she loved to tell everyone. We had so much donated paint, and I figured we could just mix it all to make enough for all the walls to match—to stretch it out. The only problem is when I mixed the paint, no matter how hard I tried, it always came out to be shades of terra-cotta. So she named the paint "Terra-cotta One," "Terra-cotta Four," "Terra-cotta Sixty-eight," etc. We knew we could never touch up the paint in the future because we would never be able to match that shade again. It was an ongoing joke about never touching the walls. "Don't use tape on the walls! Don't nail anything up!"

While Shay and I tore up the building, Melinda would work on the program curriculum. The first time I really understood the vastness of what we were doing was when I was in the lobby one day alone, sitting in the quiet. Then it was time for a class and I watched all the women laughing, hurrying to class, filing down the stairs, and coming in through doorways. I stood in the lobby just crying like a baby with tears running down my face. "Miss Brenda! What is *wrong?*" they asked as they passed. That moment was just so surreal and too good to be true, after all the struggling and blood, sweat, and tears . . . . It was just so beautiful to have been standing there at that moment. That day, I could have been standing in any college anywhere in the nation. Women who had no hope and no options were rushing to classes, committing to learning how to change their lives and were clearly *happy* about it. I was just so honored to have witnessed that beautiful moment, much less be part of it.

By the time the floors were done, we had put together a good team: individuals who felt their entire lives had led up to that moment—that it was their destiny to help other women. Who better to understand what our women were going through than those who have gone through it themselves? We did have to venture out into the job market if we needed someone with a certain degree. But even then, many times, we have tried to hire those who have gone through the program or who have had family members who were addicts and ended up finding their destiny right at Lovelady.

It's an unbelievable thing to have a team who will take on projects because we come across something that will help the women have a better footing. Our staff is the best! I learned very early in business that a leader can only be as good as those she surrounds herself with.

Building a ministry with my sweet, blue-eyed daughter reminded me of the Proverbs "iron sharpens iron" reference. I saw a forest, and she saw each tree. She saw half-empty, and I saw not only that the glass was half-full but that it actually wasn't far from the top. I drove her crazy and still do. It has become our way, and it has been what made Lovelady great.

Melinda had to be gone one day for most of the day. We had just finished the inside, and she knew I was in that mood where I wanted to make things better with wide-sweeping changes. She made me promise not to do anything drastic that day because she wasn't ready for more changes just yet.

She hadn't been gone 20 minutes that day when the Alabama Department of Corrections called, needing to know if we had 50 beds available to fill in the Supervised Release Program. We are the only women's facility in Alabama approved by the Department of Corrections to receive women from Julia Tutwiler Prison. Therefore, if we do not have room for them, they stay in prison. I wouldn't wish that on anyone. I told the Department of Corrections that I would get right back with them later that day.

Now where was I going to put those 50 women? I had an idea and headed off to a vacant part of the building—the old surgery area now used for storage! I called the Alabama Department of Corrections and told them we could take the women; I just needed three or four days to prepare. While I was talking, my heart was pounding because I knew Melinda would not be pleasantly surprised. Shay, on the other hand, was standing right in front of me listening, adding gasoline to my already blazing fire. Melinda never liked for Shay and me or Matthew and me to be together. She says they are like nitro to me. I just say we get a lot done.

I called for volunteers among the women already at the Center, and many quickly found a place to hide. Fifteen willing, able-bodied women stepped up to the challenge. I talked about how awesome it was going to be for these women to come into the program as we walked into the storage area. Their eyes almost popped out of their heads—there was so much stuff that had to be moved out. I told them, "Let's start taking this junk down to the dumpster."

It took me just a moment to know this was not going to work. It was taking too long, and I had opened my big mouth and already told them to give me a *few days*. We decided to make a human chain and just pass stuff down the line. That *still* wasn't getting the job done. I stood there with my mind running crazy through different possibilities and my sweet women suggesting things and talking over each other and I just said, *"Shhh!"*

I ran to see where the dumpster was in relation to the building, and I squealed with delight! The dumpster was right outside the windows, three floors down. We put a lady downstairs, at a safe distance, to stand guard out back so no one would get hurt, then I opened the windows and threw the first piece out. Sure enough, it dropped three stories and landed in the large dumpster. The loud bang erupted and drew staff out from everywhere, asking *"What was that?"* But it worked great. Boxes, broken pieces of furniture, all matter of what I had quickly decided was junk and had to go was dropped into the dumpster, rattling the neighborhood with noise. Not only did we save time in the obvious way, but as the various pieces fell into the dumpster, each piece broke into pieces and we did not have to knock it apart.

Then we got on the phone and one of my fast talkers helped round up 50 beds and mattresses. *Delivered within three days? Wonderful!* I was so excited. Then the phone rang. "Mother," she said, like she wasn't sure it was me. I knew in my heart some tattletale had been texting Melinda, telling her what I had been doing. I wanted to say "Wrong number," but I'm brave if nothing else.

"Yes, Melinda, how's the meeting?" I said, hoping this was a random call to see how things were going, although I knew it was not. I tried to cover the fact that I was clearly out of breath.

"Get off it, Mom, you promised *no more changes!*"

"Well something came up. DOC has a few women for the Supervised Release Program we need to help," I threw out to her.

Melinda retaliated with *"How many is a few?"* She was growing a tad loud. I told her the whole story.

"I have so many texts from scared women thinking we are closing and you are throwing everything out the windows!" I explained the entire operation of the windows, the junk, the searching for mattresses and frames—*everything*. I explained how we could not leave those women in Tutwiler if we could do anything about it. In the end, I knew she would be fine because she has her mom's heart. We *are* two peas in a pod. But one of the peas is pretty hard to handle.

Besides, the pod was getting a little crowded. Shay made three peas in a pod, and then all of a sudden I received the call I had been waiting for a long time. It was from my oldest son, Beau. I had for many years felt like he should be part of the ministry. He is a strong, quiet believer and had gotten married and settled down. He decided to give up his business at the beach and come back to Birmingham. His first project was to build out our second thrift store, and he has not looked back.

The day he called us was a particularly grueling day. He knows buildings and maintenance issues plus had so many contacts to help glue our castle together when we did not have the funding to overhaul big projects. We were expecting him to turn the place upside down, so we certainly were not disappointed. Building repairs, maintenance, and renovations are constantly happening.

What we were not expecting was what he brought to the table for the women. He saw immediately the need for the women to give back more, and he was right. We have so much food and always strive to make use of the extra. For instance, a local grocery store that donates so much may also donate just a few pork chops in a load. If we cannot spread it out over our entire population as a meal, we end up with extra and give it out as food boxes to our graduates and staff. Gradually, we began receiving more extra than we could give out. One of our strong desires is to help our neighbors, so Beau put together a food ministry outreach, The Lovelady Manna, to aid our neighborhood. We now give out over 6,000 meals a month to the impoverished community surrounding The Lovelady Center. We call it our Giving Back Program. Our

Dr. Brenda Lovelady Spahn

women are able to give back. I always say, "You don't *birth* a hero. If you raise him right, he will always be *your* hero."

The pod is getting crowded.

The Heart of Lovelady

"A beautiful heart is better than a thousand beautiful faces. Be with people who have beautiful hearts."
—Dr. Brenda Lovelady Spahn

In prior years, money has been my motivation in life or, at least, an important motivation. I was a Christian, but I never really got my hands dirty. I was a Christian from a distance. If anyone asked me if I was a believer, I absolutely would have said *"Yes."* I served on the board of directors for ministries; I knew all the important meetings to attend. But I am here to tell you that for a long time I never got fully involved. I served the Lord the way I wanted to serve Him. Everything seemed to be fine between us. He just needed to let me be me and let me live my life. I did things that I wanted to do for the Lord. The key was the letter *I*. It was all about what I wanted and what I could get for myself and my family. I would do things for others only as long as it did not get in my way or interfere with my plans.

It's fun reminiscing about the ministry and how it began, and sharing how we have put the program together to become the best we can be. *"Empowering women through faith-based initiatives, so they can return to society as well-equipped women of God"* is our mission statement. Our goal is to assist a woman to become the very best she can be. Our society is plagued with an addiction of drugs, sex, greed, mental and physical abuse, hopelessness, and a mixture of entertainment—from music to movies—that escalate desires and hinder a woman from being the best she can be.

We push forward but also hope for the day that The Lovelady Center is out of business because it is no longer a need in our society. Our social world consists of greed, sex, and lies. Morality is headed to rock bottom. I used to think we had already hit rock bottom, but all it takes is turning on the news and I know that it seems much worse than last year.

It's like the very technology that helps us so much is the same technology that is destroying us. People think I am not all that knowledgeable about technology, and they are correct. I really feel I know all that I need to know. Well, maybe I could learn a bit more. But the point is there is too much happening now. Like most everything we have that is good and useful, there will always be those who make it bad. My goodness, our children can see people have sex on prime-time television. We must be vigilant about what we allow.

With that being said, occasionally it's brought to our attention at the Center that we are too strict about what we do not allow. We monitor our television hours as well as programs, and many programs are not allowed. Certain music is not allowed. No R-rated movies or higher are allowed.

Not too long ago, I was walking down the hall of the Center. A young girl was walking past me with her earbuds on, having a jamming time listening to her music. Earbuds are not allowed in public areas, but I walked to her and asked her to let me listen to that music that had her so intrigued—and the color drained out of her face. She reluctantly handed them over to me. She had been at the Center long enough to get out of Phase One, but she was still showing slight bruising that had been healing since her admission. Her eye had been blackened severely and still showed signs of having been pummeled. She was covered in healing wounds on her arms. Clearly she had been beaten very badly before coming to us. As I listened to the music playing in her earbuds, it hurt my heart for her. Some guy was rapping about "his woman" and saying the most derogatory remarks about his woman that I have heard spoken about another human being in a long time. It was so bad.

Of course, I invited her to my office. We sat there and talked about her abusive relationship with her boyfriend, using drugs with him, and how that felt when she lost her children because of it all. We talked about how her children were affected by the violence they had witnessed against their mother. After we discussed these atrocities, we talked about how the music made them sound so good. How the sex and violence were exactly how the music described them. The music sends a message that not only is it okay but the destructive lifestyle is exciting and desirable.

I hoped she left my office with a greater understanding, and I thanked God that I had happened upon her. I kept the earbuds for a short time as a consequence. You may think we are wrong for monitoring everything they listen to, but what you have to realize is that hearing songs they once partied to takes them back to that moment of being high. It's a trigger—one we do not wish to be pulled.

That is a few minutes of how many of our days are spent. Simply explaining another way of life is what we do every day, all day. We visit the prisons and work with the system to release women, build relationships with the courts to build trust so they will send a woman to us for treatment instead of incarceration, and long to see the light bulbs go off in their heads. We teach them how to avoid returning to their previous life of crime and drugs once they are paroled or given an alternative sentence that involves finishing our program. We meet their basic needs and then some. We feed. We dress. We give out hugs and love to those without it. We help women heal physically and emotionally. We speak life into the souls of those who have given up. We introduce Jesus to those who do not know anything about Him other than maybe have heard His glorious name. We introduce new entertainment. We pour light into the dark holes left by the world and traumatic abuse. We show it is okay to have fun and enjoy life. We actually have such a good time that it's not even work. Anyone who visits the Center hears laughter and feels the very Spirit of God as soon as they enter.

More than 10,000 women have been in The Lovelady Center program. There is no way of telling all the stories. While some may sound the same, rest assured that no two are exactly alike.

We minister to the needs of each woman. Like you, the reader, did previously with Elizabeth and Cindy, in the next pages you will get to meet some more victims who have become victors. You will also read about some who did not make it. My hope is that your Spirit will be lifted, encouraged, and educated. These women may be foreign to you, or may be your next-door neighbor. I want you to see each of them as a woman who may have made a mistake but has found a new life—maybe she simply never had a chance before. Whatever the case, I want you to meet a few of our Loveladies, the *heart* of the ministry.

It has been extremely difficult to pull together the exact stories I felt would touch your heart. For each story you read, my desire would be for that story to strike a chord with you and touch you or even motivate you to be a better person and take part in changing the world around you in some way. With so many more happy stories than sad ones, I wanted to tell only the happy ones at first. But that does not seem real or fair, for each story that is less happy than another is a story of someone's daughter, mother, or sister. Even if a story is less motivational, it is equally or maybe even more important that we share it with you. Just know that every story is a heartbeat in the heart of Lovelady.

The Girl with No Name

> " 'A name isn't a person,' Ga said. 'Don't ever remember someone by their name.' "
> —Adam Johnson, *The Orphan Master's Son*

Thousands of women have come through The Lovelady Center. Every woman has a story to tell about her life. Every woman seems to think her situation is way worse than anyone else's. But isn't that understandable? Each one's level of trauma in her life is the worst thing she herself has ever been through.

One day, as I was sitting at my desk, all of a sudden, I heard an overhead page sounding out throughout the Center, requesting that "Baby Girl Primrose" report to a certain office. I almost stumbled when jumping up from my desk and running down to the lobby, demanding to see this *"Baby Girl."*

I quickly reminded my front desk staff that *no street names are allowed in our Center.* We required that everyone be called by their proper name, their given name at *birth*. The streets were not welcome in our program's world. My desk person was trying to explain something, but I wasn't hearing it, partly because I saw a woman approaching the front desk, dragging her feet, head hanging down, hair unkempt. When she raised her eyes and looked at me, they were without hope of any kind. She must have been approaching 45, and her skin was white as a sheet of paper. It looked like she had never been out in the sun. I softened a bit and asked her to come up to my office with me, but also knew I had to make sure she understood *why* we had this rule she had just broken.

When we finally made it to my office, I unloaded on her. Remember, counseling is not my strong suit, but laying down the law is. I asked her if she had not been told the rules? "Have you not read the rules, plainly laid out in the client handbook, about using your real name instead of street names?" It seemed like everything I said was falling on deaf ears. I am a very "in your face" kind of person, and I immediately saw that my approach was not working as well as I would have liked. I finally said, *"Let's begin with your given name. Tell me that."*

With her eyes looking at her hands opening and closing in her lap, she told me that she had no name. This infuriated me to no end because I knew it was impossible. I told her she'd better give me her name *right now* or she would be on her way back to Tutwiler in the next car out of there. She looked up and stared blankly and told me once again that she did not have a name. I sensed her fear, which set me back just a bit. "I can make one up if you want me to, but I really don't have one," she stated. I slowly realized *this woman is telling me the truth*.

I sat back in my chair so as not to intimidate her and began asking her questions. Little by little, it was revealed that "Baby Girl" was indeed her "given" name. Her birth certificate had "Baby Girl Primrose." Primrose was given to her as a last name—after the nurse in the delivery room. What that really meant was she was simply abandoned. I did not know what to say. I looked at her and knew that the bewildering pain that I was feeling for a minute *she had felt for a lifetime*. I wanted to cry with her but remained strong. I knew people around her had felt sorry for her, but no one had taken the time to *do* anything about it. Right then and there, I vowed to get this wrong made right. I looked at her prison information, and sure enough, the 43-year-old woman who sat before me had no real name. The only identity she owned had been prison records and prison numbers. She didn't have a driver's license or any form of identification whatsoever other than that prison ID.

I had known others who drove without a driver's license—our Miss Shay had done that for years. I could tell Baby Girl was intelligent, and once I looked past the unkempt person with no gleam in her eyes, I immediately knew why God had her with us.

I became a woman on a mission. I called out to the office across from mine. *"Melinda!"* I wanted a birth certificate from who-knows-where on the woman sitting there in front of me with who-knows-what-name. Melinda looked at me for a second and asked politely, *"You want what, Mother?"* I recounted the story to Melinda and Baby Girl's gaze moved off of her hands finally, with a hint of curiosity in her face as she watched our interaction. Still, no smile. Still, no hope.

"Just how do you expect me to fulfill that request?" Melinda asked, but I could see she was already working out the first steps in her head. My daughter is a problem solver, very intelligent.

"I guess with some of that research magic you work on the computer, my dear," I answered, and told Baby Girl to go on to her client rep's office, who had originally called her over the loudspeaker. "Pick up your feet when you walk, my dear, and return to my office in an hour." Melinda went back to her office to get started. I knew she could do it.

Within an hour, Baby Girl returned, as I had requested. I told her to return again in two hours. She looked down at the floor, and I realized that there had been many "come back and check later" instructions in her life. She had never seen her birth certificate before and was not sure she even had one. I assured her she did. I mean, she *had* to, right? In a few more minutes, I heard a loud, whooping yelp from the adjoining office, and Melinda came running in, thrilled over what she had found. *Baby Girl Primrose* indeed had a legal birth certificate.

Sure enough, she had been given no real name and was born in Arizona. Melinda retrieved my credit card and ordered the birth certificate. I had a staff member go out into the Center and find our girl instead of calling her again over the intercom. I wanted the next time that I called her to be by a real name. Someone brought her into my office, and I began to see some hope in her eyes almost immediately when she learned she did have a birth certificate. When I showed her the faxed copy she almost fainted. "I'm real, aren't I?" she asked, tearing up.

I sent her away with a task: "You need to pick out a name." She asked me over and over, "For *real*?" I told her to go decide on her favorite name, that she would need a *first name* and *second name*. "What about a last name?" she asked. I told her, "Well, yes, I guess you need that too!"

I held my tears in until she was safely out of my office and then broke down and just sobbed. I began thinking back about seeing my babies in the hospital nursery and reading the displayed signs on their little hospital beds: *baby girl this* or *baby boy that*. At least Primrose represented *someone* who had been there at her birth. She had gone through the system, been in foster care, juvenile detention centers, jails, prisons—all with no real name. I remembered how excited I had been to give each of my precious babies their names and how much thought had gone into that.

Then I thought of that woman with no help or no one to love her enough *to even name her*. And I couldn't help it—I had someone bring her right back into my office, and I offered, *"Let me help you pick out a name."* She was elated.

I would love to tell you that we came up with a name right away, but three days later, she was still undecided and we were still offering beautiful suggestions. It became an ordeal. Finally, she settled on *Danielle*. She loved it. "Okay, you will be Danielle." A little later, she announced that she wanted her second name to be *Aliyah*. Then we decided to reverse them, with Aliyah being her first name. Finally, it was time for the last name. When she was a small girl, there was a little boy who was very kind to her, and his name was Turner. She had not had much kindness in her life, so she wanted to remember him.

So her name became *Aliyah Danielle Turner*. I felt like I had named another child of my own. We did the name change and sent the birth certificate off. The entire experience was worth every cent and was priceless to Aliyah Danielle.

She had lost everything when she went to prison. So we had her hair done, had her nails done, and bought her some new clothes. To this day, it is one of the best experiences of my life.

Her graduation date came, and I still remember her up there as a smiling, hopeful, and devoted believer. "Danielle," as she chose to be called, considered herself healed by her Savior.

The women gathered in front of the devotion area and danced to a Christian song that had a great beat, as they always do before every service, graduation, or house meeting we have down there. The music faded out, and Melinda took the mic.

"We have a beautiful group of graduates this morning, and as always, before we honor them, we want to honor *Him*. So everyone up to your feet; let's worship together!" A beautiful song about miraculous change began then, and the voices singing along with it became so loud that it was difficult to make out the accompanying artist's voice from the joyous women's.

As those in attendance took their seats, the drama team performed and the entire atrium thumped with applause and screams of agreement. Our graduation services are very powerful, filled with those who see that day as their own future possibility, those who remember their own moments from the past, and those who are there proudly celebrating their daughter, sister, or mother, with tears streaming down their faces in joy. It is one of the most emotionally rapturous moments you will ever experience, if ever you decide to come visit one Friday morning. Long-term staff members do not wear makeup on those days particularly, because the tears just flow on graduation Fridays.

Once the drama concluded, a few women helped move the large cross-shaped podium to the center of the stage, and although Melinda normally leads graduation, I retrieved the mic, deciding I wouldn't miss this graduation for anything.

With Melinda by my side at the podium, I began to call name after name of women who then approached the stage and thanked everyone who played significant roles in their recovery. We call graduation Friday "the Jesus Grammys." He is thanked first and foremost, then family, staff members, friends—the emotion is off the charts. I mean, it is just *wonderful*.

"Danielle Turner!" The room erupted in applause and screams for the woman who rose from her seat and crossed the devotion area. Friends and staff members alike loved her deeply and admired her courage. Danielle hugged me and then Melinda, and I handed her graduation certificate to her in the frame, as we do with all graduates. An extra piece of paper was sitting atop the glass, and she yelped with delight when she realized what it was.

Dr. Brenda Lovelady Spahn

Aliyah Danielle Turner held the birth certificate in her new name high over her head as the room continued to erupt with joy.

I Was Baby Girl

"A mother is she who can take the place of all others but whose place no one else can take." —Cardinal Mermillod

Everyone's life begins with a birth from a mother. Ideally, life begins with a mother and a father. Some children are born to just a single mom. After the oohs, ahhs, first and middle names, footprints and photos, the mother nurtures her baby. She *naturally* loves her baby. She tries to give the child the best life she can give her or him under whatever the circumstances provide.

Occasionally, the mother cannot raise the baby, so she finds another home for the child, also an act of love. She may later think of the child and either be glad she didn't have to deal with the burden or still long for restoration with the child. Either way, she knows she did the best to give the child a life. For a tiny percentage of births, a woman is so callous and uncaring that she simply gives the baby to anyone who wants to take the child off her hands so she can move on. Or takes off and leaves them at the hospital. *That is the story of my beginning.*

Newspaper articles are written about discarded babies, but there were no articles about the one left in the hospital for just anyone to end up with. Since there were no news stories about me, no wonderful couple rushed to the hospital to save the cute little baby girl and take me home to cherish forever. I wasn't one of those babies who was given to parents who had waited years to adopt and then dedicated their lives to raising.

When finally seeing my birth certificate much later in life, we found that my mother was unwed and it was dated in early 1964. The birth certificate was for a baby girl, and so the name was just that: *Baby Girl Primrose*. So my last name was given to me by the nurse who cared for me at the hospital, Nurse Primrose. From 1964 until 2007, that was the only legal name I had.

The foster parent who wound up with me was named Anna, and she was married to a man named Gus. I was born in Arizona but was sent to live in Texas. Anna and Gus did not name me either. I suppose they could have petitioned the court to do so, but they were not interested in what was best for me, *at all*. My first memory is not of a birthday party or Christmas morning or a family vacation, but of sexual abuse. I do not remember exactly how young I was. Anna knew about Gus and other men, "uncles," abusing me and did nothing.

I was a miserable, lonely little girl. I was not of school age at that time, so I very rarely even left the house. If I didn't do anything just the way I was told, I would get a severe beating. So I was a fast learner. There were two little boys in the home also. When I was about five years old, one of the boys was run over by a train and killed. I just suffered in silence with that, too, and did as I was told.

Anna and Gus divorced in 1970, and I gained a little hope. I was sent to Oklahoma to live with someone Anna knew. I had lived with Gus and Anna for my first six years, and those years were filled with abuse and no real love. *I still had no name.* I guess if you never have something, you have no way of knowing just how much you need that something. At that point, I really thought my life was like everyone else's. Still, I was relieved to be away from smelly Gus and the uncles.

My life in Oklahoma was somewhat better. I began going to school, and the lady I was living with told me to tell the other kids my name was Diane. I liked that, and I felt so important. The feeling of importance was short-lived, and I began to realize and see all the things I didn't have in life. I was abused in that home also but not nearly as badly as before. Looking back, I believe Anna's Oklahoma friend knew I had been sold to men who wanted to have sex with a child because one of the men who came around raped me.

After Oklahoma, I served a season of my imprisoned childhood in Colorado with about the same setup, same abusive people, and then was shipped back to Texas. I was glad to see something familiar, though it was horrible to be back with Anna. *I still didn't have a name.*

And she had changed. She was no longer the purposely oblivious woman who was nice at times. She was a very mean drunk. Beatings were a regular occurrence. She seemed to have no trouble attracting men because she was married six times before I was 15. No longer were the men called "uncles." Anna would just tell them they could do whatever they wanted with me, and most of them did. If I didn't comply, I would get the belt.

When I was in the sixth grade, Anna told me to start some spaghetti noodles cooking and she would be back. In a short while, she returned and I was still cooking them. She was plastered and meaner than usual. She took one look at the noodles and began beating me all over my body with the belt. She just would not stop. Anywhere she could hit she was swinging as hard as she could, screaming at me the entire time, "You overcooked the noodles," and finally named me with every bad name she could think of. She finally grew tired and gave out. Thinking about that now, I could have really hurt her in that state, even being that young, but it just goes to show how beat down and submissive I had become. It had been survival. I began cleaning up the mess and tried to figure out how the noodles appeared overcooked. I rarely make spaghetti now. When I do, it's an accomplishment, a victory. And I have found you really cannot overcook them that easily, and especially not in appearance.

When I started high school, I still lived in that small Texas town. By then, I realized I had been given no name and that nobody cared. I realized no one loved me and it didn't matter. I had figured out I was abused and that it wasn't right. I believed no one cared and they would be angry at *me*, not the monster. It felt so wrong to tell. I had been warned for as long as I could remember to keep my mouth shut.

I was filled with a strange dread when thinking about disobeying a direct command about the abuse, but my life had become a living hell on earth. As it became even more unbearable with Drunken Monster Anna and her pick of the week, I decided to blow the whole thing wide open.

I daydreamed about how my rescue would take place: People would tell me how sorry they were that this had happened to me. I didn't care to be hugged or touched at all, but they would probably stand up, round the desk, and try to hug me. I would let them, of course, and they would pat my back and give comfort. I visualized how my new life would be and what kind of people would make me their child, give me a name, and even what my new home would look like. *I went to sleep thinking about it. I woke up thinking about it. I had to act.*

With all the confidence and practice I could muster, I went to school that morning and asked to see the vice principal. I had decided he was the one to confide in because he seemed to be a good man. I waited outside his office, went in, and told him *almost everything*—enough to act, for sure. I sat there with him staring at me blankly, mouth half-open. It was so uncomfortable waiting for him to finally speak, but I waited. *I waited for him to tell me how terrible it was and that he was so sorry. I waited for him to place me under protection in a locked office where Monster Anna couldn't find me and then he'd call the police!*

"I'll look into this. Go back to class." *What the hell?* After about a week of hoping, a week of thinking at any moment he would knock on the door and take me away, I wisened up. I walked by his office and locked eyes with him. He looked down. I knew right then, I shouldn't have counted on anyone caring.

Even though I was terrified of Monster Anna, I planned my escape. I grabbed a few things and left in the middle of the night. I simply left right out the front door. I have no idea where the courage came from, but I decided right then and there that if I was going to be scared, I would be scared without the beatings and sexual abuse. I was finished. I knew I didn't have to quit school formally, because no one cared anyway. I'm sure Anna missed the income she made off of me—from the state as well as from the men she pimped me out to.

Before long, I had hitched rides all the way to California. Sex was easier when I was in control of who and how, and I knew by then how to work the men. It was much less stressful than dodging fists and never knowing what was coming at me. I found the Sunset Strip in Hollywood, California, and made myself right at home. I actually felt more acceptance and love than I ever had before. The throw-aways, the homeless, the junkies—I felt more love with these people than I ever had before. I was 15 then.

The men who bought me made me feel so pretty, and it felt like they wanted to be with me. After a short while and especially not knowing real love at all, I fell for a pimp and decided that my life would be safer if I worked under him. He bought me pretty clothes and gave me the money I needed. He also provided protection for me.

He introduced me to a new friend that provided another happiness I had never known: *cocaine*. I had finally found the answer! I felt a semblance of comfort and peace about life. When the relationship with the pimp burnt out, I found another one, then another and another. As long as they said the right things and provided me with money and drugs, life was good. Changing into whomever they wanted me to be was so much easier for me than most of the other girls. Not having a real name, a real identity, aided me in a criminal lifestyle, for sure. I could change like a chameleon. I could camouflage and hide and do whatever I had to do. The only constant in my life had been "Baby Girl Primrose," and guess what? I didn't even have to be her anymore. Life was easy. I slept and shopped during the day and worked at night. I was very easy to control and caused my pimps no problem. I always made everyone happy. It never occurred to me that I was the one actually buying the drugs or making the money.

More and more, drugs became the center of my universe. I was arrested after a few years for prostitution. I wasn't going to live any differently. I had slept with hundreds of men and had no way to live any other way, even if I had wanted to. The State of California sent me back to Anna in Texas because I was still a minor. They thought they were sending me "home" to be cared for. I was just another runaway who should be sent back to her mother.

The problem was, I would not allow Anna Monster to be my pimp or beat me anymore. I planned to immediately leave and make my way back west as soon as I hit her door, and that's exactly what I did. I had always lived in chaos, but for the last few years, I had chosen my own chaos, and no one would take that from me. I continued along the path of chaos and drugs for many years. There were many arrests. I traveled the country with pimps that I told myself loved me. I finally went to prison in Tennessee once I was over 18 and served four years.

Prison stripped away what identity I had built. Being seen more as a number actually didn't affect me as bad as it seemed to affect the other women. Prison did not let me just choose a name like the streets had allowed. I was told again and again that I was a nobody, but what was new there? The guards made sure I knew that, and I think they had fun reminding me every day.

I vowed when I got out that I would start a new life. The plans for a new life were not involving anything worthwhile, but I had dreams and ambitions. Within a very short time of being released, I started over. The difference was that I learned a lot in prison. I became *the* pimp. The proper name for a female pimp is Madame. And "Madame" I did. I ran my girls and made money from them. I wanted a home and pretty furniture and nice clothes, and I had big plans.

I met a man and fell in love. As long as I provided for him and kept him in the style and drugs that he wanted, things were great. I had decided no man was ever going to order me around again and found one I could order around instead. He had a good mother, who began to show me the love I had never had from anyone else. She knew about my life and where all of the money came from but did not care.

Patricia was a name that I went by then. I felt it was a name with class. And I was a boss, my own boss. I made all the money from my girls and used it to support a man and the mother who was proud of us, and I called it *family*.

After a few years, my man died. Drugs had taken a toll on his body. While I always liked drugs, I had tapered off quite a bit running my business and drew much more enjoyment from acquiring *stuff* than I got from drugs.

Miss Brenda and the Lovelady Movement

I felt like a widow when he died. All the girls in our stable (the group of hookers of a particular Madame or pimp) attended the funeral. They wailed and cried along with his mother. It was the finest farewell I had seen to that point. I kept up the life for a while and expanded down into Alabama. I landed myself in prison once again.

Julia Tutwiler Prison for Women in Wetumpka, Alabama, was no joke. I may have thought I could hold my own in prison, and I actually could have in another one, but Tutwiler woke me up real quick-like. The guards in that prison were much worse to me than the ones in Tennessee. The emotional and physical abuse the women suffered at their hands made serving time worse than could ever be imagined. And that made for a horrible time with the other inmates as well. I decided that if I ever set my feet back in Tennessee, it would take being dragged naked to return to Alabama!

After three very long years, I was finally going to be released. "Baby Girl Primrose" was set free. I was looking forward to seeing that Tennessee state line when I was informed that I was going to The Lovelady Center in Birmingham. I remember walking out of that prison afraid they would pull me back in, with some unresolved, crazy, unimaginable reason to pull me back into hell like in a horror movie. I was so afraid of getting out of there immediately that I didn't think much farther than that. But when I did think about it all . . . *Birmingham?* I wanted to die but had no choice. I was 43 years old with no name, no identity, and no hope. *Birmingham? What the hell?*

I was 44 years old when I met Brenda Lovelady Spahn that day in 2007, when she marched down to the front desk to see who had the audacity to break one of her rules and use a street name in her building. She had no idea I had been planning to just end it all, no idea my head didn't hang near as low as my heart did that first time she saw me. Reliving the life of Baby Girl is very difficult for me, but knowing how extreme my circumstances were and being able to compare them to where God has me now is a story I will tell forever.

Danielle's Redemption

"Sometimes when you are in a dark place you think you have been buried, but you've actually been planted."
—Christine Caine

Danielle was so shy, with such a low self-esteem, it took a while before she could believe any worth within herself. She hated everything about herself. She knew so much about life yet nothing about normal life. She had a difficult time believing she could find any life outside of just trying to survive. Drugs had never been the issue for her; rather, *looking for love in all the wrong places* had been the main issue she had to overcome. My heart had hurt for the empty shell before me every time I encountered her. I wanted to hold her and tell her all would be fine. The truth was, how could anyone allow this to happen to someone, much less partake in the demise of another person?

I see it every day, but not to the extent of Danielle. This woman had wandered the United States looking for hope, and no one introduced it to her. As she was the first case of complexity to such a dark existence, I struggled to relate to her level of pain. I am so disappointed to admit this, but I had a hard time seeing hope for her. If ever there was a case that I truly believed would never make it, it was Danielle. I did want to help her, but I was new to this. I thought, *"Who do you think you are, Brenda? She has been all over and come into contact with so many agencies, and you are just going to get this done for her? You're in way over your head."*

I was determined to give it all I had. From the first moment I spoke to her, I loved her. I pray to see people through the eyes of Jesus, and He answers that prayer for me. I wanted to help radically change her life and was excited to see what God could do with her heart, but I knew it would take Danielle meeting the Lord halfway. *Would she?*

I would take her to Walmart and just love on her some, just treat her really special. Many of our women have at least one person in their lives that defines them as "having someone." Danielle had no one. So I made it a point to be her someone. Ever so slowly, she would come out of her shell, and I would honestly enjoy her company. I could tell she desired real life. With help, people *can* find their way out of darkness and into His Marvelous Light.

One day, as I sat with her, we began talking about real change that could only come from Jesus. I made sure she knew that every good thing happening to her was from Him, never me or even Melinda. She had listened in class so intently, and finally I started to see glimpses of realization, knowledge of who God had intended her to be.

Danielle decided it was time to relocate and began searching for employment and a place to stay in Florida. She had to have a change of scenery, a new view. Something about the vastness of the waves and endless water is soul-cleansing. Danielle would just sit for hours and watch the waves come up to her toes in the sand. She checked off her list of goals and moved south. Melinda and I just could not be more proud of her.

I visited her once she was settled into her new place, and one day as we were talking, I asked her if she felt she was ready to give her past to Jesus, Who was not concerned with anything she had ever done. He wanted to give her life, hope, love, and most of all salvation. He wanted to live in her heart. Tears began rolling down her face. As those waves rolled in and washed out, Danielle found what she was looking for. It was such a beautiful moment. It was so profound that her entire countenance changed. Danielle had found the love she had longed for, in her Savior.

Danielle truly changed from the inside out. There was no turning back for this woman. She is not really a social person, but one day I asked her about the idea of an intimate relationship in her future. She told me she had enough social companionship in her life and needed no more. She goes to church and has a few friends and is liked by those at her workplace, but frankly, she is just happy being who she is and living alone.

I have tried to talk her into moving up by the Center and working with us. She would be very good at helping the women sort through trauma and bad choices. She reminds me that she is content and does not need any change. She loves the beach and her little home.

She came back to Birmingham to speak with the women one morning during devotion time in the big atrium. She shared much of what has been shared in this book, and boy, did the women relate! There wasn't a dry eye in the house.

"And if He did it for me, He will do it for you too." Our women just could not believe that she went through life with no real name. After she gave her testimony to our women and visited with us for a while, she was ready to get back to the beach.

How many of us are really that content? She earns a good income, her home is paid for, and she has even added on to it several times—a room here, a patio there. She told me that her days begin and end with Jesus. How do I talk to someone and give them a better life? I don't. I believe with my entire being that only God gave her the life she has and you just cannot beat the happiness she experiences on a daily basis! She is a pillar in the church that she attends. She teaches classes and bakes casseroles for church picnics. She has a tremendous savings account.

Sadly, the sexual abuse rendered Danielle childless forever. But that doesn't fill her with sadness, she will tell you quickly that she has been healed. She decided to get herself a puppy—Miss Priss—and that puppy has given her so much happiness.

She has her mother down to the beach as often as she can go, that mother being the one who did finally name her, me. During my most recent visit, she had gotten her license renewed. I was looking at her license, and I did a double take. The license read *Alyah* Danielle Turner, a blatant misspelling of the name "Aliyah" or even "Alia" or "Aleah." I said, "Oh, Danielle, they misspelled your first name!" She laughed and told me that *they* didn't misspell anything, her *mom* did. (Apparently I had, on the birth certificate.) I told her we could change it and she looked at me like I had two heads. "*Never!* That's who I am and I will *never* change it. It took me 44 years to get a name and that's who I will always be. When I see Jesus, He will say, "Welcome home, *Alyah Danielle Turner.*"

Sadie

> "To be a Christian means to forgive the inexcusable, because God has forgiven the inexcusable in you."
> —C.S. Lewis

Being at The Lovelady Center in those early years taught me a lot about the absolute *need* to forgive others who have caused harm, in order to move out of the trauma they may have inflicted upon you. I came from a good home, but many of my women did not. All the stories we hear constantly leave me wondering how many stories are left untold due to shame or fear of being looked at differently.

However, Sadie was an open book concerning her years of trauma. Melinda entered my door with a strange look on her face and those beautiful blue eyes wide. She clutched in her hands several sheets of paper with drawings on them.

"What *is* it, Melinda?" I admit that sometimes I have a rough edge, though I certainly do not intend to. I had been budgeting some needed project or something and didn't like being interrupted.

"We have a client who has turned in classwork that can't be deciphered," she said, handing me the papers.

"Well, that's nothing new, Melinda, it's —"

"Mother. *Look* at it," she interrupted. I took the papers and what I found was both puzzling and remarkable. It was like hieroglyphics and shapes, small pictures. Apparently the 27-year-old woman released to us from Tutwiler had taught herself to write in the only way she knew how. She couldn't read either.

"How does something like this happen? Call her in here, Melinda," I said. I had to get to the bottom of this. I wondered if she was just pulling our chains or something. Surely to God no one makes it to adulthood without reading or writing in the 21st century! I could envision her sitting in the classroom with our sweet volunteers helping guide her future and her just doodling in some silly, rebellious manner. That just wasn't going to do it for me!

Sadie came through the door, normal size and build, brown-headed, eyes cast downward. She looked up only to find the chairs in front of my desk and seat herself in one. I immediately decided she was not just messing around with our volunteer instructors—there was a real issue.

Occasionally, a woman will be sent to The Lovelady Center because the Alabama Department of Corrections feels there is really no hope for her rehabilitation in a prison setting. They just turn her over to us to do her time and finish out her sentence. DOC does not necessarily believe *we* can rehabilitate them, but having only *one* prison for females for the whole state means it is forever overcrowded. Suddenly, like in Sadie's case, years go by and the woman grows older within that revolving door status. The woman's life seems almost worthless. Imagine being on a merry-go-round of horrors, being unable to jump off, and just having to face the next day, which is the same as the one before, with no easy way of escaping the system. Drug addiction leads to crime, crime leads to jail, jail leads to prison. Once they are released, they go back to the county in which they caught the charges, with more felonies and no one who will risk employing them for any wage that will meet even a lower standard of living. They are soon caught up in the same mess that landed them in prison in the first place.

The young woman sitting before me was one of the women from the merry-go-round. After I read her chart, my first inclination was to agree with the summary I had just read, that there was no chance of rehabilitation. Her rap sheet was pretty long. After that first thought, I reminded myself Whom I serve and immediately asked the Lord to lead me to say the right words to reach Sadie.

Many of our women are slow in sharing their stories. It just has to come out when they are ready. It takes a fair amount of time, usually. The previous stories in this book took a while for us to learn. But in her case, I needed to know Sadie's perception of her life and so I pushed her—way out of character for me, I know, right? Goodness, she gave me an earful.

Sadie was the youngest of nine children. Her mother was grossly overweight, sick, and could not ever get out of bed. Children ran wild in that house, and Sadie's father and uncles were as wild as the children, just much older. There are alcoholics, and then there are *crazy drunks*. These men were the latter.

The other school-age children attended classes and Sadie also wanted to go, but her father said that she needed to stay home to take care of her mother. So, beginning at age five, Sadie was her mother's main caregiver until the mother's death. It seemed impossible to me that a child could be kept out of school her entire life. I called my state contacts at DOC to verify, and sure enough, her story was true. Sadie could not read or write. Her dad had used the excuse that she was so mentally challenged that she could not learn, and he was teaching her basic skills.

Sadie did not eat regularly and, some nights, actually slept under the porch with the dogs, hiding. She cried when she spoke about it. She was severely abused, and it crushed me to hear her words. One day, she smelled beans cooking on the stove and asked her father if she could please have some to eat. In answering her question, he poured the boiling water from the beans on her. Of course, she had to be taken to the hospital for the burns and the father lied to hospital staff. He said she pulled the pot off on herself.

She was in the hospital for months, and if that isn't the saddest part, she told me it was the fondest memory she ever had of her childhood—*being in that hospital*. I absolutely cringed at her stories. She told me how her daddy and uncles sexually abused her. I listened with tears in my eyes. I felt hatred rising up in me for the dad and uncles and really for her whole family. I was also very honored that she trusted me so quickly and realized she had a chance with us in this program.

She had lived in absolute squalor in a country town, and no one had asked questions. Everyone just "minded their own business." I have been appalled at how many of our women fell through the cracks when it came to truancy from school or community awareness of neglect and abuse. Thankfully, things are much better now. But for poor little Sadie, years ago in a small, rural town, the system failed her miserably. Everyone in her childhood failed her miserably.

Sadie's mother died when she was 12. Understandably, her brothers and sisters moved out the minute that they could flee. Finally, someone in that small town called the health department. Sadie was 15 years old by then, however, and the torturous abuse had taken its toll. Sadie told them everything she could, and the child protection services in that little town placed her in with an aunt. She was no longer abused, but it was still a hard life to live.

Her father was sentenced to prison when she was 16. Sadie was happy to be away from him and to see him punished, but he died in prison when she was 18. She started using drugs when she was 16, while living with her aunt. The aunt put Sadie out of the house, and the streets became her home. The door was opened, and her new life began. Every day, the bitterness grew in her heart, and hate became the only emotion she felt.

Somehow, I had to find a way to help her. She did not have a relationship with any of her siblings. I wanted to help her, but this seemed way beyond my expertise. Truth be told, I had to begin a search within myself to discover if I could walk in forgiveness toward anyone evil enough to do these horrible things to *anybody*, much less a child.

There was a *very* wounded woman, in many ways still a little girl, sitting in the chair across from me—head lowered, no hope, no education. I told Sadie to return to my office the next day, that I had to pray about these things. She told me, "Don't bother, I've been prayin' for years." I just sat there.

I prayed that night and struggled. I would wake up praying and pray until I fell back asleep. I dreamed horrible dreams about trying to help some figure being hurt and screaming, just out of reach, buried in darkness. Sadie could never walk in freedom without somehow, some way, finding forgiveness for the many people who failed her and intentionally caused her harm. And I bet there were *many* people she hated.

That was a difficult night.

When Sadie came in the next day, I told her that I was trying to understand and just *process* everything, but rather than relive her abuse, we had to let go. I told her of the love God had for her, hoping to begin work on that hardened heart. At the end of a very long session, I told her that I needed her to make a list of everyone who had wronged her. I expected there'd be about 10 or so names on the list, and asked her to come see me with the list the next morning.

Sadie showed up for our appointment early the next morning. She was sitting outside my office, ready. To my surprise, she had two full pages of names. Her roommate had written them down as she called them out loud the night before. I took the papers, and we started naming the "lesser offending" people first, starting at the bottom of the list and moving up. There were teachers, preachers, neighbors, relatives, the meter reader—*the meter reader?*

"What on earth had the meter reader done?" I softly asked her.

"He came out one day and saw him hurting me through the window," she answered. She waited for days for help to come because surely he reported the incident. Help never came. He never reported it!

She was certain everyone on the list knew about her abuse. One by one, we prayed, and we spoke about each person and how they harmed her. Some harmed her with apathy, some directly with their hands and words. Some she was unsure she could forgive. We stayed there until she let it all go.

I would ask her, "Do you still want this person to hold part of your life hostage?" She would finally decide to let go of that one but telling them openly and out loud that she forgave them. We went through the brothers and sisters, the mom who didn't report the abuse and should have protected her children from monsters, the aunts who knew. Even the uncles were forgiven, but no forgiveness was there for good ol' dad. The fact that he had died during the first years of his sentence really angered her. It was obvious that she wanted him to suffer.

"I want to dig him up and stab him over and over," she explained, and I understood that anger. But it was time to be free of its hold on her mind. Finally, after a couple of days, she let go, wailing for what seemed like forever with a few of us holding her and praying over her. A different girl came out the other side of all of that rehashing of the pain. No longer was darkness around her. He had healed her where she sat.

She had a desire to learn and just soaked up everything she could in our Education Department. She learned to read and do basic math. She was smart after all. A retired teacher was so diligent in helping her and also successfully preparing her to obtain her GED. It was truly like a flower blooming. I have a greenhouse where I plant amaryllis, and she reminded me of one of the blooms. They grow so fast I always feel like I could watch them grow if I sneaked in to watch them at night. That was Sadie.

I called each brother and sister. Some were reluctant at first to see her. They did not want to be reminded of their past and what they had also lived through and turned a blind eye to in order to survive that hell. I assured them it was understandable, that she knew they had been afraid. On the day of Sadie's graduation, all of them attended. Everyone in the audience was crying when she spoke. I wish all of you could have seen the remarkable woman who emerged from that abused, timid girl.

What I saw so clearly was the power of forgiveness. I saw the love of our Father shining through and what it took for her to be able to trust a Heavenly Father after her life had been so horrible. Sadie told me she finally had the Daddy she always wanted. No one else may have stepped up to rescue her, but *He* had!

After watching firsthand just how important forgiveness is, I began to make my own list. The more I thought about it, the longer my list became. There was no sexual abuse on my list, but I had a rather long list of people to forgive. At first, my list seemed childish, but I soon realized I had some unhealed wounds myself. I also felt my list was petty compared to Sadie's, but I feel the Lord knows, and if it was brought to my attention, then it mattered. I learned how you have to go through phases to allow yourself to forgive others. I also learned that trauma isn't significant just because it is overwhelmingly horrible like Sadie's, but that my own level of trauma is just as significant and enormous to me.

Years have passed since Sadie left the Center. One of her tutors speaks with her often and told me she is doing great. She decided against marriage and cannot have children. She sends her love to me, but I feel it is better if I just let her grow on her own. After all, she knows where I am if she needs me. I have read much about forgiveness. I have studied articles about forgiveness. I know it relieves stress in our lives. I know—and you probably know—you need to forgive, but I tell you that holding onto even one little bit of bitterness will take root and be like a weed choking the love right out of you. I see in my own life how important it is.

Much of our exercises and teachings on forgiveness stemmed from Sadie. I am very happy she found freedom in her Heavenly Father.

The Atheist

"Keep your face always toward the sunshine and the shadows will fall behind you."
—Walt Whitman

I was startled as my door was suddenly flung wide open. As I looked up, I saw Shay standing in my door. "Don't you ever think about knocking? You scare me to death barging in here like that!" Shay had become an intricate part of The Lovelady Center and sure didn't feel uncomfortable barging into mine or Melinda's office anytime.

We could have never found a better person to greet the women and become our intake director than our very own Shay. She offered love, her knowledge of the streets, and the biggest smile any woman could ask for upon entering our doors. If any of the women think they have done the worst thing possible, they meet Shay, who quickly lets them know that their past does not define them.

But apparently, even Shay had a hard time relating to one woman. "I just wanted to warn you about one of our new intakes today."

"What's to warn us about, Shay? *We've seen it all, haven't we?*" I chuckled, as if there was nothing else on the planet that could surprise me. Because there really wasn't.

"We haven't seen *this*, Ma," as she affectionately called me. "We have a bona fide crazy, badass *atheist* on our hands."

"Shay, *stop using language like that!*" I replied. "There are plenty of words in the English language you can use to describe—"

"Well, there's not another word for *this*, Ma!" she interjected.

I sighed and said, "Give me the details." I wasn't really concerned, because this intake director of ours sometimes blew things out of proportion. There wasn't anything we had not encountered before. No one was *truly* an atheist, I had come to decide. How could one *not* know there is a Creator? The woman was probably just wearing atheism like a mantel—for *image*'s sake.

"I'm not going to give details, I'm going to let you meet her for yourself, 'cause she is gonna cause us *trouble*." Shay widened her eyes as if that would help me understand the trouble we were about to face. She nodded to make her point stronger. I was unmoved.

"Go ahead and bring her in, Shay. Let me meet this bona-fide, badass *atheist*."

Shay escorted a thin blonde through my door. She didn't seem like much of a problem to me; in fact, I had known plenty of "badass" women who actually *had* given me pause over the years. This woman who stood before me now just was not scary to me at all.

I very kindly said, "Have a seat." She quickly answered, "I'll stand." I looked into cold eyes. She was agitated, but I had learned enough to know defensive moves when I saw them. Every now and then, she scanned the room, perhaps in paranoia—I was not sure yet.

"I'm Miss Brenda—" I tried.

"I know who you are," she interrupted, almost spitting at me. "I'm sure everyone here knows who *you* are. All this BS about your beliefs on how to get clean is a joke. No one here has really been clean for years, Ma'am, not *really*. They're just waiting for a safe time to use again. Turn your head a moment and see what happens."

"Well, at least you're honest," I threw back at her. Just as I was wanting to tell her what she could do with herself, I took a breath and said, "Why don't you go get settled in." She glared back, as if my kindness was a joke. She looked as if she were trying to figure out what I was up to. As she left the room, Shay whispered back, "I told you, I told you. I've already warned Sissy about her too."

Sissy was what Shay called Melinda because you could not convince Shay that she was not my child, thus making Melinda her *Sissy*. Truth of the matter is, I would've never tried to change how she viewed that. I loved this softened, albeit dramatic woman as if she were my own. I narrowed my eyes so she would take in my seriousness and softly stated, "If God can change *you*, He can change anybody, Shay." Her eyes met mine. She seemed to think about that for a moment. "Well, I'm going to check her bags and walk her to her room. I don't want anybody else having to deal with her," she huffed as she turned on her heels and left the office.

A few weeks later, Shay came bursting into my office, yet again. "*Jeanne* wants to talk to you." I had warned Shay not to pester her about her beliefs—or *disbeliefs*, rather—and to let who we are in our actions speak the truth to her. Shay had made her determination already and seemed excited for me to have to face this woman again. Jeanne had started in housekeeping, under Shay's direction. She was a hard worker and seemed not to be able to sit down for very long, and I was happy that she used hard work to wear herself out enough to sleep instead of trying to find drugs to combat her restlessness.

"Yes, Sweetie, can I help you?" I asked the young woman. She rolled her eyes, probably because I used an affectionate term to address her.

"I have a question for you, *Miss Brenda.*" The cynicism and sarcasm was so thick, I could've stirred it with a stick. I wanted to get up and just slap her cheek. Remember, counseling is not my strong suit. But there was something else there, right under the surface. I couldn't pinpoint it at the time because of her insolence, but looking back, Jeanne *needed* that answer. She was searching and disguising it as criticisms.

"Why wasn't Eve *surprised* when an animal talked to her in the Garden of Eden? Come on, Miss Brenda. A snake walks up to me and talks, I know what's happening just isn't real. I'm probably high," she said with a laugh. "But I tell you this—I'd definitely be *surprised*. No doubt I would at least be surprised. Your book is based on mythical stories."

I leaned forward for effect and asked a question back: "And just how do you know she *wasn't* surprised?" Jeanne began to answer that, probably was going to say something rude, and then just sat back in her chair, thinking. We began a back-and-forth conversation. Jeanne would state what she believed were contradictions of the Bible and the Christian faith, and I would counter. I realized in that conversation that she would reason every possibility other than the one I was delivering—and this wasn't an image game to her. She really didn't believe the existence of God could be *proven*. And she needed to know the truth more than anything else. She agreed that it was equally as difficult to *disprove* Him. I believe she needed this foundational truth in order to believe in and trust the staff who proclaimed it so continually. I decided right then and there that she was more agnostic than atheist.

Other conversations with her involved such questions as "How much money are you and your daughter racking up in this?" I laughed at that one. I laughed *really* hard, actually. Jeanne rose to leave, and I noticed she didn't scan the room anymore, looking for something. She closed the door behind her.

Shay popped right in, of course, "What'd she say, what'd she say?"

"She told me you are tremendously overpaid. She also said I should do something about your attitude and that wig you always wear." With that last remark, she said, "Keep on, Ma, she's going to get us into some stupid trouble—she's the type to call City Hall on you with lies." She knew what she could say to upset me, but this time I just laughed. This woman wasn't the type to *make up* a lie. She was the type to uncover and expose them. The problem was, Jeanne needed *Truth* in order to recognize the lies of the real enemy—the one who had been playing with her mind the whole time when she was high on opiates and methamphetamine.

Shay mumbled something about allowing crazies in the building, and I said, "Quit worrying about her; we have hundreds of women to worry about. Now go on."

I sat in silence and said to myself, "Lord, Shay isn't far off the mark, really. Meth is shaking these women's minds apart."

Every few days, Jeanne would come in with new questions. Sometimes they would be technical or administrative, but mostly, she would ask questions that I had never previously encountered. Somehow, my answers seemed to soften her over time.

"How did a man survive three days in the belly of a whale? How did Noah fit all those animals on the ark? Where did the animals poop, and how'd only eight people stay on top of all that? What happened to the dinosaurs? Why did God create Satan if He knew it was going to be evil? If God is love, how could He just watch all the cruelty happening?" The questions went on and on. I signed her up for a Bible study at my house, where the questions continued. I did notice the deep questions were reserved for when we were alone, and I decided it was good that she was considerate of the effect her questions may have on others around her. If she was doing *that*, it just might be due to considering that the Gospel *may* be the truth, and she did not wish to derail another woman's beliefs. That was encouraging.

It seems like her last major question that I remember was one that I had heard almost daily, because it is such a revelation when a hardened criminal realizes they still have value. *"Why do y'all do this?"* I saw a tear fall from her eye as I answered her: "Maybe just for *you*."

During the deep conversations, I learned that her disbelief began with the horrible world of drug-induced delusions. Sitting in a jail cell on maximum security in Jefferson County, she had a horrible break with reality coming off methamphetamine and opiates. In fact, she had been delusional from hard drug use for a while before being arrested. Once in the cell block after her arrest, the television had told her to just walk out of the slider and go home when it rolled open. She tried that as soon as the big sliding door rolled open, as the doors slid open throughout the day for various reasons. That particular time, it was for a trustee to enter. Jeanne shot out the slider and found herself standing in front of a central cubicle that housed guards. She could not make it to the elevators to her left, as there were additional large, sliding iron doors, which were closed.

"Me and my partner's about to make a difference for *you*," the female deputy yelled from the cubicle. Another door rolled. It was to the maximum-security block, and Jeanne was escorted by two large, female deputies toward a cell. The cell door opened, and she was led inside and left there. The 8- by 8-foot cement cell had two empty, iron bunk beds, a stainless-steel toilet/sink combination, a one-seater table combination attached to the cement wall, and a vent at the top of the wall, out of which a continual stream of strange voices roared. Jeanne had been so confused already about the voices in the walls, not being able to rationalize that it was inmates speaking to each other through the ventilation.

In the following days, on an iron bunk alone, Jeanne decided that the old delusion that started during methadone withdrawals years earlier was indeed true. She had been adopted by an organization that had filmed every moment of her life since birth and broadcast it to an awaiting world audience. But what was worse than that was the realization that came to her sitting on that bunk in Jefferson County Jail: *those are the same people who showed me the Bible. The Bible must also be based on myth.*

Jeanne recounts that in the years following that arrest, many times she would embrace that ideology hard, deciding that if there really was a God, she didn't need to meet Him. The life she was living was filled with the possibility of death, and it was easier for her to decide there would be no answering for any of her sins to a Holy God.

Tell It Like It Is

"Turn your wounds into wisdom."
—Oprah Winfrey

Jeanne's two daughters are beautiful. I have had the privilege of getting to know these remarkable young women. I have talked to the elder, Monica, many times about her younger life. I sometimes watch Jeanne doting on her *seven* grandchildren and just cannot believe that, years ago, this woman was so strung out she actually went days without feeding her children anything.

I know the story of Jeanne, Monica, and Megan and have such a difficult time recognizing the person Monica describes to me. It is mind-blowing and a testament to what God does. I consider it such an honor that He has allowed Melinda and me to have the roles in their lives that we have had.

Sometimes people talk about how blessed the women at the Center are to have us. We are blessed even more so because we feel called to this ministry. I feel it is so important for everyone to know that to change a woman's life affects her entire family. It's like a new path in time is created, veering off the bad trajectory and into what God already had for them all along.

There are countless victims in the world of addiction. Monica and Megan were victims who now have victory.

Monica's Story, in Her Own Words

When I was a small girl, we had to play outside a lot because our mom was *sick*. What we didn't know then was that she had a psychotic break while withdrawing from methadone, a drug that is supposed to help a person stop using opiates by blocking the opiate receptors in the brain. The problem is, methadone made her higher than the pain pills she was trying to be freed from, and the withdrawals from methadone were much worse than the withdrawals from the pain pills she was hooked on, known then as Lortab.

When she broke with reality, paranoia seeped in. About that time, the previews to the movie "The Truman Show," starring Jim Carrey, was airing on the television she sat in front of day in and day out, believing the television would give her a clue needed to "figure out what is *really* going on." She no longer realized she was just withdrawing from a very hard drug. In that movie, Jim Carrey portrays a man who is slowly finding out he has been secretly filmed his entire life, and is the main protagonist in a television show that millions across the world watch daily. My mama grabbed hold of the delusion that she, herself, was a victim of that very same thing. She believed there were cameras hidden everywhere, and began whispering every time she spoke, as if every word was being recorded and played on a television show to the entire world. Now it is known that Truman Syndrome is a type of delusion in which the person believes that their life is a staged reality show—obviously a symptom of psychosis. What made matters worse was that the methadone clinic would not help her. They told my father that she must be using other drugs, that methadone withdrawals would not cause her a psychosis. Nothing could have been further from the truth, but she was too far gone to submit a urinalysis to them, believing everyone in the world would see her pee in a cup.

Her eyes would grow wide when she said to my little sister and me, *"I know you're a paid actor in my life."* I was eight years old then. I could never describe with mere words the fear and bewilderment that filled me in that moment.

My daddy worked in the maintenance department at the apartment complex where we lived. We were out of school for the summer. He would check in on us during the days he had to work and, of course, was with us nights and weekends when he was on call. He didn't use drugs back then; he just worked all the time to support us *and my mama's habit*. He explained to us that Mama's illness made her think things that were not really true. What can you tell eight- and six-year-old girls about mental illness? Everyone told him to "put her somewhere," but he just couldn't. Her eyes would fill with fear and confusion over the most normal things, and he loved her very much.

One day my little sister and I spent hours sitting on the living room floor with my mom, lights and television off, blinds closed, banging on pots and pans to "give the world their stupid show." We just banged away, happy that something made a little sense *without making any sense*, I guess. Mama laughed while we banged away, and so I was happy that *she* was happy for a change.

Then she got worse. She was convinced that the entire apartment complex was a prop for the show. I don't know what she was thinking, but she would lock us outside frequently. We would just sit and wait for our dad to come by and let us back in and feed us. We made a game out of it ourselves and played outside. I became my sister's mom, trying to take care of her when she wasn't hiding in her room. We eventually had to go stay with relatives, and my dad had to take off work an entire month to sit with her. And after successfully stopping methadone, about two months later, her mental state improved. Six months later, she started using it again and went back to the clinic. I cannot remember all the excuses and lies about "her medicine," but I knew she was going to the clinic every day once again.

After a while, we moved to a house out in the country, on land that my dad's family owned. Mama had distanced all of us from her own family out of shame. At least we had plenty of room to play. I was a dreamer and loved playing outside with my sister and friends in the neighborhood. We moved to the house around the end of my third grade year in school. By the time school rolled around again, my dad had started using drugs too, to cope with the new life my mother chose over him and us, I guess. Looking back, it got bad very quickly, with both of them using and my dad dealing drugs to support both of their drug habits. They started meth about that time.

I still didn't know yet that my life was not normal. My paternal grandmother lived behind us and was a mean-spirited alcoholic who hated my mother even years before she started using drugs. While my parents were crashed-out after a five- or six-day run, we would go out to my grandmother's and eat. If Mama and Granny were at odds, Mom would forbid us to go there, which became a problem during one of their three-day crashes. They slept so hard that there was no waking them, and there was no one to go get us hamburgers or honey buns from the gas station, common meals for us when we couldn't go out to Granny's and eat. And we couldn't go out to Granny's, Mama had said. *That was a long three days.*

My mother did not get up in the morning and clean or can vegetables or create summer memories with us anymore, a hard contrast to the memories of making mud pies with her when I was very young, reading books, singing through the house—*having a normal mother.* We didn't have a lot anyway because my parents married young and had children right away, but life had still been wonderful prior to drugs. But being in fourth grade with addicts for parents and little to nothing already meant life was bad, I was soon to find out.

I was happy that school was finally going to start after the long, hot summer. We didn't have new clothes or a clean home to get ready in, but I didn't know the difference. I was just glad to get to go. We would catch the bus right out front. After a few days of school, it was quickly brought to my attention that my life was most definitely *not normal.* I did not smell good. I was not clean, my clothes did not fit, and my hair was filthy. The first week or so, we had lunch money, but that tapered off too.

Now that I have children of my own, I appreciate all the great teachers who pour into my daughter's and two sons' lives. The school that they attend is wonderful, and I thank God for all the good educators. But the hateful teacher I had during the worst days of my life would actually run me away from her desk because, to quote her, *I smelled bad.* She would say it in front of the class, and everyone would laugh. She probably has no idea just how much trauma she contributed to my already hard childhood. *Maybe she does now.*

If my sister and I missed the bus, which happened frequently once my zeal for going to school that year declined, I had to remind someone to take us. Finally, I had had enough and decided to be a school dropout in the fourth grade. It wasn't hard for us to stop going. I attended school in the fourth grade for only 50 days, and no one in authority back then really cared, I guess.

Many times, my Granny's husband, who I considered a grandfather, left us snacks and goodies in a box in the driveway and honked. We would watch movies and play outside while other kids went to school. It was better than going to school and being bullied by everyone. Nights were filled with noise from outside while my parents built a bonfire and had parties. There were a lot of cars pulling in and out all through the day and night.

One night, I heard my father yelling, "We all die, tonight!" You know that feeling you get when a roller coaster drops you down? That's what happened when I heard that. My sister and I ran to the window to look outside. My mom and dad were both pointing guns at three guys who also had guns drawn. *"We're all going to die tonight,"* my dad was yelling. I pushed my little sister into the bottom of the linen closet to hide and pushed my way in beside her. We were as quiet as we could possibly be. I am not sure how long we were hidden in there.

We came out to check on things a little while later, and all was well. The bad men were gone, and my parents were working on a car in the driveway. I know now that the men had come to collect on a bad drug deal and my parents were tuning up the car to be able to take off. The men had traveled from California to find the five people who had messed them over, and my parents, being two of those people, were armed and waiting.

It was a few days later and almost the end of the school year when the Jefferson County Sheriff's Department pulled up to inquire about our truancy. My parents lost custody of us shortly afterwards, and we were sent to live with Granny. My mom and dad went to the family court hearing but could not pass a drug test. My mother cried and cried. My mother's father, my Pawpaw she had estranged us from, attended the court hearing to make sure they didn't turn us over to the State. They didn't know Granny was so difficult but thought it better we remained in the same school zone—as little upset as possible.

Miss Brenda and the Lovelady Movement

Shortly after, Mama and Daddy went "on the run," being hunted by bad guys *and* good guys, due to drug-trafficking warrants. Our phone calls to speak with them because we were even more miserable with my alcoholic grandmother went unanswered. They were just *gone*.

I missed them so much. When school started in the fall, I enrolled in the fourth grade again and was taller than the other kids. I had seen more than most adults. I settled into a new normal and made pretty good grades, considering. *I had another teacher, and this one liked me.*

As I said before, my mother's parents were good people who had been kept in the dark about everything their daughter was doing. She had pushed them away hard, ashamed of the choices she was making. In the late 90s, people did not understand addiction like they do now. No one could fathom what we were living through. Still, they bought us clothes and shoes and helped Granny financially all they could.

Around Christmas of the first year at my Granny's, Mom and Dad came to see us. They were going to take us shopping for Christmas presents but instead drove us down to a church parking lot and sat, talking, watching the rearview and side mirrors, paranoid and high. Then they took us back to my Granny's after an hour or so. It was like they couldn't remember from one moment to the next what we were actually doing in the first place. It was very strange. They were so far removed from the parents I had known in my early life, and my sister and I blamed ourselves for how they acted, like every child who cannot grasp that being an adult does not mean you are a perfectly good person.

The next summer, Mawmaw and Pawpaw sent me to a Christian summer camp with their church. Their Sunday School class and several members of their church had been praying for my parents for years, and did so for many more. During a prayer service, the camp counselors asked me if I had any prayer requests.

"I want God to make my parents stop using drugs," I answered.

"Let's pray that God does whatever it takes to get your parents to stop using drugs," the counselor said. Everyone gathered around and prayed with me.

One week later, they were picked up on drug-trafficking warrants. The next time I saw them was through the thick glass of the jail's visitation area. After six months in the county, my dad went to prison and my mother was court-ordered to a women's shelter program, out of the county, for six months. It was not a drug program, but they did the best they could. She conformed.

When Mom got back home, it was wonderful. She had already been clean for a year, between jail and the women's program. She worked a real job and was finally coming back to her old self. We would go to school, she would go to work, and we all were happy. She spent time in the law library downtown, looking for a way to help get my father out of prison. When she finally found out the judge retained jurisdiction on a mandatory split sentence, she approached my dad's judge, and he released my father from his sentence six months early. We had a "welcome home" party for him.

Unfortunately, prison is like college for criminals and when my parents were together, they were going to find a way to use drugs and get away with it. I know now that my mother was just waiting for "a safe time to use again." And they did—*for years.* When I was a teenager, it was common for drug deals to be happening in the garage while my friends and I hung out in the living room upstairs. They were as low-key as they could be, but no one can control a drug addiction, and yes, we knew what was happening. Eventually, the trips to jail and prison started again and continued for years. We spent a whole summer living in a motel, adjoining rooms with my mom and dad. They built a group of people they could trust, and my sister and I were carted around and "protected" by a biker and a Hispanic man. We grew to love them both, and they treated us like gold; however, it was an experience far removed from any normal teen years.

By my early twenties, I had two beautiful children and no resources at all. My father was sitting in prison after a manufacturing raid, facing "life without parole" due to being a habitual offender, having been raided while still on parole from other sentences.

My mom had picked up more charges and was released from jail, and immediately used the "Oh, I'll never be with my husband again, poor me" as an excuse to start shooting up Methamphetamine and Dilaudid, a super-strong opiate usually reserved for extreme pain management in terminal cancer cases. I wasn't sure where she was and worried about her constantly. I remember sitting on the floor of the bedroom, folding laundry and praying that God would just let her overdose so she would be at peace—so *I would be at peace*. I had been trying to take care of my parents for so long. I had been fighting her to keep her safe and alive and to keep track of her most of my life.

My Pawpaw and I went out looking for her. I didn't know it then, but she had hidden from us that day in order to stay at the drug house where she was turning tricks and using. Any limits that she had prior to the precious four or five months since my dad was told he will never leave prison were all gone. My father had never allowed her to shoot up drugs, and now that he was gone, she did that just as hard as she could.

When I finally saw her again, I told her that if she didn't get into a program and off the street, she would never see me, my sister, or our children again. (Megan had a daughter by then also.) I know she loved us somehow, in some strange, distorted way, and I heard it in her voice that this ultimatum rocked her.

My mother entered The Lovelady Center program to placate us all—me and Megan, her parents, her sister Connie, my dad from prison—*everyone* had pleaded with her to get off the streets and get help. She had charges she was facing also and was living with the fact that my dad may never leave prison, a path she felt she unintentionally and carelessly started him down many years before.

She was not the same woman anymore. I wondered if she would ever come back to us mentally, and the only point of reference with which to compare her was that measly little clean stretch of a year or so about eight years prior. I knew deep down she was only at Lovelady to placate us. It would just be a matter of time before she bailed. Nothing would work on someone that far gone.

Bury the Past

"It's no use going back to yesterday, because I was a different person then."
—Lewis Carrol

Jeanne proved to be one of the most intelligent people I had ever met. She asked me so many questions. Many times I would have to say, "I do not know the answer to that question, but I *will* find the answer." I think she respected that I never tried to give her a cliché and send her on her way. "You just gotta have faith" didn't make sense to her.

She finally grabbed hold of Intelligent Design Theory and could logically believe in a Creator. Her sweet parents took her to the Ark Encounter and the Creation Museum in Kentucky, and she told me all about the trip. "The last of my questions have been answered," she said, a new joy apparent in her face.

I also watched her pine for her husband, who was in prison. She felt tremendous guilt about his doing time for crimes they had committed together. She wanted him to be free, too, and finally, he was released from prison. She was so excited! I was mortified because the established fact is that a former drug partner and the new person in recovery cannot easily coexist.

But this is a problem for us, the addicted men who are left behind when a woman gets clean. I'm sure if you spoke with a men's program director, they would say, "My guys can't be around the woman they used drugs with." It's just how addiction works. The percentage of those who successfully quit drugs is so low, and two people in recovery together lowers the percentage of success even more. After a few years, Jeanne and her husband just could not relate to each other any longer, having done so much to each other during the drug years. They divorced.

Jeanne works with us in the ministry and has for almost 13 years now. As far as being an atheist, that's all over with. She is a believer, through and through. She is devastated that drugs were such a big part of her and her children's lives, and I have no doubt she will remain drug free until she meets Jesus face to face. I uncovered the worst parts of her daughter's stories while doing research for this book. Jeanne had been so high throughout their lives that she completely remembered things her children went through as "not so bad, just a chaotic, crazy party, so to speak," and that she had successfully protected her children from the lifestyle she and their father were living. My heart hurt for her when she was faced with the truth about her children's stories. She had no recollection of them being hungry, and did not remember the horrible way the teacher treated Monica. She remembered her youngest, Megan, leaving voicemail after voicemail, crying for her mother to please call her. Jeanne had tormented herself for years over that and what she could remember of it. I found myself thanking God she was more than a decade clean when she learned just how absolutely horrible she, in fact, *had* been as a mother.

Monica is the only client representative working for us who has never had a substance abuse problem and never graduated from The Lovelady Center program. She parented her parents for so long through their addiction that she has a real knack for giving out tough love and relating to our women. She is the director of our Supervised Release Program and gets so excited when she receives the call from the Alabama Department of Corrections telling her that inmates are ready for pickup at Julia Tutwiler Prison, about an hour and a half away from Birmingham. She immediately calls our In-Kind Resource Director, Donna, and lets her know she will be needing hygiene gift bags for however many inmates she is picking up the next day. We provide everything needed for a woman's complete stay with us: deodorant, razors, soaps, toothpaste, clothing . . . . There is no limit to what we will provide a woman in order to create an environment where she can easily heal and grow.

When Monica is not sewing kindness and hope into the lives of the women at the Center, she is with her children and husband. They own a home on the outskirts of Birmingham. Jeanne's other daughter and family live not far away and have very successful lives also.

Sometimes, especially when we have guests at the Center and I wish to explain how radically Jesus can change someone's life, I ask Jeanne to talk about her former self—the one our Sheriff at the time referred to as *"the Devil"* when he learned she was in our program.

"It's difficult to speak about the old me because, truthfully, she is *dead*. She is someone I can no longer relate to. She is someone who will never resurrect." Jeanne immediately tells people she entered The Lovelady Center to pacify her children and family and truly did not believe, all those years ago, that the program would work. "I didn't believe there was any joy beyond substances. I thought I had gone too far and had done too much to ever come back to being myself. Now, the person I have become, I love, and I know a Real Christ does as well."

The Client Rep

"I've learned over the years that when you have really good people, you don't have to baby them. By expecting them to do great things, you can get them to do great things."
—Steve Jobs

Melinda called me to her office and told me we needed to hire a new "client rep." A Client Representative is a Lovelady program graduate who has excelled in all areas and then chosen to come on board as a staff member and lead other women through the program. A good way to describe a client rep is "a healed woman who pulls other women from the pit that someone pulled her from." Our client reps return to the fire with drinks of water for those who are still burning. They are the most important staff members, alongside the counseling department. Most client reps guide and maintain a schedule for around 30 clients each. People often wonder how so many women are overseen by one person—the same way you eat an elephant: one bite at a time. That's what a client rep does: They solve one problem at a time. They are elephant eaters. And yet another analogy is this: Jesus changed the world with 12 disciples. Each client rep is to help us meet all the needs of each woman. Each client rep disciples a woman throughout the program. That is how we can change prison recidivism—*one woman at a time.*

So when Melinda asked me for a name for the open client rep position, I immediately thought of Cynthia, a perfect example of someone who has a past but has risen—against all odds—to become a functioning member of society. We are so blessed to have her on our staff. She is someone who found her destiny, the reason she was born. She is a bit tough, but our clients need that unbending authority through certain phases of our program.

Cynthia's Story, in Her Own Words

I am from a very small town in Alabama. My mother was a good woman but could neither read nor write. I was the youngest of seven children. My mom and dad divorced when I was only two years old. My father had barely left when my mother married another man because she had so many kids to support. The second man was wealthy. He was also the most selfish, greedy individual you could ever imagine, as well as an alcoholic. He was a complete miser. I actually witnessed this man ironing his money.

Most of the time, we did not have groceries, and very seldom did we have utilities. I used to pray that he would go get drunk because when he did, he would take us all shopping, get the utilities turned back on, and provide us plenty to eat. Then he would sober up, and within a couple of months we were back to having no utilities and being hungry again. My childhood was a cycle of complete and utter poverty contrasted with out-of-control spending.

My brothers and sisters were all considerably older than me, and most had left home by the time I was 12. At around that same time, I started sleeping with all the boys. I was the "bad girl" in town. I got married at age 15. You must have a parent's signature to get married that young in Alabama, and my mother gladly signed for me because she could not do anything with me.

I had two sons, back to back. When I was 22, separated from my husband and running wild again, I was in a terrible motorcycle accident. I lay in traction for five months in the hospital, underwent five surgeries, and became addicted to morphine. My mother took in my sons when I was hospitalized, but then got more than she bargained for, ending up having them for many years. I was so addicted to morphine that it became my entire life.

I became an intravenous user, and it became my first love. When I could not find morphine, I used heroin.

For the next few decades, I had no life outside of drugs. Every day merged with the next, and I lost time—*I lost years, actually.* Christmas, holidays, birthdays, no matter—every day was the same for me. My rap sheet would be a few feet long if printed. Three times judges ordered me to rehab, and I would complete the 28-day or 3-month programs and use again within 24 hours of my release. Detoxing was very bad, but even the horror of withdrawals was completely overpowered by my love for the drug. I knew I was eventually going to run out or be jailed and be very sick, but that did not deter me.

A few times when I was arrested, I faked a heart attack in the police car so an ambulance would be called to take me away, and I would jump out at a red light and run. The cops began riding in the ambulance with me so I could not escape. They all knew me and were so fed up.

Both of my boys became avid drug users also. We used to laugh and say, "The family that shoots up together stays together." I am ashamed to say I actually used drugs intravenously with my children, if that is any indication of the depth of depravity to which I had succumbed. It is also an indication of the power of transformation that is found in a life led by Christ!

My mother died, never seeing me become a sober, successful, or even happy adult. She left all her children money. I immediately went out and bought a mobile home with my inheritance and moved into it along with both my boys. We blew the rest on drugs, of course.

One of my sons had become a crystal methamphetamine manufacturer. Not long after moving into our *home sweet home,* we were particularly paranoid from the meth, which I had begun shooting along with the morphine, speed-balling—the simultaneous use of an upper and a downer. I had found a way to stay up—way up—and enjoy my morphine without nodding out. But the paranoia . . . . We dismantled the interior of the mobile home, looking for listening devices that we were positive the Feds had planted there to catch us in criminal activity. Methamphetamine use causes extreme paranoia and delusional thinking. After a few days, we came down from the high and realized what we had done to the inside of our home. It was no longer livable, really. Every single appliance was taken apart and left in pieces. So we decided it would be a good idea to just torch it. The insurance gave me $21,000 for the mobile home and contents, which we immediately used to get high again. I did buy a car, but after a couple of weeks, I flipped it three times, completely totaling it. I left the accident relatively unharmed, but I looked at my wrecked car and realized I was homeless with no transportation. I started walking and did not look back.

For the next 10 years, I walked the streets as a prostitute. I would stay with my sons occasionally, but mostly I lived on the street. Eventually, I was arrested for prostitution. "You've been a busy lady, haven't you?" the judge asked me, ordering me to yet another short-term rehab. I completed that program, went to my son's house, and began shooting up again. Within a few days, the police came, busted through the door, and arrested all of us. Both of my sons went to prison. There I stood, before that same judge, 48 years old, no hope, no family, no home. I once again had a court-appointed attorney.

The judge peered over his glasses and looked at me, "Miss Ledkins, your life as you now know it, has ended. I am going to send you to a long-term facility to see if there is any hope at all for you." That day, the judge sent me to The Lovelady Center. That court-appointed attorney delivered me to the Center himself, and I later found out that he had paid my intake fee into the program. A few months later, that same attorney paid for me to get my GED. That young man wanted to make a difference for someone, and I can never thank him enough.

I stood before that judge 14 years ago, and everything he said that day was completely true: *My life, as I knew it back then, ended.* I have a wonderful job. Every day I get to help women find their way, the way Lovelady helped me find mine. That court-appointed attorney also gave me a car, and I drove it for years. When I finally traded it in for a brand-new car, it had 315,000 miles on it! Many of those miles were accumulated by driving back and forth visiting both sons in prison. After years of renting, I also am now a homeowner through Habitat for Humanity.

Today, both of my boys have served their sentences and been released from prison. They are faster learners than their mom and have remained clean, and both have good jobs. I was able to give them both a stable home when they got out of prison.

I now have four grandchildren who keep me extremely busy during my off-time. I see them every chance I get. They are adorable, and I cherish them in more ways than anyone could imagine. I could not envision a future for myself for most of my life. I could not see past my present circumstances when I stood before the judge that day. Now I know the future holds life for me.

I once had absolutely no hope—now I am *full* of hope. I once was strung out—now my mind is *clear*. I repeatedly was homeless for many years—now I have a beautiful *home*. I like to tell people that I was an IV user but now am *an NIV user*, referring to the New International Version of the Bible.

Even though we are a women's facility, Miss Brenda and Miss Melinda helped me learn to be a mother to my boys and a grandmother to their children. The only reminder left of the old me is my heart. I have to be very careful because my heart is weaker than it should be. Doctors tell me I caused all the damage from years of shooting up drugs. I guess my heart got tired from all those years of a high and a low plunged into my system together. I love the Lord with every fiber of my being, and if I die tomorrow, I will die a content woman.

Michelle

"Nothing is impossible, the word itself says 'I'm possible.'"
—Audrey Hepburn

"Mom, I need you to come here please," Melinda called, asking me to visit her office. I can't stand it when she does that. I am roaming the building, minding my own business or, rather, minding everyone else's, if truth be known. One of the best ways of taking the pulse of The Lovelady Center is simply by visiting the natural habitats of our residents. It's similar to children—if parents visit them in their bedrooms or any other place where most of their time is spent, much can be learned. Also, many of our women tend to be hoarders, and even though we have a limit on clothing pieces, there have been times where our pop-ins keep a room less cluttered. They have spent years without cleaning sometimes or picking up food to prevent a bug or rodent problem, so we really have to teach or reteach them how to live in cleanliness again. Many years of living one way in addiction may mean, for example, forgoing the habit of making your bed each morning. We really don't have to say much; our presence speaks volumes. But that day, I had just begun roaming.

When I returned to the "oval office," as the women love to call Melinda's and my offices, my sweet daughter wanted to talk to me about a teaching position for the summer program that we were putting together for the children living in the Center. Children had never been meant, at least in my eyes, to be part of the program, originally. It is a huge undertaking to house children, much less those who have been through the ringer, though our hearts did go out to them. We simply didn't know if we could help them the way they needed to be helped! Soon enough, we learned that reuniting mothers and children was absolutely necessary to help a woman really rebuild her life. So we'd better get to learning how to help the precious little ones that addiction affects the most.

Every day, more problems seemed to arise. I grew weary of all the surprises we faced over and over again. Often, people tell me that we are pioneers in the field of rebuilding lives, a field which is needed and rapidly growing with so many good people. Being called a pioneer by any of those soldiers of good is really a cool compliment, but wow, the surprises and the learning curves that come along with it!

"We've got to hire a teacher for our children," she started.

"You have an idea?" I knew full well that she did, being one who rarely proposed a problem without a few ideas for a solution. Melinda is one determined soul, let me tell you. I wonder where she gets that from! What she was really saying is this: I got this problem worked out, and I just need you to sign off on it. All of my children know my rule: "If there is a problem, then there is a solution. Bring me the problem and solution at the same time."

"I think we should give Michelle from Georgia the opportunity," Melinda said. "She will be graduating in a few weeks, she has a teaching certificate, and she loves kids. She loves *our* kids." She added that line in because our kids, those belonging to the mothers in our program, are often difficult, understandably. As stated before, they've been through a lot for their young ages. "Hunter even likes her," Melinda added. Hunter, my adopted son, was and still *is* hard to handle. But that is another story, a book unto itself.

"Surely you are kidding! She was a *terror*. Hunter probably likes her because they are just alike," I chuckled. "I'm just not feeling it, Melinda."

"You have a better answer?" she stated actually with respect, as she always does with me, being the absolute definition of one who honors her parents. But she knew full well that I probably did not have an answer. I relented and told her to ask Michelle about it and get back with me. Who am I to say someone cannot change? I certainly didn't have any of my own ideas, so what could be the harm? Besides, Melinda told me that Michelle had more patience than anyone she had ever seen. Gee whiz, we always need someone with patience for our kids. She might have been a terror to herself and other adults, but she had a warmth for children that could be seen. About that time a young boy around six years old came strolling in. His dad had driven him up from Mobile. Tears welled up in my eyes as I looked at him. He had a swastika shaved in his hair. That little boy didn't even know what he had on him. He was so ragged and dirty. Suddenly I was glad we had him in our program.

As I looked over Michelle's file, I thought my daughter really must be seeing beyond the file for her to be considering this young woman. The truth is, I trust Melinda's instincts as much as I trust my own. She was correct when she told me I needed to look at the new person, not the file. I knew she was right. People make me so mad, not willing to give "my women" a second chance, and I felt small when she pointed out my mistake.

A little while later, Melinda walked back into my office with Michelle in tow. Most of the women are a little intimidated if I jump in and start questioning them, so I attempted just small talk with Michelle. I'm not really known for being a good small-talker, to say the least. However, Michelle opened right up. She knew she was being considered for a summer job with our kids. Maybe her story wasn't as bad as I thought it had been. She told me "No, you have the right story, just the wrong girl. I'm not her anymore." Well, I *love* that way of thinking! And she loved all the children in the building and spoke about them by name. As Michelle's story unfolded, I was totally captivated by it. She had lived through five Lifetime movies and was only 28 years old. She did have her teaching certificate for kindergarten and seemed totally fit and qualified for the program. She had everything we needed, but was it what *she* needed? Only time could tell that.

However, we were having to make a decision that day about Michelle setting up a children's summer program at the Center. We decided it would be in everyone's best interest to let

Michelle give it a go and see how things came together. She was absolutely devoted to the children, and the program turned out to be so good that volunteers who came to the Center actually were talking about how good our program was. After school started, we let her continue and work with the children in an after-school program.

We discovered Michelle had many more talents than we had seen. That first day, Michelle took it upon herself to tutor the clients in math. She loved algebra and had a good personality that seemed to minister to the women. Over the years, we learned to trust Michelle with other jobs. If we needed someone to oversee and keep an eye on things for us, Michelle proved to be our girl. Over the next 12 years, she would become family and a valuable member of our staff. Michelle served as a personal assistant to Melinda and me and freed up much of our time so we could do other things that only we could do. However, that first day I met Michelle, as I listened to her story, I would never have believed she would prove to be such a valuable member of Lovelady for over a decade.

Michelle was 28 years old and had come to us from a small town on the Alabama/Georgia line. She was an only child. Her mother and father were never married, and their relationship had been a one-sided love affair. Michelle's mom, Betty, was not known for choosing good men; on the contrary, she chose men with problems who ended up abusing her. When the guy found out Betty was pregnant with Michelle, he beat her up, hoping she would lose the baby. Abortion by beating, I suppose. Geez, what a good man he was.

Betty did not lose the baby, fortunately, and healed from the beating. Little Michelle was born. The new mother had been a long-haul truck driver, but she had quit upon learning of her pregnancy and began a career with Sony music in the production department. In spite of her "wild nightlife," Betty stayed with Sony for over 22 years. She had been a great employee with a stellar record. She had been determined to raise her daughter and give her anything she could ever want, the dedicated mother who was also the partying, good-time girl.

Betty's first marriage had been at the age of 14, and the other three marriages happened at various times in her life—Michelle being the only consistent figure throughout. Betty really wanted Michelle to have a father, so when she married someone, a requirement would be for Michelle to be adopted. Consequently, Michelle changed names along with her mom. As far as I could tell, Betty never refused Michelle anything. It was both of them against the world. There were a host of "uncles and friends" in Michelle's life from birth to 18 years old. Michelle sat there in front of Melinda and me and listed about nine different men who Betty hooked up with who had been a big part of her daughter's life.

One of the men Betty married sexually molested Michelle when she was only six years old. The abuse continued until she was about 10 years of age when a sex education class was taught at school, and Michelle realized how wrong and perverse it was. Charges were brought against the man, but Michelle did not want to testify, and Betty dropped the case.

A short time later, at age 12, Michelle met a cute 15-year-old kid she really liked named Jay. Michelle became sexually active, and her mother simply looked the other way and allowed her to be with Jay. All Michelle had to do was ask if Jay could stay over. Jay introduced Betty to his father, Randy, and the double-dating started. Jay and Michelle lived in one end of the house, and Betty and Randy at the other end. About that time, Betty's stepfather and his partner moved in. It wasn't long before cocaine was introduced into the mix by the stepfather.

Things just rolled on, and Jay became totally obsessed with Michelle. Neither of them were mature enough for a relationship of that nature, and Michelle had begun changing her mind about Jay. That threw a kink into the whole living situation of the household. They argued a great deal. Michelle began going places to stay away from home, away from Jay. He assumed she was seeing another boy. The more she pulled away from the relationship, the more he went downhill, mentally. One night, they had a particularly horrible argument when Michelle finally returned home late. Jay was ranting and howling, just out of his *mind*. Right in front of Michelle, Jay shot himself in the head. He died at the hospital 2 days later, at only 18 years old.

Most of us have a difficult time accepting things the way they actually are. When Michelle and I were talking and we addressed this suicide issue, she absolutely believed she had been in love with Jay. I had no right to tell her she was not, but we decided to shelve that subject for the time being. I'm of the belief that she was filled with guilt and regret and was mistaking that for love. Jay's dad could not believe his son would shoot himself in the head and decided Michelle must have shot Jay, and so it was investigated. The law deemed her innocent, due to Jay's fingerprints and the residue on his hands. That in itself had been extremely traumatic. I know if I was being investigated for murder, I would definitely have been traumatized.

"My life really spun out of control after that," she relayed as she continued her story. Of course, I had been steadily trying to cover my shock over her childhood. I *"fixed my face,"* as we commonly say at Lovelady. It is important for us to meet the women where they are and I was really trying, but sometimes I just cannot process what I learn about some of our women.

In spite of all the craziness, Michelle graduated high school. She was and is extremely intelligent. That, in itself, was shocking to me. Some people are very smart but still do dumb things. Michelle was smart with no chance to live a sober, grounded life, but still saw education as something she needed. That was Michelle. Michelle and Betty strayed farther apart after the suicide. Betty was disillusioned and in love, and Michelle went from one relationship to another.

Within a year, Michelle was using every kind of drug around she could use. Betty was self-proclaimed anti-drugs, although she smoked pot on a daily basis and had used cocaine with her daughter years before. But Michelle left Betty and simply went to the streets to live, helping people manufacture methamphetamine and steadily selling and using it.

She had her first son at age 21, and made a decision to stay straight to raise him and give him every possible thing he could ever want. But that same cycle Betty had been caught in was pulling Michelle into the same black hole. I call it generational curses, or one could say, "it runs in the family."

Things were going decently as they could under the circumstances for Michelle and her son at first, and she was attending night classes at a local college, determined to break the cycle. She also had an apartment for them. She got pregnant with her second child and had a beautiful daughter. She was ecstatic, even though she knew it was going to be hard to be a single mom. Michelle was 24.

That sweet baby girl died of SIDS when she was a few weeks old. Torn apart with grief, Michelle drove her son to Betty's house, left him, and just took off. She spiraled down farther than she had ever been before, making meth in her own car and then burning the car to destroy evidence when she thought the cops were getting too close to her. When she got pregnant a third time, her attention was once more redirected. She went to a rehab when DHR began to close in on her. She was terrified of her son being put in a foster home, but DHR was reluctant to leave the son with Betty. She was hoping the rehab would be just what she needed to change her life permanently.

When the baby arrived, constant fear of losing another baby to SIDS engulfed her. Unable to sleep and full of anxiety, she went to a doctor and he gave her a prescription for Xanax. She took too many, though, and developed an addiction. Betty was allowed to take custody of the second son then, and also decided to get her own life in order to better take care of both her grandsons.

Michelle found herself standing before a judge for manufacturing methamphetamine. The judge she was standing in front of was in Alabama, because she had crossed state lines and the judge had just heard about "that new women's facility" in Birmingham. He decided to send Michelle there. "If they can help *her*, they can help anyone."

Michelle walked through our doors 13 years ago for the first time. She entered our program having just found out that her mom had moved her own baby's father in with her and was in a relationship with him. That was a hard fact to accept and yet another clue telling us what life must have been like for her.

For the most part, Michelle was very standoffish. She seemed hesitant to talk with anyone. She wanted a new life but was used to having everything she could want; she wanted the new life on her own terms. It doesn't work that way at Lovelady. Have you ever watched a Western where they are breaking a horse? That is how we had to handle Michelle. She absolutely was successful in every job she was asked to perform. She graduated from the program. She married "her knight in shining armor," and eventually gained custody of her two wonderful boys.

Michelle's mom, Betty, after having broken up with the grandson's dad, spent a great deal of time with Michelle. They actually formed a stronger bond than they ever had before. When Betty was diagnosed with cancer, Michelle was right by her side, accompanying her to treatments and taking care of her in her own home. From her years at Sony, Betty had managed to save and, combined with her stock options, had built a nice nest egg for her daughter. She passed away with Michelle lying right next to her. Michelle got all of the money over the next few months.

I became a little concerned when I saw her husband and Michelle buy two new trucks. Michelle paid for her home and put money in accounts for both boys. I saw some good decisions being made, as well as some terrible ones. The money was drained quickly. Then hubby got a girlfriend and asked Michelle for a divorce. Going through the divorce was extremely hard on Michelle. After her mom's death, with the money spent and a husband who left her, it was heartbreaking and all happened so fast. Some of the things she was experiencing were just life moments that everyone experiences. She was not handling life the way she had learned to handle things in the program. We see every day that life throws us curveballs. That is something out of our control. How we handle the unpleasant things thrown at us is the key. We all have them every day, and how we handle them is the key to staying sober and overcoming.

Michelle handled the curveballs by allowing herself to spiral out of control. Thirteen years and a whole new life slowly disappeared before our eyes. It did not take 13 years for the fall. I watched her begin to spiral: drinking at first, then a failed drug test for pot, all like a stack of dominoes tumbling down. Rather than throwing her away, we talked, we counseled, we did all we could do to stop the insanity. Losing her job was the final straw, but we really had no choice. I especially spent time with Michelle to see if a bridge could be built to bring her back into the fold. It was not the drugs but rather the power she was after. She wanted to be in control of something after having lost control of so much, when you boiled it all down. She had taken a hard left turn, and then she took a complete dive into harder drugs again. It was a slow, steady fall.

She went back to selling drugs, running across the state lines of Georgia and Alabama and leaving her beloved boys by themselves. The old Michelle was back, front and center. Her older son was so hurt he quit speaking to her. She quit answering my phone calls. The rumor mill was working overtime. She was spotted with people she should never have been around.

Eventually, she was in jail in Georgia and in a big legal mess. She did not call me for several months during that period. I was dealing with the aftermath of her actions. I thought about our own clients' families. I was trying to help her older son get through his senior year. He was awarded a full scholarship to Auburn University. We helped him find an apartment in Auburn and furnished it. The more I dealt with her children, the more I saw how deeply wounded her boys were. Her younger son went to live with Michelle's cousin in Georgia. Michelle was so embarrassed and simply gave up on life. Her older son stayed with my family when he was not in Auburn. She has lost him for now, but maybe she will reunite with him at some later time. Michelle is a case that baffles all of us, and how this could happen right before our eyes was difficult for the entire staff.

Magnifying the destruction for the boys is the fact that Michelle had left on Christmas Eve after the boys had gone to bed. She had told them she would be home and they would spend Christmas Day together. She had their gifts in her truck. She was arrested that evening and, of course, never made it back to the Christmas Day plans. Those boys had been home alone that Christmas with no gifts, no mom, and no groceries—and they did not want anyone to know. They didn't know their mother's whereabouts or even if she was alive or dead. It was Christmas Day and they were all alone. Here is a bird's-eye view into the addict's lifestyle: Many children on holidays are lonely and without. Drugs steal Christmas just like every other day. Drugs don't take holidays. Drugs steal the very life of the user and everyone touching the user, especially the innocents. Unlike users, the innocent ones have no escape from the sadness.

I finally decided I would take Michelle's call from jail. When we spoke for the first time, she was crying so hard I could barely understand her. I listened that day, and many days after that. I did not attempt to get her out of jail no matter how she asked, and honestly she did not ask much at all. I watched up close and personal the destruction of those two young boys' lives, lost to their mother using drugs. I have watched so much the aftermath of families torn apart by drugs and I felt the pain of so many moms and dads, brothers, sisters, and friends who have begged and pleaded with their loved ones—but drugs were so much a part of their life that they would give up everything and everyone. Her sons were devastated, and I described everything in grueling detail to Michelle. I watched and waited a full year.

The drug supplier was gone; the drug friends were gone. At the end of a year, the judge set bail, and I got her out. We walked with her through her legal issues. It was like trying to get a knot out of an extra-thin gold chain. Alabama and Georgia, with Georgia having some of the nation's hardest drug laws, proved to be a real issue. Michelle lived at Hob Hill with my family for 10 months, and I worked with her every day. It was difficult for me to watch her slowly discover the emotions she had buried for all those years. She finally could talk about the unusual relationship with her mom, mentioning how most women do not date their daughter's boyfriends while their daughter is in rehab. I did not want to rob her of her love for her mom. She just needed to see the truth in their relationship.

I was able to navigate the waters in Alabama, and Michelle was able to walk out with probation. But Georgia courts are not particularly understanding with drug traffickers. As the judge told me, "Miss Brenda, my job is to put them away; *yours* is to rehabilitate."

It wasn't pretty, but was lenient, considering. No one could expect better, realistically. This young woman with a bright future was going to prison. Well, at least her home was paid for, right? Wrong. She had put a small mortgage on it during the spiral, and ended up losing the house also. When I say bottom, it was the *bottom* she hit.

"What happened? How could you let this happen?" I asked her.

"I guess I thought, being clean for so long and knowing everything I know, that I could do what I want and not lose control. I was so wrong," she stated.

She sure was. Without a doubt, God forgave her for returning to that life, but the State of Georgia demanded consequences.

"Any way you can show her mercy?" I found myself asking the DA in the courtroom, one more time, offering alternative ideas and responsibility to oversee ankle monitoring and house arrest options in my own home. Alabama knows Lovelady, but Georgia does not. The district attorney and I discussed her case many times. In his defense, elected officials must clean up the streets. When they looked at Michelle, they did not see the past she had lived, the pain she had endured, even the child abuse; they saw a person who was running heavy drugs and lots of it through Georgia.

"The mercy has been shown, in that she will come up for parole in three or four years. That's the mercy." Indeed, they had done everything they could on two drug-trafficking charges and a slew of little possession and paraphernalia charges.

I understand the State's position, really I do. But sometimes I want to stand on a mountain and yell to the whole world that most addicts are covering pain when they start getting high—and of those, most wouldn't ever commit a crime if not for the drug use that they need treatment for, so where do we step in and start to treat that cycle instead of sending them to the depths of yet another pit altogether that doesn't help them heal from the main illness? And so it is with most programs that specialize in addiction—addiction is a *beast*.

At first, I initially thought about not including Michelle's story in this book. I wanted to talk just about our thousands of success stories and how wonderfully the women have done. But that's not my way. I would feel dishonest to give you just the good and none of the bad, and this is a bad true story. It is filled with my tears, those boys' tears, and tears of the Lovelady staff who are still in shock. Michelle has plans to minister to the girls in prison. We look forward to keeping in touch and hearing how she is able to help other women in the prison where she is sent. She certainly can return to the Lovelady family when she is finally released in a few years, and begin the process of starting over. Again.

Michelle left for jail, where she will await being picked up by the State for prison, just a few days ago. I have cried a true river of tears. Melinda actually has become a little irritated with me because I have carried on so much about it. I talk about the consequences of our actions and how they affect people. It is so difficult to write about my feelings in this. I am so angry about what Michelle has done. So many have been wounded by her actions. Addiction leaves so many wounded people who suffer, through no fault of their own. We grieve for our lost ones.

But as I listened to Michelle talk about how life will be when she is allowed to leave prison, I am keenly aware that I may no longer be that spry mother figure to whom she has grown accustomed. This last year with her has brought some understanding, but I am growing older. I may not be able to hop in the car and go shopping with her ever again. It also makes me realize that it's the same in each one of their lives. Women believe they can come out of prison and just pick back up right where they were when they went in. They grow older in prison. They lose another day of life and then another and then another. Every day brings a few more gray hairs. Life doesn't seem to advance past the hard, continual routine, and time moves pretty slowly. If only they would remember that we lose life when we forget the consequences of our actions.

My tears are not just for Michelle; rather, they are for all the lost lives, and for so much lost time. My tears are for the children who have suffered through the pain of drugs and destruction. This experience has been extremely difficult. It has made me more conscientious about every word I say to the women in our charge. My prayer and hope is Michelle will do what it takes to get out on parole as soon as circumstances allow, and I will be just as I am now.

Michelle had to be delivered to the county jail for them to house her for 30 days before she actually goes to the state prison. She does not know which one will house her. Unlike Alabama, which only has one women's prison, Georgia has six. Michelle could be housed all the way across the state. She left for her 30-day stay at the county jail. Through my tears, I watched her limp to the car with her head down, crying every step of the way. When she was a little girl, she had hurt her foot and arthritis developed there. So to the car she limped. She had been told to enter with no makeup on or hair products in her hair, and no jewelry with the exception of a solid cross. I gave her one of mine last week so she would have that.

While in prison, a woman has to buy any shampoo, conditioner, and other hygiene from the commissary. Things are expensive in the store, so it actually costs to live in prison. That just amazes me. The Feds have taken over the operations of Tutwiler in Alabama, so it is much more reasonable now. I don't know about the Georgia prison system. At best, Michelle will need about $300 a month to maintain any sort of normalcy. With no family or other friends, that will have to come from me. For the women who have no one, life can be very hard. The system itself sets up women for all types of behavior and criminal activity to survive. Contraband is rampant in the prisons. Cell phones are not allowed, but at least half of the women somehow obtain a cell phone they keep hidden. Most of the contraband comes from the officers watching over the women. The whole system is corrupted from within. The women with nothing are easy prey for the ones "making store." The indigent women get a bar of soap to use for their body and hair. Michelle and I spoke at length about all of these things.

She knows we help her sons financially, and I know she is worried that I will not help her. Many of our women have declared their desire to send money that will be put on an account for her. What happens, though, is time is never on your side in prison. After a while, people forget people. Prescriptions needed seem to take forever to get to you. Michelle has asthma, so she was so concerned about that. Georgia prisons are air-conditioned, which is always a major concern in the South. One time we had a client who got her throat cut in an argument over a fan in Tutwiler, as it is not air-conditioned. My goodness, I would not want to live there.

Miss Brenda and the Lovelady Movement

We sat up several nights talking about prison before Michelle had to leave. She was extremely afraid. Her youngest son would not get out of bed to go to school for several days. She has expressed concern he might run away. What would a mother do if she received notice one of her children ran away? She could do nothing. Someone dies? She might or might not be able to attend the funeral. An officer has to go with her and the State has to be paid by the family before the officer can escort. All of these things were raging in her mind. I sat there and listened to her as she cried, and I could visibly see her shaking. Her voice was shaking, and she was so miserable. I knew the enticements of the world were not looking so good to her anymore. Power, drugs, men, or money meant nothing to her anymore compared to the freedom she had lost. I used to take freedom for granted, but not anymore.

I have not seen or spoken to her since she left last week. Until she is settled in the prison where she will spend the next few years, she will not have phone privileges. I watched Michelle limp into the back seat, wiping her eyes, and once the door closed, she was no longer visible to me.

That old, familiar anxiety—much closer to physical pain, actually—washed over me in that moment as the car pulled away. It's the same intensity that floods through us when we lose a woman to overdose. *Could I have done something different? Could I have hollered at her more? Could I have been silent and listened more?*

A feeling of dread unless I do something right then comes with it, sort of like a panic, and then I remind myself I cannot make their choices for them. I remind myself of all the sound teaching, of all the moments. And I take from it just a bit more wisdom for the next woman.

This morning, I actually received a call from her. She was allowed to call me for exactly five minutes. She was in the county jail where she had spent the year prior to her release on bond, and most of the deputies knew her. She had been a trustee. I was so shocked when she called. She was crying so hard I could barely understand her. She was just overwhelmed with her fate, not being able to see her sons, and being far away from her home here in Birmingham with us.

"I can't do this." She was saying so much, and just wailing into the phone. I actually grew aggravated. I became very stern with her and told her to get it together. I told her that this was her opportunity to allow God to use her, and this was her consequence and she needed to just "woman up." We spoke a few more minutes and then had to disconnect. I felt bad for Michelle, but my feelings were so conflicted. I felt so angry at the same time. I asked myself the question yet once more. The question I had asked her repeatedly. The question her sons had asked her. *Why?*

Most Wanted, in Carmen's Own Words

"It is never too late to be what you might have been."
—George Eliot

My name is Carmen. I am so excited to tell the story of my terrible past, incredible present, and unbelievable future. I was born in Alabama 38 years ago. I was a special child, a real daddy's girl. He was into sports, and he put me in them like I was a son. I strived to be everything he wanted me to be.

    He was such a good father to my family but showed favoritism to me. Sometimes I would feel a small amount of sympathy for my younger sister, but I always thought, "Oh well, she has Mom." We were from Alabama, but my dad got transferred with his job to the East Coast. We kept moving up the coast until we got to the very top. The higher we went up the coast, the higher Dad went up the ladder of success. Before long, the man who started at the bottom was at the top.

    We lived in nice houses, had great cars, and wore the best clothes. Life was great. Oddly enough, my mother never cared that much about money and the things that money could buy. She was as introverted as my dad was extroverted. Dad would try to get her motivated because he said he needed a wife who could help him make it to the top. There were parties she didn't want to attend, conferences she didn't care about, and eventually the list of their differences began to grow. She would not act the part and especially would not dress the part. She was not and has never been materialistic. She only cared about her kids.

So Dad met the kind of woman that he thought he needed. She was a little older than Dad, but she acted like him with the parties, clothes, and the rest of the high life. Daddy left my mother. Really, he didn't go anywhere; he just gave her a nice big divorce settlement. I told myself then and still believe that he felt guilty and the settlement was conscience money. He was more than fair with her. She didn't even say a whole lot. She just took it in stride. She packed up my sister and me, and back to Alabama we came. Gosh, I hated to leave my daddy. He was my life. We spoke almost daily, though, so I managed. I kept up my sports, so I thought everything was fine. I would have bet my life that my dad and I were tied together at the hip with a tie that could not be broken.

I went to a medium-size high school in Alabama, got excellent grades, and dated a big-time football player from a larger school across town. He was just great in my eyes. I must have had bad vision back then and should have had some glasses as my vision wasn't very good. I don't know why so many women who have problems always pick the wrong man. Wrong men are like magnets; I guess it's that "bad boy" thing we women like.

I just loved that man. His name was Jimmy, and he was so fine. We dated through our senior year of high school and then right on through the University of Alabama. He dropped out of school and went into the construction business with his family. I had always dreamed of being a nurse. My mind was set on that dream, and I never wavered.

Thank goodness my dad paid for my education and was still giving me the money I needed to live on so I didn't have to work. Toward the end of school, Jimmy and I decided we just had to get married. Dad did not care for Jimmy at all, and the decision to marry him was the first time Dad and I had a major difference. In hindsight, Dad was so right. Jimmy was as spoiled as I was. He was just as much of a mama's boy as I was a daddy's girl, and for us, that was a dangerous combination. His family was upper-middle class, and they had everything they wanted and then some. His mother and I had a lot in common as she was an RN and worked for a local medical clinic.

The wedding was a small but beautiful ceremony. I was so hurt that my father did not attend my wedding ceremony. I was hurt to my core over that. He paid for everything but would not attend. I had always envisioned him walking me down the aisle and having the first dance with me. Daddy was still being most generous.

My mother became even more introverted. She loved and longed for my father. Most of the time, when a man falls in love with another woman at my dad's age, they fall in love with a younger woman. In Dad's case, the other woman was older, dressed flamboyantly, and laughed a lot. She was just more fun. She was someone who understood his ambition. I feel it just hit my mom harder because it looks like to her, he got an older model with more miles on it. I laughed and told her he wasn't trading cars. At any rate, between the retirement from her former job and the money from her marriage to Dad, she was in very good shape financially.

My younger sister had a baby, and Mom doted on her as much as she doted on anything, so I thought Mom would be fine. However, she never started dating again. She did get another job, but it did not last long. The divorce seemed so easy and friendly. I learned that divorce generally leaves a broken heart with one of the parties. I ache for my mother and will always have a home for her.

After Jimmy and I got married, I continued going to school. It was hard being married and being a full-time student. Money became much tighter with only Jimmy working. I never imagined Jimmy being so demanding. He would want me home the minute he got there. Finally, I finished nursing school and got my dream nursing assignment. You can finish nursing school and get a two-year degree to be an RN. I really considered that but had always excelled at school and love to learn. There was something so important to me to get my master's degree. I am an overachiever by nature and I love to learn, so school agreed with me.

All good things seem to end. I felt let down after finishing school. Things really got hard with Jimmy then. First-year nurses don't get the best hours in the hospital. It didn't matter to me, but if the weather did not permit construction on a certain day and he couldn't work, then he would call over and over for me to come home. Of course, I could not just leave work, nor did I want to. However, when I got home that great big football hero would scream and act like a crazy person. It was awful. I was already getting fed up with him before I found out I was pregnant. Oh, my goodness, I was going to have a baby! I was so thrilled. Even Jimmy could not rain on my excitement. Carmen was having a baby! My enthusiasm was contagious. Everyone knew within a few days of my knowing.

Pregnancy added a dimension to my life that I was not expecting. We worked on the nursery, and it was so beautiful. My life was beyond any of my expectations. It was wonderful. My dad was calling his little girl to check on her. When my baby boy was born, we were ecstatic. We named him Bradley. He was so cute and sweet. He was a good baby. I thought I knew what love was but the second they laid him in my arms I learned I had never truly known what it was before that moment. My life was so perfect.

There was one little problem. After Bradley's birth, I began to have migraines. They started with one the first month and then I had two the next month. After that, they began every week. One day, Jimmy asked if I wanted a couple of his pain pills. He had been hurt at work, and the emergency doctor had given him a prescription for hydrocodone, an opiate. I was surprised he had any left and told him that. He just laughed and threw the bottle at me. I looked at it and saw the prescription was for 90 and it was written by the doctor his mom worked for. I said "Sure! I've got to feed Bradley, clean up, get dressed, take him to nursery school, and then go to work for a 12-hour shift!"

Jimmy had quit caring when I got off as he had begun to ask how many hours I was working and calculated in his head how much I was making. He had begun not even going to work all the time because I was earning so much money. He especially loved my overtime. It was so much money for two young people, and that four-year degree really paid off for us. I started to hand him back the bottle, and he told me to keep half of them in case I had another headache.

Miss Brenda and the Lovelady Movement

In a few days, I felt a headache coming on so I went to the bottle in my purse to get a pill so it would go away. A few days later, I thought I might have a headache, so I went to my purse. A few days after that, I was tired and thought the answer would be a pill. Finally, one day I had, or thought I had, or might be going to have, or might just need a pick-me-up; I went to the fountain of "feeling better" in the bottle in my purse and the fountain was dry. I couldn't wait to get off that day. I was supposed to work overtime, but I told the head nurse on my shift that something had come up and I couldn't work. I hurried home and Jimmy and several of his friends were sitting around, drinking beer. Jimmy looked up and said, "What are you doing at home? I thought you were working a double."

"Why don't you go work a double, or even a single, or even just an hour?" I shot back at him. I walked into the bedroom, and he followed me, and as I turned around, he held out a bottle of pills. I snatched them, took two, and put the rest in my purse. He asked me, "You feel better?" I did not answer but knew in my heart I was a long way from better. I had never been worse in my life. Another kind of birth had been given that day, the birth of an addiction.

Jimmy's mom kept us in all the pills we could take for a long while. She finally got caught. She really didn't know we all were so addicted. We thought we were just coping with our lives. She lost her job. When Bradley was two, Jimmy had a car accident and they did not even test him. During those years, addiction just wasn't talked about in the medical profession like it is today.

Goodness, we got so bad Jimmy would stab himself to go to the ER and get sewn up to get a bottle of pills. I have seen him do that so many times. It is just ingrained in my memory. We wanted the prescription rather than to get them on the street. We were still paying our bills and could not afford to buy them from the dealers. We never sold them—we couldn't because we needed them for ourselves. We had fallen into a deep well and did not see a way out.

I hurt all over and thought I was at the end of my life. I went to the ER and told them something bad was wrong with me, that I hurt all over and nothing was helping. I thought they were going to start therapy and psychotic help. I couldn't even sit up. They came and hooked up my IV of fluids and were putting my meds in the line. I asked what they were giving me, and they gave me a list of medications; in that list they gave me Dilaudid, one of the strongest opiates there is. Well, that certainly made me feel better! My flu flew right out the window. It was like gasoline to an empty car. I was able to walk right out of that hospital. I really was naïve about opiates, even though I was a nurse. I am not making excuses for myself, but I was pretty dumb about it.

Eventually, my mother-in-law was able to get Dilaudid in pill form, and we learned how to break it down so we could use it intravenously. Any life as we had known it was over then. We were in too deep and there was no getting out. I look back on that time period and it has taken so many years for me not to just loathe myself.

My nursing license was gone. The profession I loved with every fiber of my being was just gone. My dad, who I had called for help, flew down and with one big swoop one day, filed an emergency petition and left with my son. I cried until my eyes were literally swollen shut. That's not just a saying—they were really swollen where I could not open them. Jimmy was arrested on a robbery charge, went to jail, and was sentenced to prison. We lost our house and our cars. Every possession we had was gone. All our clothes were donated to a charity. I thought I had hit "rock bottom," but in fact, I wasn't even close.

I was arrested eleven times. The happy nurse who loved life so much overdosed four times. EMTs brought me around every time. One time my "boyfriend of the hour" dropped my overdosed body at the emergency room door, and they even told my mom I was gone, and some doctor was determined to bring me back and when he did, I wanted to know why. I hurt so bad. I wanted to die.

I went to prison for a year for shoplifting to support my habit. As bad as Tutwiler was, it didn't compare with my father taking my son. I called him for help and he came and took my son forever. He moved so I could not talk to him or my son. I had made a terrible mistake, but to take my baby forever was beyond my understanding. I guess he finally got the son he always wanted.

I got out of prison and went right back to shoplifting. I would shoplift and take the items back for cash refunds. Of course, I was such an inexperienced criminal that I got arrested soon after I started. Some guy picked me up, and I started driving his car. The police pulled us over and arrested me for driving a car used in a robbery!

I was released on bond and sent to Lovelady. I never even listened to anything they had to teach me. I would leave the program and be arrested, go back to jail, get back out to go back to Lovelady, and the routine would just continue again. One day, I stood before a judge, and he gave me this long lecture while I just stared at him. I had known him in the past, and when he asked me where the happy, loving nurse was, I told him, "She died." They were taking me to the bus to load us to go to prison. I simply walked off in another direction. I didn't even run, I just walked. They arrested me and put my picture in the paper under MOST WANTED.

No one really wanted to be around me. When I thought none of the bad people wanted to be near me, it made me so sad. They put me back in jail, and the judge gave me 20 to life with escape in the first degree. For all you good normal people, that's really bad. All of this adds to the fact that I've been on parole, probation, and placed in the Supervised Release Program at Lovelady. The judge said I had less than a 1% chance of survival if I did not listen to someone. Lovelady never gave up on me, so I decided maybe I should try. I did not expect it to work at all. I would just kill myself later.

Carmen's Redemption

"When I see the Ten Most Wanted Lists, I always have this thought: If we'd made them feel wanted earlier, they wouldn't be wanted now."
—Eddie Cantor

I had seen Carmen in Lovelady several times. It was so sad to see her come and go like she had. Sometimes someone would say, "There's Carmen—now you see her, now you don't." Seldom do we let anyone come in and leave and then come back over and over, but we want to be careful to show enough grace until a woman *does get it*.

Everyone seemed to love Carmen. People talked about how smart she was. Therefore, I knew who she was but did not know anything about her. She came across as almost happy-go-lucky. I was so intrigued, observing her and listening to the clients laughing and talking about her; then she'd have those vacant eyes. I just saw those dead eyes and knew they had to have life somewhere deep down inside. Sometimes, I can read a person if I just watch her from a distance more than if I sit and talk to her. On one of her trips back to Lovelady, Carmen's mother brought her, and as I watched her mother, my heart ached for her. I chose not to introduce myself. I knew her mother was wanting to hear some great heroic story of hope with Carmen getting a new life with all that we could do, but the truth was I did not hold out much hope for Carmen.

One day, Carmen just walked back through our doors, actually wanting our help. She said she really wanted it this time. No one held out much hope for her. Melinda and I talked and decided we would give her one more opportunity, but it would be the final one. Carmen started the program once more. I watched her. She had been to the Center so many times before that she could probably teach the classes. She actually loved the classes.

I had some time one day and passed her in the hallway so I asked her to sit with me a while and tell me all about herself. As I listened to her and she answered my questions, I immediately saw what others had seen. Her personality was quite infectious. She was laughing, which I had never seen her do before. She was witty. I asked about her children, and I knew that was her Achilles heel. Her smile turned to a frown, and her eyes welled up with tears.

She told me she lost him. The way she expressed it to me made me think for a minute that her sweet child had died, but she told me he was still living. She had not seen or talked to him for a very long time—years. He was a toddler when she had last seen him. I asked her who had him, and the tears ran down her face as she told me that it was her dad keeping her from him. She said she had called him for help and her dad came and took him. As I asked more questions, it was like turning on a faucet of flowing words rather than water. She told me about her parents divorcing, her school and nursing, her marriage, her lost son, her addiction, and finally the mighty rejection from her dad, a trauma that was apparent in her face. When the faucet was turned on, there was no turning it off. She was finally afraid to die, but even worse, she was afraid to live. I took one more look at her and asked, "Are you ready to live?" Without hesitation, she said, "Only if I can *really* live." I responded demandingly, *"Then go pack your things."*

We got to Hob Hill, and I told Carmen she should go to the guest bedroom. We would start in the morning. The very next day, I went to the Center and she stayed at home and followed Tiffany every step. Tiffany (aka "Suga Suga") has worked with me since we began the program at Hob Hill. She was one step behind Shay as the girls came the first day, although she says Shay was behind her.

I bowed out of that argument years ago. Tiffany said, "If I stopped too fast, she would have run right into me."

I loved it. We were on the right path. When someone has been on drugs as long as Carmen had been, when she tried to make a decision, she did not have the capacity to make even the most mundane one. It was really sad to watch her thought processes. Drugs had stolen so much from Carmen, as they do from anyone who has taken them for any length. She was slow in her speech. I did my best to just listen and lead her to a better way of understanding. After a few weeks, we began to see who she was. It was not long before she and I were best friends.

That was not a good thing on my part, nor is it something I normally do. In Carmen's case, it just happened naturally. She had to have so much one-on-one time within a family environment, and it turned out that was just what she needed. She thrived in it, maybe because of her daddy and how much he had meant to her. She would go to the Center for counseling, but she had been to so many classes at the Center, we didn't see the necessity of her doing something she could already lead on her own. She also is very personable. And she did not need to be in a place where it was easier for her to take off. I did not allow her around the other girls until about six months in, and without making it obvious I monitored her moving around. Carmen simply was not anyone I wanted to lose, which reminds me of the verse in Matthew when Jesus talks about the Good Shepherd leaving the 99 and going after the one. So that is what I did, and I gave much time to Carmen's transition. We went to church every Sunday. She went on a pass to her mother's home. Previously she had not been allowed at her mom's because of her problem with stealing. Her mother was hesitant at first, but after about three times, she was excited to see her.

Carmen got baptized. She began her walk with Jesus, and it was awesome to watch. At the end of two years, we began talking about Carmen leaving. I began talking with Carmen about her plans for the future. At first, all she could see was that I was trying to get rid of her. I explained to her that part of learning was to plan for the future and to live it out. Many of our women do not want to leave. They dig their heels in and decide they will be with us for the rest of their lives. God does lead us to hire some of them. We cannot hire them all, not because they would not be great employees but because we need only a few with certain skill sets. One thing about Carmen, she is a caregiver and a person who has no boundaries. She wants to help everyone. We have so many women at the Center, and she would give the shirt off her back wanting to help each and every one. Such is the difference between Carmen and many of the women. She had money in the beginning of her drug days and then would latch on to just one man. She had not done any of the things some of our women had done to get finances. Since she had always had easy access to money, she was too free with it. Teaching her boundaries with money was a harder problem to solve. I had not let her have her own money for about six months. There are always different teaching strategies.

The truth of the matter is, I would have loved to keep her right where she was: right there beside me, helping me, for as long as I worked. Everyone thought that would be what I wanted and would do. She was so efficient with everything I asked her to do. She could get things done faster and better than anyone who had ever worked with me. However, God had a better plan for Carmen. He had called her to be a nurse years ago. She thought that would be impossible. She felt she had damaged that beyond repair. I had heard Carmen talk about this patient or that patient, and oh, how she loved them! How she loved medicine. She had a paper printed in a medical journal. She was so excited! She told me over and over about all the plans she had for her medical career.

I became extremely sick in November. Jeff had gone to California to see his mother. I felt terrible. I had something like the flu. Old people get sick and just don't do well. Carmen was happier than I had ever seen her. She took care of me and slept in bed with me. After a week of being in bed, I got better and really could have gotten up and done some work, but it was the weekend, so I just stayed in bed. I really believe that is when the ideas I had began to grow legs.

I was praying about several situations that were forming, and none of them were that good when suddenly I thought about Carmen and her nursing license. We work closely with a church in Birmingham that has a medical clinic, which was growing fast. It is a modern clinic with great doctors in two locations. I think it has some of the more innovative ideas in Birmingham. I couldn't wait to present my idea. Our Board Chairman is good friends with the head doctor there. They have worked with us and know our reputation with our clients. I was sitting at John's desk Monday morning at 8:00 a.m., ready to present my brilliant idea. I just put the whole plan out there.

"John, you know my Carmen. Did you know she used to be the best nurse in the whole city?" I barely breathed and John just kind of looked at me. "Best in the whole city, Brenda?" He knows me! "Yes, John, but I meant to say the entire state. I think that sweet, wonderful Dr. Record needs to hire Carmen. For her to get her nursing license back, there are a few hoops she must jump through. We could help her. When she becomes a nurse practitioner, she could come back to us. He just needs to keep her for a few years. Can you please just talk to him about it? I believe this is one of my best ideas ever. I'm not saying God said it, but I was praying when I thought of it. When will you go talk to him?" I asked as I handed him his phone. I just walked out at that. He came to me in a few minutes and said he was meeting him the next day. I smiled at him and said, "Thank you, John."

"For the record, no pun intended, I believe in her too," he said as he walked out. Then he added, "No promises. This is the medical field, Brenda; they cannot afford mistakes." I would be lying if I told you I did not get a tad queasy when he said that. I was putting an awful lot on the line for some girl who had relapsed many times. Did I really believe in my soul that Carmen was walking the walk? Yes, I did! I smiled at John and said, "I know. She's a new person." Jesus had changed Carmen. Miss Brenda was just hands that God had used. I silently asked God if she was ready to make this happen. If she wasn't, shut it down.

The next day John gave me an application for Carmen and for her to write an addendum to the application about losing her license. I was so excited. Carmen did not know a thing about this entire plan of mine. I handed her the application and gave her a 10-word explanation of what had transpired. Did I mention earlier how excited Carmen can get? Well, if I didn't mention it then, I'm telling you now: She can get excited. She cried and cried and hugged and hugged. It was so cool. I was so happy for her. I explained she would not be paid like her nurse's pay. She couldn't care less. It was so great. Her mother went and got her new nurse's shoes and a stethoscope. You would have thought she was performing brain surgery. All it was was an application. Of course, she got her job. That was over five years ago. She is a right hand at the clinic. She has met every requirement to get her license, and we expect it any day. John talked to Dr. Record, and he does not want to send her back to me. I figured that was coming, but she's taking care of our clients at the clinic. Our life is so much easier. For her once to be listed as MOST WANTED on the television as a criminal, she is now MOST WANTED as one of the most remarkable nurses ever.

In a major turn of events, in December of 2022, I got pneumonia and went septic. I was close to death. I was in the hospital under the doctors there, who are good doctors. Carmen sent in a special team of the best doctors they have at the clinic. They made a few changes, and obviously I lived through it. I honestly believe that God used her in my life at that moment to help me live.

I love Carmen so much. We laugh more than I have laughed with anyone since high school. She has a husband who has never had any drug problem—he is just a hardworking, good guy. She has an adorable baby boy. Her mom lives with her in her beautiful house. No, she still is not able to talk to her dad. She still does not have a relationship with her son. She still cries about those losses, and we have decided that's okay. I truly believe the relationship with her first son will be restored one day. She may miss out on it for now, but God is the God of restoration. Carmen has learned to accept that which she cannot change, until the Lord changes it.

In the meantime, Carmen enjoys all the many miracles God has given her. She is certainly one of the many miracles I have seen in my life, and I am so thankful to God that He has allowed me to serve Him by serving so many wonderful women, including Carmen. Thank you, Lord!

Vivian

"A good friend is like a four-leaf clover: hard to find and lucky to have."
—Irish proverb

Vivian was born in Tuscaloosa in 1965 to a mother who already had four children. She was the baby. When Vivian was nine months old, her mom found herself pregnant again and decided to have an abortion. She died from complications with the abortion. Of course, Vivian doesn't remember these things. When we were talking about her life, I remember specifically thinking, "I'm sure glad she didn't abort Vivian."

Vivian and her brother went to live with their father, who was married to a very good lady who adopted Vivian and her brother. The other three children went with an aunt. For some reason, and although his new wife was a good woman, Vivian's father decided that she was the child to beat on. She was abused constantly. Occasionally, her adopted mother would try to intervene in the beatings and the father would turn on her and she would get walloped too. One would define Vivian's childhood as being *extremely* troubled.

Vivian's father would give her part of the check he received because of his veteran's disability—he had been shell-shocked in the Vietnam War. Maybe that had something to do with his violent temper. When I said that to Vivian, it seemed to help her find a dab of peace with it. I also explained to her he most likely was trying to buy himself a little peace by giving her some of the check earmarked for her.

By 13, she had already been shooting drugs for three years. She was shooting opioids by the age of 10, a powerful combination from the seventies called t's and blue's. She left home and lived on the streets, going back to visit her father's house to pick up the check he allotted her. She went to the fifth grade in school and then never went back. When she told me that, I was surprised because Vivian is very smart and, in conversation, seems educated. She is a self-taught person. Her life from 10 on consisted of drugs, stealing, robbing, and prostituting. She was in and out of juvenile detention homes several times. Finally, when the law caught up with her, she had so many years of violence and darkness in her soul that prison was a relief. As I listened to Vivian talk, I could see the sorrow in her eyes for lost years. I recognized the look, as we see it all the time. If I'm thinking about my own life as I look in a mirror, I can see the same look. I may not have been in prison, but I consider I have wasted years for my refusal to do the things I knew in my heart the Lord had called me to do for Him.

So Vivian found solace in one of the worst prisons in the United States. She quickly learned how to survive there. It takes settling in and accepting one's fate to make it in there. I'm a survivor and persistent by nature, but when I visited the prison, I ascertained that I would have a difficult time accepting my new home for one week, and Vivian's first run in Tutwiler was 10 long years.

She was disgusted with men after her dad's beatings and years of prostitution and dealing with bad men, so being around just women suited her. She quickly formed bonds with the women for friendship and love. Many of the women look to other women for intimate relations for the first time. However, in the drug world, women addicts also fall into the trap of doing whatever they need to do to fill the need for drugs.

Vivian had girlfriends, and some of them cheated on her. With her violent streak, that wasn't very smart, I thought. She ended up stabbing two of her cheating girlfriends. They both survived, but time was added on to Vivian's sentence. The whole prison culture is very sad. People just want to be loved and accepted.

Vivian finally got out of prison and vowed not to go back. She returned to the same friends and the same places, so her vow didn't last long. She was caught sitting in a stolen car and was charged for stealing the car. She told me she did not steal the car. Vivian is brutally honest, so if she said she didn't steal it, then she didn't steal it—but still, she was sitting in it and thus "in possession" of the stolen car. She gave Tutwiler another four years of her life.

When Vivian got out of prison the last time, she immediately fell back into her old ways. But this time, the Equal Justice Center had contacted her. An attorney from Selma, Alabama, saw the same special thing in Vivian that I immediately saw. Vivian decided on her own to come to Lovelady. She walked through the door with the same determination she had on the street.

Another interesting thing to me is that in the women's prisons—and even somewhat in the men's prisons too—is that the inmates will form their own families. When Vivian first came to Lovelady, she was excited to see her "dad." "Oh, we only have women here," I told her. She told me that her "dad" was at Lovelady. Her "dad" was the one and only ... my best friend Shay. I almost fainted when I heard that. Then she told me who her brothers and sisters were, and lo and behold it was like we had a family reunion right there at Lovelady. I could not wait to talk to Shay about this newfound "daughter" of hers.

Shay was so embarrassed she looked like she wanted to fall through the floor. I naturally wondered if Vivian's "mom" was in Lovelady as well. They both looked at me like I was the dumbest person in the world. "Well, there's lots of moms—whoever dad was with at the time was 'mom,' " Vivian told me. I was just shocked right out of my mind, and believe me, it takes a lot to shock me. After the women get out of prison, the family culture from the inside fades and someone she treated as her aunt or father is no longer considered such, no longer contacted. Vivian has explained it to me, and I just find it fascinating. We have so many ways to exist and to find our ways in the human mind.

So when she came to Lovelady, it seemed most everyone knew her, but she let everyone know she was coming to change her life. And that's exactly what she did. Every class she could take, every counseling appointment she made, and everything she could do to change she did. Everyone was astounded. At age 43, she had never had a legitimate job. She excelled at Lovelady, and I became extremely fond of her. Old girlfriends would come through, and she told them upfront she was done with that life. I asked her one day how she did that because same-sex relationships as well as relationships with men seem to be even harder to break than some other issues. At Lovelady we ask everyone to put relationships down until you know who you are. There are no relationships with other clients allowed to be expressed in the Center. No men are allowed in the building except with our approval, and there is no approval given other than men required for work, ministry, or law enforcement.

Vivian graduated and was content to work at the Center. She had gotten her driver's license and had a car given to her by Brian, the Equal Justice attorney. She was happy and in a great place mentally, but The Lovelady Center is not meant to be a forever home.

One day a lady came in who was looking for a supervisor for homes for special needs individuals. These people lived in several houses, and the supervisor was to oversee the homes. She also needed some house moms for various shifts. I gave her a list of clients to interview at the Center, and I asked Vivian to interview for the supervisor job. She did and got the job on the spot. I was so happy for her that I failed to realize that she might not be as happy as I was with her spreading her wings. She worked there for years and did very well for herself.

Vivian has several health issues now. No matter how forgiving God is, and He is all-forgiving, bodies still suffer, wear, and tear. The wear and tear of street life is tremendous. It did not take me long to figure that one out. Stress on bones, undiagnosed diabetes, tooth decay, many days without food, dehydration—the list goes on and on. The stroke certainly took a toll also.

Vivian, no longer able to work, moved back home to The Lovelady Center to be with us. Beau and I take her to her treatments for lung cancer. We love her very much and will prayerfully have her with us for many years to come.

Changed, in the Changed Woman's Own Words

"The important thing in life is to have a great aim, and the determination to attain it."
—Johann Wolfgang von Goethe

My name is Brenda, just like Miss Brenda. However, my life could not have been more different than hers. My two sisters and I lived with our mom and dad very happily. My sisters were much older than I was. Being the baby, I was a daddy's girl, through and through. My sisters were 12 and 14 when I was born. We were not very well off and lived in a very poor neighborhood. Everyone would say "She's from the hood." I hated that. It made me feel less than and put a name on me that I did not deserve. No one can help where they are born, but when people are talking about you, they act like I chose to be a hood kid. Nevertheless, I was a relatively happy kid. My daddy would spoil me, so I had everything I needed. He had a job at the papermill, and my mom didn't work.

    I was held back in the third grade, and that hurt me a lot. I was already a big kid and it made me even bigger in comparison to the other children. I stayed stressed out about it, and bitterness started growing in me right then and there. One day in third grade I got a headache. The school nurse called my mom, and she came right after me. Instead of giving me regular headache medication, my mom gave me hydrocodone, which is an opiate. My headache just disappeared, and it made me feel so much better—even my anger subsided.

Miss Brenda and the Lovelady Movement

What a wonderful drug! It just seemed to solve all my problems, so I fell in love with the pills. As often as I felt I could get away with it, I would get an ache here or a pain there. Mom would dutifully hand out my "medicine" to me. I look back on it now and see how twisted it was to do that to a little child.

By the time I was 14, alcohol, pills, pot, and occasionally meth were all my way of life. I had a boyfriend, but sex was not limited to him. I ran wild but was home most nights. My sweet daddy was so worried about me, but even that was not enough to get me to stop my wayward living.

One day my dad took a day off to take our family fishing. Me, my mom, dad, and nephew went. In spite of our life without much money, my mom loved my dad so much. She was as excited as I was to go fishing. You would have thought we were going to the beach the way we acted. Off we went, all piled in the truck, with the rest of the family following. We were singing good ol' time songs when Daddy stopped the truck at a stop sign with a jerk. We kept sitting there. After a few minutes, we said, "Come on, Daddy, let's go." He didn't move. Right then was the worst moment of my life. I knew my daddy was dead.

We were all screaming, acting up, I don't even know who called the ambulance. We moved Dad around, and when we did the truck started rolling back. Then we were screaming about that. The men behind our truck stopped the rolling. The ambulance arrived, and they put my dad in it. They were working on him, and as they loaded him up, I thought he was breathing. They took him to the hospital and I really thought there was hope and was feeling better about it. After we were at the hospital a short while, a doctor came out and told us Dad was gone. I didn't see him breathe, I just thought I had. He was 47 years old. He had just worked too hard, and it was over for him. Mom received a large sum of money, but I never saw a dime of it.

In our neighborhood there was a lady who sold candy, sodas, and a sundry of other items out of her home. We called her "the Candy Lady." My mom went to her house all the time. When I got older, I realized that the Candy Lady was Mom's dealer. I loved the Candy Lady after I knew what she sold. I found the way to

"Candyland" and went there often. I grew even more distant from my mom. Sometimes I would go away for several days at a time.

Once, I finally decided I would get off pills for good. Addicts like to tell themselves they are not addicted, but they are. I decided to kick opiates, and I cannot begin to express how bad I felt. I gave up and just decided to go to the streets. I look at that now and think how stupid I was. Life on the streets is hell on earth. I finished the sixth grade and never looked back.

It was not long before my boyfriend and I decided to get an apartment. I was almost 19 and found myself to be pregnant. I have never been able to figure out how I spent all those years and never got pregnant and then BOOM. Suddenly, I had a desire to get clean. It was not hard this time, and I did get clean. I had my son, and I was happy for the first time since my dad died. We were working and being "normal" people for once. Then we began using drugs for recreation only. We "recreated" often. I joke about it, but it was actually very sad. Then we moved and I got pregnant again. Then we had to move, and I got pregnant again. And again. And again. That's five BOOMS. That's right, we had five children in eight years. We moved so many times we had trouble finding new places to take us. We were spiraling out of control. We simply could not control all that was happening to us. We began cooking up meth and selling it. We made a lot of money, but instead of paying rent, we bought different drugs. It was like a ride at a fair that spun out of control and threw the riders off into the crowds.

My mom had remarried and decided to save the day. She let us move in with her. That should have been my wake-up call, but all it did was give me an excuse to go out because I had a babysitter. DHR came in and gave custody of the children to my mother. In the beginning, I made a half-hearted attempt to see the children, but it did not help them or me. It was easier to just cry, whine about it, and let my mother do what she wanted. She ended up adopting my son, someone else got two, someone else got one, and my cousin got my daughter. My mom moved and changed her number. I have spoken to my daughter but other than that, I have never heard from my mom or my children again. My mother gave me my first drugs in the third grade, and DHR let her find the homes for my children. That's ironic, isn't it? You probably are thinking that would be my bottom, but at that time, I was still far from bottom. My life had made me so mean.

I left everything and just went to the streets again. It pains me to even write about my life after that time—I prostituted, stole anything that was movable, got into countless fights, sold a great deal of drugs, and went to jail many times. I could not put a number on my jail visits. I stabbed a guy with scissors who tried to rape me. He had me arrested for robbing him at gunpoint. I cut him up pretty bad with the scissors. Even as I tell these stories I can't believe this all was me. I fought at least one time a day, with anyone, anytime. I hated everyone, and I hated the world. I hated my mom and my sisters. Most of all, I hated myself so much. When you don't care if you die, you do some crazy things. You don't care what or who because you don't care about the consequences. You don't care if you get arrested—at least you would have a place to sleep if you did. I hated the cold weather much worse than the hot weather.

One day a girl needed some money, and I gave it to her. I really wanted a room that night to sleep. I was so tired and wanted to shower. I told her I would give her the money she wanted if she would take me to a guy's house later on so I could spend the night there. I wanted to go to his house because he owed me much more than I gave her. And I'd be able to settle up. When it was time for me to go to his house, I found her and told her it was time to go. "I'm not going anywhere, b****," she screamed at me like a mad woman. I could not see, I was so mad! We were screaming at each other. There was a crowd of people standing around. They were feeding my adrenaline, and that woman got in her car and started it. I was furious.

I tried to pull her out of the car, but she was determined to leave. I got in front of her car, screaming at her. "You're not leaving unless you run over me!" I screamed over and over. She must have believed me. She ran right over me and did not look back. I did not see anything else. Everything went black. I woke up in the hospital after surgery. I had a cast up to my hip. It seemed to weigh a ton. The hospital put me right on the street in a wheelchair when they released me.

Dr. Brenda Lovelady Spahn

For a year and a half, I had the cast. I had to roll everywhere I went. If I was sleeping on a park bench, I had to scoot over to it. If I was going to prostitute, he would have to scoot me out onto a bed. I was wheelchair-bound. I would roll to the doctor, see him, and roll out. My arms would get so tired they would burn. If you looked up "misery" in the dictionary, it would say "Brenda getting run over and being confined in a wheelchair for 18 long months with no place to go." I cannot express to anyone how bad it was. I would still try to fight, and people would just look at me and turn away shaking their heads. It's bad when homeless drug addicts think you're sad and pitiful. Well, that's where I was.

Finally, I got the cast off but discovered I no longer could walk. I had to learn to walk all over again. I had lots of cuts, bruises, and scrapes. At last, I could walk the street again. Oh, happy day—I was home! I almost felt good about my situation. But happiness on the street hit a stop sign, and I was arrested and went to jail. The judge was really fed up with me. He was sending me to prison. I had been arrested, and life as I knew it was over. As an afterthought, he was sending me to a place I had never heard of, a place called The Lovelady Center in Birmingham. They shackled me up nice and tight, threw me in a cop car, and off we went.

When we finally got to our destination, they pulled me out of the car and walked me up to the door. If you have never walked shackled up, let me tell you, it's not easy. It's especially hard when you are being pulled and dragged by two big burly cops who are angry anyway because they have had to drive a crazy woman over a hundred miles. I was dirty in jail clothes. My hair had not been washed. I was a mess.

That was three years ago. I found life. I found Jesus. I found love. I found hope. I found a family. I found a home. I am the happiest person who ever lived! I couldn't get mad at someone now if I tried. If you looked up "a changed woman" in the dictionary, it would say "Brenda." I am transformed by the love shown to me. Not long ago, one of my children found me. I know I will see them all in due time. I may not have my birth mom or sisters anymore in my life, but I *do* have a family.

When I walked in that first day, the girl at the desk looked at the police and their court order and said, "*Sir, you can take those shackles off of her. She's ours now.*"

Weeping

"Weeping may endure for a night, but joy cometh in the morning."
Psalm 30:5

The day I met Miss Brenda was a rainy day in April of 2006. I had been living in juvenile hall for a while, and then finally the judge said I could go live with my mom at The Lovelady Center. I had just turned 16, and I was so happy because I felt that I finally belonged somewhere and would have a real home. I loved it the minute I walked through the doors. I had my mom back, and for a time I thought my entire life had changed forever. Happiness filled my soul. We had a room, two beds, clothes, and plenty of food.

Miss Brenda called me into her office and asked me a bunch of questions about my life. She sat with tears in her eyes, and it made me mad because I thought she felt like I was a nobody. I had a real chip on my shoulder. I had been in five foster homes and had spent the last year in juvenile detention. I was one angry person.

I told her my life story, which wasn't really much to tell. I lived with my dad when I was a little younger. Social services took me from my father when they found out we had no electricity or running water. We hadn't had either for over a year, actually, but I didn't tell them that. I hardly ever went to school, but no one seemed to care. Daddy drank all the time and let me start drinking with him when I was 12.

When I was 13, he taught me how to smoke marijuana. I thought I was something. Every once in a while, my mother would come by and see me and promise me that she was working on getting us a home together. I always believed her. She didn't mean to lie; she just couldn't quit using dope.

That's why I was so happy to be at The Lovelady Center. I got to see my mom all the time, and she was sober. She made me all kinds of promises, and I believed every single one. All I ever wanted was a mom and her love. I learned what had been in Miss Brenda's eyes that day was not pity—my life had truly made her sad to hear about it. She asked me to tell her about the last time I had been truly happy. I told her I could not remember *ever* being happy for very long. Miss Brenda said the system had failed me miserably. She wanted so much more for me than the life I had been dealt up to then.

Mom did something to get kicked out of the Center the day after my first good Christmas ever. They tried to keep her there instead of dismissing her, because of me. They wanted to just give her consequences so I could stay in a safe environment, but she just wouldn't—or couldn't—get it together. She took me with her and left. In no time at all, I was smoking crack and shooting drugs with her, I guess trying to hold on to our strange bond, which was all I had with my parents: getting altered together.

I met her drug dealer's son and got pregnant. I really wanted something different for my baby. I was actually excited about being pregnant because I would finally have someone of my own to love and to be loved by.

I went to see Miss Brenda, and she let me come home to the Center. I even had my own room. It felt so good. I stayed clean and had my precious little girl. I even gave my life to Jesus and got baptized. I was working at the Lovelady Thrift Store, joined the drama team, and was doing pretty good. I felt real love there. I tried so hard to change.

Mom came back to the Center for a while, but something was different and she and I fought like crazy people. She was dismissed from the program and asked to leave. I felt so guilty. No matter what anyone said, I thought it was my fault. Somehow, we got our roles confused and I had become my mom's mom. I wanted to help her. Even hearing myself say that makes no sense now. I was still only about 12, mentally, in a woman's body. The staff at the Center begged me to stay away from my mom, but how could I? She needed me.

We ended up doing drugs one night while I was on pass, when my baby was nine months old. I really messed up then. I ended up leaving my baby, and the Lovelady staff called protective services. Me and my mom started using anything we could find all the time.

Mom taught me how to turn tricks, and soon I was funding both of our drug habits. I would go to the Center and beg for help over and over and they would try to help me, but I just couldn't let my mom and the drugs go, so out the door I would have to go. After a while, I was so tired of all the men and giving Mom all the money I made. I decided to turn tricks on my own. She got so mad, so I gradually had to let her go. Funny, how I would let her go for drugs but not for my own sake. I simply could not earn enough money for us both anymore. We were using so much.

I finally became too ashamed to go back to Miss Brenda because of all I had done then. One day, five guys locked me up in a room for two weeks. They beat me, raped me, and kept me shot up with heroin. I just knew they were going to kill me. Finally, they asked me where I wanted to be dropped off. I wanted to go home to the Center. They drove there and threw me out on the street like an animal. Sure enough, Miss Brenda and her staff came rushing out and cleaned me up. She begged me to stay, but there was no place for me by myself anymore. I wanted my own room. She said I could go to her home and stay with her, but I didn't want to do that either. The pull of escaping reality through drugs was just too strong, and I had done it for so long—I just did not want to stop using. I promised her I would be back soon. I didn't want to sleep on one of the couches in front of everybody while they sorted the space out either. I was full of many excuses as to why I could not stay—the biggest reason I would not tell them was that I just wanted to get high one more time.

"Let me get myself together, and I promise I'll be back." I think I even meant that. I would get high just *one more time* and then I'd be back to turn my life around at the Center. That's the last thing I said to her.

On October 10, 2011, I kept my promise. I made my last journey back to the Center to see Miss Brenda. I arrived at the Center in my funeral urn. They had a memorial service for me at the Center, and my mom couldn't even attend. She was too strung out. They showed all of these pictures of me smiling and looking happy. One thing was so special—they gathered 21 white balloons to represent my life and one red balloon to symbolize the blood of Jesus that covered me. Everyone was crying, and Miss Brenda took the people and the balloons outside on the front steps of the Center. They let all the white balloons go that day, like they were releasing me to God, and then Miss Brenda let the red one go and it floated up to the sky. The white ones had been released way before the red one because she was saying a prayer and telling the crying people what everything represented. "This one represents the blood of Jesus, who loved her. She did accept His free gift of salvation," she said. Funny thing is, that red balloon was let go after all the white ones, but it soared up to the heavens ahead of all the others. She hoped I was finally free. I *am* finally free.

Losing Shay

> "Death must exist for life to have meaning."
> —Neal Shusterman

"Come on, Shay, we're not listening to this nonsense," I told her, pulling her out of the chair. She was shocked and had begun to cry. "Stop it," I said, a little too harshly. "He doesn't know what he is talking about." I explained to her that we were going to believe in God for a miracle and that she would be healed.

We had just learned the doctor felt Shay had only about six months to live. She had developed cirrhosis of the liver. Shay was my best friend, confidante, daughter, royal pain in the butt, and always feisty and bossy to me. But, oh my *goodness*, how I loved her! Shay had the honor of being the first woman to enter The Lovelady Center, 14 years earlier. She came to us kicking and screaming on the ride to the house, not wanting to be assigned to that "crazy white woman" straight from prison. She had spent the bulk of her life in Tutwiler and trusted no one.

When I felt led to begin the Whole-Way House at Hob Hill, Shay was the first to enter our doors. She was the most reluctant houseguest anyone could have ever imagined. However, after a few months, she became an intricate member of our organization. She became our "professor of the streets." Melinda and I listened to and learned from Shay. We knew nothing back then about street life or prison culture, and Shay had taken it upon herself to educate us. And what an education we received during those first few years! She was the undisputed professor of the underworld.

Shay had turned to drugs to hide her pain from years of childhood sexual abuse. She had spent more than 20 years in various incarceration settings since her early teens. She never had the first chance at any life resembling the one that I took for granted every single day. When we first met, we were polar opposites in almost everything, or at least that was how most people saw us.

She was black; I am white. She was short; I was tall—though I seem to be shrinking yearly, now. She clipped her hair very short; mine was long. She spoke very rough and used slang; I didn't even know what she was saying much of the time. I had been protected by my daddy growing up; no one had protected Shay. And our relationship was deeper than could be seen with normal eyes. It was birthed in our spirits in that unseen place within us, bonded together through the reliving of her trauma. Within a few months, Shay and I were best friends. Within another month, I was "Ma." Jeff, my husband, was "Pa," and Melinda was "Sissy." Beau, Matthew, and Miranda, my other children, were also her siblings. And Hunter, my youngest, was her favorite of them all. She was family. When he was older, he would take her to the grocery store and anywhere she needed when she was sick. Times when I would have to threaten to throw cold water on him to get him up, his phone would ring and say Shay and he would hit the floor and be wide awake.

I normally do not take well to bossy individuals, but I allowed Shay to order the girls around. Once in a while, I would remind her from where she had come, just like they had, and how we had to look at others with the eyes of God. She would call me all day long and I never ignored her calls, out of respect. How could anyone not respect someone who allowed God to change them to the extent that Shay allowed?

I was in awe at the changes taking place in her. She found a deep peace and happiness that most never find. When Shay first came to Hob Hill, she was miserable. She knew she wanted a different life, but like so many of our women, she had no confidence that she could have one. Bit by bit, I watched the icy cocoon in which she had enveloped herself just melt away. I became her protector, and before I knew it, she was mine. I discovered a friendship that I cherished to the core of my being.

When we moved into the old hospital, it was more work than I could have ever imagined. Shay was with us from the first day until she could no longer work. She was strong and never seemed to tire, until years later when her sickness came. We pulled up carpet, painted, cleaned everything, and led women by example. She and I together could get more done in a day than any two other women could accomplish in a week. We were a force.

One day, she and I decided we were going to make a day camp for the children, and we cleaned the entire parking deck. When Shay and I called for volunteers, people would run the *opposite* way. Working with us was no picnic, in reflection; I would most likely have run also.

"I'm going to have to stay to help y'all. You probably can't do it without me." We knew in our hearts she was right, and that God had sent her to us. She and Tiffany, another original Whole-Way House Lovelady, would argue all day long who was the "first Lovelady" to come to us. I would always remind them that I was the first. I believe Tiffany came right behind Shay and could be called the *second* Lovelady. "The first Lovelady" was Shay's title, and every woman who entered our doors was quickly made aware of it—by Shay herself. She dressed like a diva, every nail and hair in place, but worked like a contractor. We would agree to meet for any certain task. She would show up all diva-like, and I would show up, well, to work. I would ask her why she would be all dressed up like she was, and she would quickly tell me I needed to go change and dress appropriately, that I looked like I just rolled out of bed. After all, that's probably what I had done. I'd be mostly covered in paint, hair in a ponytail, and eyes barely opened.

She always wanted to get started at daybreak. Shay and Melinda loved those early hours. Now I get started at a reasonable 5:00 a.m. Those two would one-up each other at an unreasonable 4:00. In those first few years, there were so many hard hours we put into doing all manner of moving and construction work, painting and the like.

Shay became the Director of Intake in our new home base at the hospital and welcomed each lady who entered our doors.

We called that position her day job. Women came in with no hope, feeling no love or joy, and she would dish all three up like progressing them through a buffet line. I would stand amazed. The new women could not get away with any of the games they were used to playing on people. They couldn't manipulate Shay. She taught Melinda and me the necessary skills to help someone, as we taught them how to live a new life. If I was not feeling well, she would come climb in the bed beside me and tell me I had to get well for her. It always seemed to rally me back to health. I have lupus, which brings some downtime. Shay would tell me God gave me lupus to slow me down so she could catch me, but I would always argue that God did not intentionally give me lupus.

In the beginning, when we would baptize, Shay would squirm and run around like crazy. I knew she was so ready, but once again her reluctance held her back. One day, I finally asked her to join us and get baptized because I just could tell how much she wanted to. However, Shay had decided she just had to get baptized in the ocean. Before that day, we had already taken the girls to the Gulf a few times, down south to the property we still owned. There was no changing her mind. She told me she and God had worked it all out. She would get so angry with me when I would remind her that it was the *Gulf of Mexico not the Ocean of Mexico*. However, we had a trip planned for an upcoming October and, without really thinking, I told her she could get baptized then. October came and we loaded up about 20 women and off we went in two large passenger vans to the "ocean."

It was a very cool, windy day in late fall, much cooler than I had expected it was going to be. It had rained the night before, and the waves were higher and more turbulent than usual. Never one to shy away from an opportunity to serve, I decided we would go ahead as planned and I would just "grin and bear it." Several women had decided to join in the baptism. We had a church service on the beach, and I was shivering because it was getting so cold. Most of the women were hesitant to get into that cold water, where waves were rolling in higher than we stood. I suggested we wait and have a nice service in Birmingham. I explained that our new portable baptistry would have arrived within the week, and they could be the first baptized. "What an honor," I explained, trying to build it up in their minds because I was so cold. Everyone was buying into my dinner and baptizing plan. It sounded so warm and inviting to me.

Everyone really looked quite content to wait a few days when they glanced at the waves crashing in and felt the wind whipping around us. Thinking I had convinced everyone, I was ready to get out of there. Suddenly, Shay began to wail: *"You promised me I could be baptized in the ocean!"* Oh, it took everything in me not to go jerk her up. I saw Jeff and Beau look at each other, and I believe their thoughts were the same as mine.

I explained that it was never cold like it was that day and it would be harder on all of us. Actually, I was mostly thinking about myself. *"It's just the Devil trying to stop me from my dream baptism,"* she wailed loudly. I mean, what does a minister say to something like that? *"What if I die on the way home?"* she added.

I felt so small and looked around at the other women. By that time, the others had come together and wanted to be baptized right then also. I sighed and took off my coat and in I went, praying I would not drown in that freezing, salty surf. One at a time, the women came, and of course I was overjoyed at how awesome it was to be standing there with the opportunity I had. I will admit I was cold, but I was overcome emotionally. Shay insisted on being last, and it was her turn. I stood there waiting . . . waiting . . . and waiting.

Shay talked with her hands, and I watched as she was flinging her arms, explaining something to Jeff and Beau, my son who lived at the beach. I had no idea what she was saying. I could see they were explaining something and shaking their head *no*. I then saw my sweet husband and son look at each other, both smile and finally begin to peel off their coats and shirts. What was going on?

They both had been baptized and were both strong Christians, so I knew they weren't getting baptized. By this time, all the other women were wrapped in blankets and were heading to the warm van. I was positively turning blue when all three finally began walking toward me. Jeff on one side, Beau on the other, and Shay between them, smiling from ear to ear, clinging for dear life to them.

Dr. Brenda Lovelady Spahn

They finally reached me. "What in the world are y'all doing?" I asked. Jeff and Beau shook their heads, looking frazzled, and Shay answered, "Ma, I'm so afraid of the water." I laughed so hard and said, "Why in the world are we doing it this way then?" "You taught me I have to overcome my fears, and I reckon this is a way for me to show God how much I love Him. I want to serve Him forever." *I loved it.*

I held her nose and began to immerse her in the water. At first, her natural instincts were to fight against going under, then all at once her body just relaxed and under the water she went. As she came out of the water, she was crying hard. I looked at Beau and Jeff and saw the same. I knew that my face looked the same too. We all wept, all the way back to the shore. Of course, I am human though and my tears felt like razor blades as the salt and cold cut my skin.

Shay talked about that day so often, and I'm thankful that good sense didn't prevail. I'm so happy that we followed through with her "dream baptism." We lived another day to tell her story over and over. It became a beacon of hope for so many Loveladies who followed. It was also tucked away in my memory bank, and I pull it out ever so often when thinking about my best friend, Shay.

Shay has been such an inspiration to Melinda and me. She liked to think she kept me straight, but it worked both ways. She was my first call in the morning and my last one at night. Darn, she loved a phone! About 30 years ago, or even longer, I got my first cell phone. For sentimental reasons, I kept that phone number. Shay begged me to let her have that number. Of course I let her have that number. After she passed away, I got that number and gave it to another best friend. Whenever she called someone the phone would pop up that Shay was calling and it would freak people out. Shay would have loved that! I did it on purpose.

My daddy always insisted on trying to "keep me in line," and Shay was the same way. I was an only child, and she was the sister I never had. She didn't have a mother—I was her mother. We filled voids in each other's lives. I loved her unconditionally. We watched television together. We shopped together. She taught us all manner of things, some I wish we didn't have to learn, but we did. Our friendship went way beyond any normal friendship. She quit only one time and was a nervous wreck to get with Melinda and make sure I didn't replace her. She and I argued one time and I fired her. I called her back before she got home. You simply cannot fire a daughter, and she had become that to me. When Shay had visitors in her home, they would comment that her home looked like a "mini" Hob Hill. Shay would never miss a beat and would tell everyone that she taught me all about decorating and gave me things she no longer needed. I just smiled and said, "That's right."

Shay and I would travel and talk about the Center and her transformation from the old to the new Shay. She loved it. We had a way of communicating with each other that was infectious to those around us. Together, we made a very good team. Everyone would laugh and really enjoyed our appearances, and soon we were known locally. It was fun and so encouraging to many. I don't think there were over 20 days in all our years that we did not see each other.

The doctor had given us that grim prognosis about nine years ago. I immediately found other doctors who gave us much more hope. We prayed, we cried, and then we fought. One time she was in the hospital and the doctors told me we should simply let her go. I looked at her in that bed through their eyes that day but could not accept what they were saying. The doctors were kind but were giving up.

Shay had lost her hair and looked so frail. I went and got a picture of Shay with her wig and all diva'd up and laid it beside her head. In a few minutes, when the doctors returned, they got the message and continued her treatment. She left the hospital a few days later. I have no idea how many times she was hospitalized, receiving no hope from anyone, and bounced back. I have been called to the hospital a great deal with calls telling me she might not make it. She had one of the strongest wills to live I have ever known. She was on the liver and kidney transplant list. Years of substance abuse had taken their toll on her body, but her spirit was strong. You can't start using heroin at 11 years old and continue it a few decades and live a long, healthy life. There are always consequences to our actions.

At times Shay would tell me she was tired and couldn't fight on her own. I would fight for her. When someone has cirrhosis, toxins can build up in the liver and cause so much confusion. Many days I would have to call an ambulance to help me get her to the hospital. So many times I sat with her on her front porch, waiting on her levels to come down after she had taken more of her medicine. We waited on spaceships, men on horses, wagons, and other forms of transportation to pick us up. Some days things would go back to normal, and some days things would accelerate to an emergency situation. At the beginning of the decline, she would be upset and embarrassed, but I worked to put her mind at ease. After a while we learned to just laugh about it. I would give her a play by play of what had happened. I will admit, sometimes I would tone it down because there were some episodes better left burned in my mind rather than burned in hers.

One day stands out in my mind above most others concerning what Shay would call "when the cheese slides off my cracker." Shay looked fine but was making no sense at all and just would *not* listen to me. I usually could talk her down and get her to unlock whatever door she had locked herself behind or get into a car with me if she happened to be at the Center when the ammonia levels rose, but not on that day—I absolutely could not make her understand anything. Her husband would even have to call me to help get her together. At any rate, I had been trying to get her to go into her house from the porch where she had been sitting too long. We called the ambulance, and I sat on the porch and listened to her rambling. When the paramedics came, they began asking Shay questions about day-to-day affairs so they could assess her mental frame of mind. She answered with wrong answers, but they didn't know that except that I interjected and told them, but they were really looking at me like I had called them for no good reason. She told them she was *not* going to the hospital. They said she probably would not have to go. I told them they needed to ask more questions.

One of the paramedics looked at her and asked her name. Shay never missed a beat and spoke right up: "Miss Brenda Lovelady Spahn, Founder and Executive Director of The Lovelady Center." The guy asked her for her birth date. She fired right back with some crazy date. The guy looked at me and said, "Seems okay to me." I just sighed and showed him my driver's license. He looked at her and said she had to go get some help. When he went to assist her, she tore into him.

Oh, my goodness, how that broke my heart. Her wig fell off in the hustle, and there I was, chasing the stretcher trying to put her wig on her head because I knew she would be so upset when she got her mind back on track. I would always stay with her until the hospital drew the toxins from her body. Shay loved this story. She thought it was so funny! She would make me do the imitation for her. After a few times, I would exaggerate the story to make her laugh hard—kind of like the "how big of a fish did you catch" story where every time the fisherman tells it, the fish gets bigger.

In October of 2018, I received a call from one of her neighbors that she had been seen being loaded up in an ambulance. I was frantic and tore out to go to the hospital where we always took her. She was not there! We called around but could not find her. Finally, we located a Jane Doe who had been brought into another local ER. I hurried over there and sure enough, there she lay. I was reminded of the times she and I had gone to identify girls in the hospitals when we had been searching for someone missing. They stabilized her, and I called in her husband and daughter. She was eventually moved to a private room where I visited her daily.

Then one day I was called because she had decided she was leaving. She had left the hospital before against medical advice, understandably tired of being there, and I knew this time she *should not leave*. I immediately went and calmed her down, but I could tell she was irritated with me for not rescuing her and taking her home.

That very night the phone rang and we were told Shay had taken a real turn for the worse. I arrived at the hospital in a matter of minutes. I remember standing at the elevator, hitting the buttons rapidly, trying to get to her. The doctors told me they had brought her around, but it was not good. They brought her around two more times. Finally, with her family there, reality began to sink in. We were all so devastated. She just kept fighting. I was holding her hand, and I finally mustered up everything in me and told her, "I love you, but if you are so tired then go on. I will miss you, but we will all be fine." Shay's spirit left her body within a few minutes.

Shay had lived seven more years, not six months. Every day that she lived was a testimony to her will to survive, to stay on this earth because her work here was not finished. She was remarkable. Even today, I can hear her voice and some of the things she would say. I'll find myself laughing out loud. She had such an influence on so many people.

I was going through Jeff's desk searching for a document one evening. As I turned over some papers, there lay a letter from Shay to Jeff. It was such a beautiful letter, telling him about what a genuine male friendship had meant to her, and how it showed her there are good men on earth. It meant the world to "Pa," as she affectionately called him, right up to the end.

Shay and I had spoken about her memorial service many times. She would want me to plan every single detail, and I just really did not feel it. I told her we would plan it when the time drew closer. She was nervous that I would die before her and Melinda would have to handle it. She was nervous Melinda would be "too upset" to prepare it accordingly. She actually had it turned around. And she wanted her service to reflect on who she was at the time rather than some cracked-up lady.

"Where in the world is that video of the two of you lip syncing," I asked Jeanne, sitting in her office as we pored through the many photos of Shay's family, friends, and life. This meeting was a few days after Shay's passing. Five of us had traveled to Missouri to speak at a conference a few years prior, and all of us had acted so silly the entire trip. "She's not so bad," Shay had decided, after Jeanne surrendered her life to the Lord. But she never stopped asking Jeanne, "What is *wrong* with you, Diva?" Jeanne is a very pretty person but strictly not diva-like. She is more of a classic beauty. Shay wanted to spruce her up to be flashy rather than classic and Jeanne wasn't having it.

Jeanne had become our digital marketer, along with wearing other nonprofit development hats, and loved to create videos and promotional media that told the stories of God transforming the lives of women and children. Compiling media for memorial services also fell under her purview. "I've dreaded this one," she said about making a memorial video for Shay. Everyone had been dreading this particular memorial service more than most. Memorials are never easy.

Years before, we had a special celebration for a grand opening of some kind. I had ordered butterflies to be released on that day. I decided again to order butterflies to be flown in and had them delivered the morning of Shay's service. We gave small silver boxes with the butterflies in them to each of the grandchildren and put them under their chairs. Melinda and I created a timeline and message. All Lovelady leadership members had a role in the service, and there were eight female pallbearers, close friends of Shay and graduates of The Lovelady Center, some of them from the Whole-Way House at Hob Hill in the beginning, others who served under her in Intake. We brought her body to the Center and kept the casket open for the duration of the service. Shay's body looked so peaceful and full of life.

"I want a spectacular send-off, Ma," she had requested, and we did everything within our power to meet that request. I feel like we did. She had the kind of service she would have loved and in fact had described. We released beautiful butterflies because she loved butterflies so much. The words and memories spoken brought everyone to laughter as well as tears. There were so many stories told, and just when the pain would be so hard to handle, someone would have a funny story. A soloist sang, and the celebration of life video was played. I could envision the angelic choir standing and singing behind where she lay, filling the space. We have skylights high above in our atrium, and the sunlight just poured in on her body. The area above her casket seemed to be full of life as the butterflies were released.

Her entire family was there. Her grandsons looked so handsome, sitting with their mother. We wanted everything to be fit for royalty, befitting someone who called herself the Daughter of the King. She was and *is*. She looked at peace, a peace like I had not seen in a long time, almost as if she was smiling. I remembered her baptism so many years before and how happy she was in the water. She had the same, peaceful look on her face.

"The very first *prisoner to princess*, indeed, one of our pioneers, has moved on to meet the One Who freed her of her shackles and placed a crown upon her head. Until we see you again, Miss Shay, we love you," and with that, Chap, our Director of Counseling, closed out the service in prayer. The butterflies were released, and the area above the casket was filled with light, the actual butterflies, and the envisioned choir just singing away. Butterflies landed on the body, and one landed right on her hand. It was beautiful.

Shay left a legacy of love few people ever leave. I miss my Shay. She would have loved all the growth and change at the Center since her passing. Of course, she would have felt she was an important part of the growth. You know what? I would have to agree with that. Shay wanted her service to reflect her later years, the years that counted, not the former. And it did.

Some voids are meant not ever to be filled. They are just voids that are there. We find ways to maintain and go on about this thing called life. We have to live, we want to live, and yet we know the void is there. The void left with Shay's passing is one of those voids meant to remain empty.

Epilogue

"When you wake up, get excited for the morning ahead of you.
You can start over from the day before."
—Dr. Brenda Lovelady Spahn

Melinda and I settled into our separate yet necessary roles. Now we have over 150 full-time staff at the Center and thrift stores. When we first began a program and set up class scheduling, I would stand at the top of the stairs in awe that this organization was running so smoothly, though I take absolutely no credit or recognition for how well things run at the Center.

We give tours daily, and I am always so happy because at least four out of five people always comment that they are shocked how happy everyone in this place is and how much love they feel when they come here. "I can feel the Holy Spirit in this building," many people say. We know what they are talking about, right away—the peace that falls over us when we walk in is obvious also. Without God, none of this would be possible. This Center and ministry have become what it is today not because of us but rather because of *Jesus*. It is an amazing place. The staff at the Center are the hardest working, most dedicated group of people you could ever meet.

Melinda is the most loving, serving person I have ever seen. In the beginning, she was easily fooled by all the women because she is so trusting. She would bring every problem to me. Now she is as equipped to tell the truth from untruth as anyone else I know. With Shay's constant guidance, Melinda became as "street smart" as if she had lived in the streets herself.

One day, we were listening to a young woman trying to convince us of a lie concerning her "boyfriend." Melinda sounded just like me with her "You think we are crazy?" and I looked at her and thought *"She is so ready for this."* Having her as a daughter has been the most wonderful experience you can imagine. Teachers used to ask me what I did to make her the way she is. I tell them that if I had known, I would have done the same to my other four. Our entire family is amazed by Melinda. She is pleasant and loving and quick to forgive. Now, don't get me wrong, she walks in authority. She knows what needs to be done and gets it done. She is a force to be reckoned with. In those early days, I would feel torn between what I felt God was leading us to do and what I could see before me with my own eyes as impossibility. It's one thing for me to go down the rapids without oars or life jackets or really without even a canoe, but to take hundreds of women and a beautiful daughter whom I loved so much with me was really hard on some days.

Melinda is educated, talented, a wonderful mom and wife, and she excels at so many things. At times, I could almost imagine how Abraham felt with Isaac. Was I sacrificing my daughter for what I felt was my mission from the Lord? But then I would watch her and know she was meant to be with me on this mission. She loved it! This abnormal life we were creating had become very normal for us. I honestly don't think it ever crossed her mind to quit, even though I had doubts myself. She was with me from day one. Even if she didn't agree with some of my decisions, which honestly happened quite frequently. I have raised my children to be independent, and often I wondered if I might have over-taught them independence. But the scriptures say iron sharpens iron, so we seem to sharpen each other.

Not many people can keep up with my next idea, especially since I come up with multiple ideas at once, but Melinda has always been able to. I'll realize the women need something—a certain class or a partnership with an organization that can help us help them—and before I can turn around, it seems, she hands me a well-thought-out curriculum or plans for a workshop happening on the weekend to benefit our ladies. Young people are so much more tech savvy than some of our older generation. I can say that because I am of that latter sect of people. However, she has taught me enough on the computer to get myself in trouble.

Our media department was handling my social media page. Melinda begged me not to get on and post anything, for fear of what I might say. I already refuse to turn anyone away and try to throw our waiting list right out the window. If someone needs us, I want to give them the chance. Well, not knowing how this particular social media platform worked, one night I decided to give it a whirl. I signed on and saw that about a thousand people wanted to be my "friend." I accepted every single one of them. I also answered private messages, and some of them were requests for a bed in the program. Jeanne almost strangled me for accepting "friends," who weren't really actual people or something, and Melinda was just as mad. Melinda prissed herself right in front of my desk and told me that's why I needed to stay off social media. We had so many people coming into the program, my social media management career was over. I think social media can be great for so many wonderful reasons, especially "free marketing and promotion," as Jeanne says, but in the wrong hands, it can be disastrous. I understand that now. In *my* hands, it can be disastrous.

Melinda has instead taught me all about search engines. People call me "Doctor Google," and if you need to know about any kind of ailment, I am your girl. I will diagnose your symptoms faster than House.

One of the first questions people ask me about Lovelady is "What will happen when you retire?" I always just shake my head because the way I perceive what they are saying is "Gosh, you look old. Who's going to run this thing when you leave?" I always just introduce them to Melinda, and within a few minutes they are no longer worried and are ready for me to move on. Well, maybe they want me to finish the day, at least.

The truth is, after the pandemic, Melinda and Beau handled the Center themselves with me being off-premises. They did such a capable job, I felt it only fair that Melinda moved into her rightful position of Executive Director and Beau became Presi-

Dr. Brenda Lovelady Spahn

dent of Operations. Between them, things are better than ever. I am their trusted consultant, the Founder, and I serve on the Board of Directors. That gives me time to write and do other things I feel led to do. Plus, my speaking engagements take up some time, and I just *love* to talk. But I bet you have already figured that out for yourself.

It Takes a Village: An Acknowledgement to Our Volunteers

"Volunteers do not necessarily have the time; they just have the heart."
—Elizabeth Andrew

I am convinced that Lovelady has the most wonderful volunteers in the world. You may think that is a bold statement, but it is the truth. Without them, we could not do what we do every day. Like the staff, I believe they are called by God to help our women. They work on the building and our large transportation fleet, they teach classes, they rock our many babies, they change countless diapers, they read to our children, and at Christmastime, well, they bring in the season at Lovelady like you wouldn't believe. They distribute toys in the "Santa Shop," help our women choose toys for their children, host hygiene item drives, help out in our thrift stores, and over 400 women sit down at 52 tables at the same time for Christmas dinner, all because of volunteers. Church youth groups come by bus from all over the South to volunteer with us for a few days, and our annual event for Lovelady Alumni would not happen without volunteers manning festival booths or placing hot dog wieners in buns.

We have one spry gentleman who is close to 90 years old and plays golf every day. He was an absolute star in the legal community and is a complete gentleman. On Mondays, he parks outside our KidZone Department (where the Intake Department was when we first started) and comes in to read to our little ones.

Dr. Brenda Lovelady Spahn

They love "Mr. Bob," as everyone calls him, and they look forward to seeing him. Cheers are loud and pronounced when Mr. Bob enters the door, book in hand.

A group of women from a local church brings homemade cupcakes to every class they lead, teaching the women how to live a Christian life and showing them what it means to be a follower of Jesus Christ. They have been coming to teach that class for years, and boy, do they know the subject matter!

Another group of women from a local Sunday school class shows up every time they are asked by our Development Department to fold brochures and invitations, stuff goody bags for holidays, and host a table for Christmas dinner. Sometimes our women assigned to admin-related office jobs sit down to help them when they come, and we are overjoyed that our women can experience community relations with other women who accept them wherever they are in life.

Another cooperative group from two of the top universities in Alabama educate our women on gardening, building beautiful rooftop gardens and sensory areas for the kids. Every single volunteer brings love, hope, and inspiration. They celebrate victories, comfort and pray for the women during life's battles, attend graduations, and love our women with the love of Jesus. They are warriors' warriors. We have more than 400 active volunteers—the heartbeat of Lovelady. They give of themselves and their finances, and we applaud them.

We have one very special volunteer, Father William. Well, let me tell you, a more special person does not exist. He's like a "Father Teresa of Calcutta." He is an Anglican priest with a wife and family. He took a vow of silence and was a hermitage monk for many years before meeting his sweet wife. He founded an orphanage in Bolivia and speaks very quietly, I believe because of the long vow of silence. He is very humble, and I do not think he could raise his voice in anger if he tried.

One very stressful day years ago, everything had just become too much for me. I had been thinking about quitting this whole thing for days. I had decided to tell my sweet daughter that her mom could not take it anymore and was quitting. I had it all worked out in my mind. I felt bad for all the women and children, but I was just too tired and downtrodden to continue. I had spent several nights in the chapel on a mattress praying for the Center's finances, and my heart was heavy. *It just wasn't supposed to be this hard!* Having that many women and children looking to you for everything they needed and the bills needing to be paid is a very heavy weight.

As I sat at my desk preparing what I was to say to Melinda, there was a knock at my door. I thought to myself, *Oh good grief, what now?* "Who's there?" I asked, as Father William opened the door a few inches and peered in. "May I come in?" There was no way I would ever say no to him, but wow I sure wanted to at that moment. "Yes, Father William." He came right in then, carrying a picnic basket. *Oh, good grief! He means to have lunch right here in the office!*

"I thought we might have a nice picnic in your office since you can never leave the building and go out for lunch," he quietly said. He made a beeline to the table in my office and spread out a tablecloth, plates, and silverware. There was no paper or plastic like I would've done, only glass and silverware for this picnic. I was somewhere between aggravated and touched but was thinking what I would also tell this great man, who had become such a good friend, that I was loading everything up and going home for good. Then he pulled the Eucharist items from the basket and set up for Holy Communion. I told the Lord I was sorry right then and there for wishing Father William had not come in. But I was still determined to leave the Center behind and end this daily struggle.

I was so weary of the everyday struggle. It seemed all I did each day was argue and fight to be able to continue to help the women. And then helping them see their own worth was also a fight. City Hall, my family, the women—there was some kind of drama brewing every which way I turned.

I moved to the table, and he began the Communion ceremony that he leads so well. He is so soft-spoken and full of passion in his words—I can feel his heart every time he speaks about the Lord Jesus blessing the bread and telling the disciples, *"Take, eat, all of you. Do this in remembrance of me."*

By the time he reached the last "The Lord be with you," and I answered, "And also with you," Father William Wilson turned to me. "As I walked in my garden this morning, speaking with the Lord, He told me to come tell you that if He was on the earth today, He would be roaming these halls with you." I wiped the tears from my eyes and thanked him. After a moment, we began eating the fine picnic lunch he had prepared, and I decided right then and there that I would not quit on these women and children. If Jesus was willing to come roam these halls with me, nothing was going to keep me from staying right here with Him. I knew without a shadow of doubt that the Lord had sent Father William to speak to me that day.

"Many years ago," he continued, "when I lived in the Andes Mountains, I had to walk to the mission, many miles from my little house. The snow covered a cow pasture, but it was the shortest route so I climbed the fence and kept walking. It was like a beautiful white blanket covering the field. I stayed at the mission for several weeks, and when it was time to head back home, I climbed that same fence and walked back through that same pasture. Well, that beautiful white blanket of snow was melting, and this time I could see all the cow patties beginning to show through the melting, white blanket. It was beginning to look so dreary, and I avoided stepping in the cow manure as best I could. Then, *there*—in the midst of all that cow manure—was a single yellow daffodil growing out of the middle of one of the piles. It was not yet time for flowers to bloom, but there it was, pretty and yellow and strong. That daffodil reminds me so much of you and of The Lovelady Center." No one had ever told me before that I reminded them of a flower growing in a field of cow dung. But those words coming from Father William's beautiful heart touched me deeply.

Reverend Carson Franklin has been volunteering with us the longest. All the women love him, and it is so healthy for them to see a good Christian man with no ulterior motive other than just loving them because the Lord commands it. He is a great, compassionate listener. He is always so tender-hearted and motivational. He has given so much time to the Center and led many of our ladies to the Lord. He is a full-time pastor, and his flock feels the same about him as we do. He is very respected in the community. When he teaches at Lovelady, every woman listens, which is really uncommon for classes with our women. His grasp of the scriptures is very insightful and honest.

Not long ago, he unexpectedly lost his wife. When I spoke to him on the phone at the time of her passing, he told me it would help him to just keep teaching. He showed up right on time. We passed him on the way, taking food to his house. I begged him to tell me other things we might do to help him, but he simply asked me to pray and asked my women to pray for him. So we all prayed.

We have had the most wonderful psychiatrist you could ever imagine. He came to us by recommendation of a donor. He actually came for a tour 14 years ago and called us back the next day and said he could give us one day a week. As I look back and see where we were, I am amazed that this fine doctor believed in us enough to come on board and help. He would see the women who needed psychotropic drugs. Mental decline and drug addiction go hand in hand, unfortunately.

Many rehab facilities, especially faith based, do not think a rehab should ever allow those drugs to be given. In the beginning, I could not decide and I prayed and prayed about it. I came to the conclusion that if I had a diabetic person, I would surely allow her to take insulin. If someone was prescribed medication to lower her blood pressure, I would surely allow her to take that. God made us body, soul, and spirit, and we must take care of all three. I feel the same way about taking care of the mind. Dr. Hall believed this along with me. He is a godly man who is very careful what he prescribes. He was so faithful to the Center.

When Dr. Hall retired, he maintained his license for Lovelady only. The precious man must have given up much of his retirement time. When Covid came in like a hurricane, he began a virtual appointment day for us and all his appointments were online. Even after Covid slowed down and regulations declined, he continued online. However all good things must end, and he reached an age where he needed to retire. This year, 2023, we had a celebration and said goodbye to our beloved Dr. Hall. God will certainly send us another one. It takes a special person to see through someone who has self-medicated and used way more drugs than should have been used. Dr. Hall was especially good with treating addiction and, of course, that made him so efficient for us. Occasionally, we would have someone who refused to use him because he would not give her what she "needed," when in fact, her previous doctors were overprescribing medications for her or she was tricking them with fake symptoms, doc shopping. We would have to work to correct the problem. Doctor Hall was absolutely the best, and he will be missed.

Equally as great is our wonderful Dr. Combs. He is a truly great general practitioner, and that is just what we need. He has saved us countless trips to the emergency room. The same women who were living on the street at times and had not been to a doctor for years walk into the Center and all of a sudden they are hurting everywhere. Once the drugs begin to leave their system, they can feel everything they have been doing to their body, sometimes for many years. Pain is intensified, and they have so many things going haywire in their system. We can do simple detoxes at the Center, and we watch over them 24/7 for their first three days. Doctor Combs has set all of this up for us.

He comes every other Wednesday, and every appointment is always booked. We have his cell number and can call him with many questions. When he finds something that needs tests or scans, he tries to find a friend who specializes in the particular need. One day a girl was talking about what he had done for her getting her to a specialist and I thought I bet Dr. Combs' friends get tired of his "referrals." He is just a good person, and we are so fortunate to have him.

When Dr. Combs comes to the Center, he rides a bicycle. That man rides his bike rain or shine. At first, we all were just amazed, now it's very normal to us. I guess he does it for exercise. He is a physician at the University of Alabama in Birmingham (UAB) so rides about 10 miles to get to us, and I don't know where he goes when he leaves, but it has to be 10 miles away from us.

Dr. Combs never asks for anything other than to have things in perfect order when he arrives. When he leaves, we hand him his special order of chicken fingers and fries. Now that's something, only asking for a meal, and maybe that's why he rides the bicycle to us. I don't question any of this; I am just so glad to know him and have him with us. He has been with us for 14 years. I look forward to many more, but I realize that time wears on a person. Dr. Combs is a Lovelady through and through.

It's still simply amazing to me how God brings people together, even after all the miracles and all the "right on times" and all the transformations. The Christian community, once they saw God was truly in this thing, came together in full force, serving and nurturing, making quilts for our women and donating goods, supporting financially and painting walls. What they may not realize is that they are impacting our women through acceptance—our women see people who show up just to love on them awhile—for no reason other than serving Jesus by serving them. It is one of the most beautiful displays of love I have ever seen.

John F. Kennedy once said, "We must find time to stop and thank those who have made a difference in our lives." When we started the Center, I had never even been around a ministry like ours. I had never been around halfway houses or the people who ran them. I entered this field only because I felt, and still feel, led by God to do this. I never had a desire to go in this direction with my life at all. This is such a hard feeling to tell some people because people tend to judge what they don't understand.

Who in their right mind does such a thing like this unless there is an ulterior motive? I assure you, there was no motive at all other than doing what I believed God would have me do. Before, I had been so selfish and had been striving for more material wealth every day. For someone like that to give it all up because they felt like God was directing them to do so, you can count on *that* being the reason. It took God to get me where I needed to be. Addiction comes at you from every corner. I wanted *stuff*. That was *my* addiction.

There were times during the first 10 years that I felt like some child attempting to put a puzzle together. I felt like I was on an emotional roller-coaster ride. Up-down-up-down. I wanted to just run away at times. When I prayed, all I could hear was, *"Be still."*

I asked the board to put in an individual to take the temperature of the ministry. I only wanted what was best for us. Melinda felt like I was giving up, which was not the case at all. I was at the point that if God wanted someone else to manage it, that was fine with me. I could be done, and in truth, I was a little put back. We had grown so fast. If God wanted me for this ministry, then He had me, but if I was just to birth it and leave it for someone else, then that was fine with me also. After all, this ministry belongs to Him.

The first day the brilliant John McNeil showed up, I met with him for several hours. Melinda met us too, and we all sat and talked. I felt if I was at the Center, no one would speak truthfully to John about how they felt about those leading the ministry, so I had decided to leave. After our meeting, I told them I was going to go to the beach and would be back in a week or so. Melinda was so taken aback and distraught. She saw the need for me to stay behind during his study of us. I explained my feelings to Melinda. I had no fear any longer. It was God's way or not at all for me. And off to the beach I went. Melinda would call me several times a day. John would call with questions.

Finally, he called me and asked me when I might come home. I told him I would leave in the next hour. I was at the Center the next morning, bright and early. "Brenda, I want you to always remember this statement: *Perception is reality*. The way people perceive a situation with anyone is how they believe it to be. People don't care enough or have enough time to really look into the heart of things. You are a very complicated person, and you have allowed yourself to become a mystery to people. This is without a doubt one of the most holistic and worthy programs I've ever seen. You and your wonderful daughter have done an incredible job of putting this giant program together. I will be giving the report on Lovelady to the board this week." John looked me directly in the eyes and told me he knew God had called me and he doubted the ministry would make it without my leadership. I felt so much better.

John became one of our valued volunteers and another great mentor for me. I really did not know much about John in the beginning. As usual, it was one of my gut instincts. John showed up. He immediately began to talk to his friends. I had no idea who he was and whom he knew. Oh, my goodness, the man knows everyone, and everyone loves him! John has done more for me than anyone could imagine. He has brought people in to meet me, and he takes people on tours. John is now Chairman of the Board and has been with us over 11 years. He is incredible. The only negative thing I can say about John is that he likes Melinda more than he likes me. He is always on her side in everything.

With John, we really got two people, a package deal: John and his wife, Beverly. If there was someone John did not know, Beverly did. She owns an art gallery and has such an impressive group of artists whose work she represents. She has put together the most amazing book, *Portraits of Hope*. Beverly asked some nationally renowned artists to paint portraits of some of our women. Those portraits, along with the story of each woman, make up the beautiful art book. It is such a great representation of Lovelady. All the proceeds are used in our aftercare program, assisting graduates with necessary fees like old power bills preventing them from having power turned on in their new lives, or being able to get their drivers' licenses in good standing in order to drive again.

Beverly also oversees our largest annual fundraiser, the Legacy of Love. Every year, we have more than 600 guests attend. She is the most incredible person ever. She and John are a real force, a power couple. Sometimes when I think about what all John and Beverly could be doing and yet God sent them to Lovelady for us, I am so very humbled and so very thankful. They have such a strong heart for our troubled women. The girls call them Ms. Beverly and Mr. John. I am eternally grateful for these two people and have come to call them some of my best friends.

I could go on and on about hundreds of volunteers. The phrase *It takes a village* applies to The Lovelady Center like no other description I know. And we certainly could use help—*your* help.

Dr. Brenda Lovelady Spahn

Will you commit to changing the life of a woman and child through financial support of the program? Visit www.loveladycenter.org/donate.

Will you commit to coming into the Center and loving these women and children right where they are? Visit www.loveladycenter.org and fill out the online application to volunteer.

Want to come see what we do on an average day or attend a graduation ceremony one Friday? Email tours@loveladycenter.org for information.

The Lovelady Center is located at: 7916 2nd Avenue South, Birmingham, AL, 35206.

Lovelady Life in Pictures

Melinda MeGahee and Brenda Spahn, 2023

Dr. Brenda Lovelady Spahn

A 2019 Graduation

Melinda McGahee with children at a graduation service, 2019

Shay Curry, Intake Director

Elizabeth and her son being baptized at Lovelady Center

Jeanne, Elizabeth, Matthew (Miss Brenda's son and Miss Melinda's twin brother, and Pam, a Lovelady, 2018>

John McNeil and Elizabeth, 2021

Miss Brenda and the Lovelady Movement

Miss Brenda and Miss Melinda, 2010

Beau takes the boys to the movies

Dr. Brenda Lovelady Spahn

Brenda, the Lovelady

Carmen and her husband, Brent

Cynthia and her son, Jonah

Miss Brenda and the Lovelady Movement

Vivian, painted by Teresa Mattos

Monica, painted by Mary Morvant

Dr. Brenda Lovelady Spahn

Lovelady Salon to restore outer beauty

Shay Curry and Tiffany Gulledge, original participants in the Lovelady Whole-way House

Miss Brenda and the Lovelady Movement

Tablescapes Annual Christmas Dinner Event for Loveladies

Miss Brenda decorates for Christmas every year

Dr. Brenda Lovelady Spahn

Lovelady Thrift Store Grand Opening, 2010

Children's Thanksgiving Play, 2008

Miss Brenda and the Lovelady Movement

Miss Teresa and Dr. Debra "Chap" Jones, D.Min., A.F.S. Psych

Rt. Rev. Dr. William Wilson and Dr. Debra "Chap" Jones, D.Min., A.F.S. Psych